Brooklyn Jew

Brooklyn Jew
Journey of an American Sports Writer
Copyright © 2025 by Lowell Cohn

All rights reserved. No part of this book may be reproduced or transmitted in any form or by any means without written permission from the publisher and author.

Additional copies may be ordered from the publisher for educational, business, promotional or premium use.
For information, contact ALIVE Book Publishing at:
alivebookpublishing.com

Book design by Alex P. Johnson

ISBN 13
978-1-63132-258-7 Paperback
978-1-63132-259-4 Hardcover

Library of Congress Control Number: 2025913056

Library of Congress Cataloging-in-Publication Data
is available upon request.

First Edition

Published in the United States of America by ALIVE Book Publishing
an imprint of Advanced Publishing LLC
3200 A Danville Blvd., Suite 204, Alamo, California 94507
alivebookpublishing.com

PRINTED IN THE UNITED STATES OF AMERICA

10 9 8 7 6 5 4 3 2 1

Brooklyn Jew

Journey of an American Sports Writer

Lowell Cohn

Alive Book Publishing

To my wife, Dawn

"Without interrupting each other, we both said at the same time, 'Let's never get out of touch with each other.' And we never have, although her death has come between us."
—*A River Runs Through It* by Norman Maclean.

CONTENTS

Preface IX
Lowell Cohn Biography XI

Chapter 1 Judaism Is the World's Largest Religion 13
Chapter 2 Stevie 19
Chapter 3 Oh, the Pretty Flowers 25
Chapter 4 Library Card 35
Chapter 5 How I Became a Sports Writer 39
Chapter 6 The Vacuum Cleaner Salesman 43
Chapter 7 The I-Cash Man 47
Chapter 8 The Cha-Cha King 53
Chapter 9 Step Off 61
Chapter 10 Farbissener 69
Chapter 11 Sex on the Go 73
Chapter 12 A Fast-Moving Car 77
Chapter 13 Bar Mitzvah Season 81
Chapter 14 The Never-Ending Importance of the Bunny Hop 91
Chapter 15 The Price of a Pea Coat 97
Chapter 16 Death Knell for Old MacDonald 109
Chapter 17 Christ Descending 115
Chapter 18 Subway Token 125
Chapter 19 Twenty-Year-Old Virgin 129
Chapter 20 On Reading Aldous Huxley 137
Chapter 21 The Dip Master 145
Chapter 22 Carl and the Jewish Huckleberry Finn 149
Chapter 23 Kindergarten Baby 161
Chapter 24 My Catholic Jewish Father 173
Chapter 25 My First Christmas Dinner 183
Chapter 26 Bill 187

Chapter 27	My Introduction to Linguistics	193
Chapter 28	An Honest Bloke	201
Chapter 29	Smart-Ass Jew	205
Chapter 30	I Married a Shiksa	213
Chapter 31	The Can	225
Chapter 32	Horseshit vs. Bullshit	229
Chapter 33	I Take on the Hearst Empire	237
Chapter 34	Jew 'Em	253
Chapter 35	Gravestone	259
Chapter 36	The Prisoner of Waldbaum's	267
Chapter 37	The Flood in 4B	277
Chapter 38	Alimentary Jew	287
Chapter 39	Jewish Intellectual	295
Chapter 40	Why Judge Judy is Essential	303
Chapter 41	Poland	309
Chapter 42	Spaldeen, Meet Paul Tillich	315
Chapter 43	Heaven	321
Acknowledgments		331

Preface

I am a Brooklyn Jew, born and raised in the Flatbush section of Brooklyn. I talk Brooklyn Jew and think Brooklyn Jew even though I have lived in California since age twenty. I am approaching my ninth decade on Earth. Until I went away to Lafayette College in Pennsylvania at sixteen, I thought mother and father were pronounced *mudda* and *fadda*. I still say *chawcolate* instead of chocolate, *cawfee* instead of coffee, *Yooston* instead of Houston and *sistuh* instead of sister. I talk like a Brooklyn Jew. I proudly carry that with me.

I went to California in 1966 at age twenty for graduate studies in English Literature at Stanford. At Stanford I was exposed to a world I never imagined—brilliant professors and students from all over the planet, people smarter than me, certainly more sophisticated.

I realized I had grown up in a *shtetl*. I was from the biggest city in the United States, but the Midwood enclave of Flatbush, almost all Jewish, was a small ghetto which I thought was big. People from my parents' generation were bilingual, spoke English and Yiddish. Some wore tattoos from the death camps. I bought pickles from the local deli on Avenue M from a huge barrel. They cost a nickel. My father was legally blind and took the subway every day from Brooklyn to Manhattan to eke out a living in his small law practice. My mother and two of her sisters were teachers in the New York City school system. They believed education was their entry to America and that a good education guaranteed a happy life.

In California I learned how to overcome the limitations

of my upbringing, so parochial, how to navigate a larger America I didn't understand, how to become part of that country without losing the me who grew up in Flatbush.

I wrote this memoir for people of my generation and for their children and grandchildren to learn who they are and where they came from, to show why we are scholarly and successful, and funny and sad, and aggressive and afraid, and verbally savage.

It begins in my childhood and ends in old age, shows what I learned and suffered along the way and how my Jewish background sustained and sometimes hurt me, how it is still the lens through which I see and judge life. I am a Brooklyn Jew.

Lowell Cohn Biography

Ethnicity: 99 percent Jewish Peoples of Europe. 1 percent The Balkans according to Ancestry.com

Born: 1945

Grew up: Brooklyn, New York. P.S. 193 Elementary School, Andries Hudde Junior High School, Midwood High School, Ocean Avenue Synagogue Hebrew School

Advanced Education: Lafayette College, B.A. English Literature 1966. Stanford University, M.A. English Literature 1968. Ph.D. English Literature 1972

Occupation: Sports columnist for the *San Francisco Chronicle* and *Santa Rosa Press Democrat* 1979 to 2016

Books: *Rough Magic: Bill Walsh's Return to Stanford Football* (HarperCollins 1994); *Gloves Off: 40 Years of Unfiltered Sports Writing,* a 2020 memoir (Roundtree Press, an imprint of Cameron Books, which is an imprint of Abrams Books)

Elected to Northern California Jewish Sports Hall of Fame in 2022.

Current Status: Retired

Residence: Oakland, California

Married: 1985 to 2022 to Dawn Elaine Rounseville

Chapter 1
Judaism Is the World's Largest Religion

I knew for a fact Judaism was the world's largest religion. Not only the most important but definitely the largest. And not by a little bit. The world was overwhelmingly Jewish.

I knew this from my experience in the 1950s. The food stores on Brooklyn's Avenue M, our shopping street, were kosher, had the word *kosher* written in Hebrew on the store windows. My teachers were Jewish. The school principals were Jewish. Our neighbors were Jewish. My friends were Jewish. They closed the schools on Rosh Hashanah and Yom Kippur because almost no one attended—we all went to temple. Walk down any street in the Midwood section of Flatbush—my neighborhood—and we saw synagogues everywhere, Orthodox, Conservative and Reform. My dad would say, "There are more synagogues around here than you can shake a stick at."

In my neighborhood there was only one bar, the Elm Tavern. It was considered a sin to be *shikker* (drunk), and Jewish men of my father's generation didn't drink, wouldn't go to a bar after work to unwind. They came home to their families and read or watched Sid Caesar on television. Nowhere on Christmas did we see lawn reindeer or the wise men with the little child. Christmas didn't exist.

I was a kid and it felt great to know we Jews were in charge. That's what being the Chosen People was all about, right?

When I was eight my parents bought the *Encyclopedia*

Britannica Junior. They wanted my brother, sister and me to be educated, to have all the world's facts at our tiny fingertips so we could attend prestigious colleges when we grew up. The *Encyclopedia Britannica Junior* was impressive, fifteen volumes as I recall, and it was bound in red leather—or was it faux leather?—and everything about it shrieked sophistication, class, tradition. My parents placed it prominently on a bookshelf in the living room right next to the faux fireplace in our apartment. Walk into the living room, we couldn't avoid the *Encyclopedia Britannica Junior.*

I would flip through the volumes from time to time. I was not a reader, and I wasn't a curious child, but I would look up *World Series* or *Heavyweight Championship Fights,* sports stuff. One day, and for no apparent reason, I found myself in *Graphs.* I read some of the article, but mostly studied illustrations of the various kinds of graphs until I came to pie charts. I was unfamiliar with pie charts, although I had eaten a slice of blueberry pie, so I had a running start.

This particular pie chart dealt with the world's religions, gave every religion its appropriate share of the pie, each slice a different color. And inside the slice written over the color was the name of the religion. When I looked at the chart, really looked, I was sure the graph was wrong. Christianity, Islam and Hinduism had big hunks of the pie.

I couldn't even find Judaism. Weird. I searched all over the chart. Finally, I noticed a slice near the top. You couldn't exactly call it a slice. A slice you could sink your teeth into. This was a sliver—barely a taste of pie. A crumb. I saw no words in the sliver itself because the sliver was too small to contain print. A thin line pointed from the sliver to outside the pie graph to the indefinite world of the margin. At the

Chapter 1

end of that thin line, I read the word *Jews*. We were relegated to the margin of world religions. In terms of population, we were bottom feeders along with "Other religions," which must have included Zoroastrianism and Neo-Paganism. We were even below "Folk" religions.

This gave me a big laugh. I brought the "G" book of the *Encyclopedia Britannica Junior* to my dad and told him the famous encyclopedia made a big mistake in the graph about world religions. How could that happen when we are the Chosen People?

A sad expression seized my father's face. He sat me down, said we needed to talk, said sure we Jews are the Chosen People and that's great and that's also a big responsibility, but God couldn't make everyone the Chosen People. He chose a select few for the job. He said when I would grow up and go away to college, I'd see firsthand Jews are a very small group in the whole world. He said we weren't big to begin with, but the German bastards killed six million of us in World War II. He mentioned the Holocaust. He hated to tell me all this, he said. His eyes were red.

I walked into my bedroom and shut the door, needed to think this over. I felt wounded, scared, displaced, angry, ripped off. I've never lost these feelings although they've become less intense.

In the playground across the street, I played with kids my age, mostly Jewish. But there was a group of kids from Sicilian and Neapolitan families who lived among us, shopped at the kosher stores. They spoke Italian in the house and ate baked ziti, pizza and lasagna, delicious stuff we never glimpsed in our apartment where chopped liver and knishes were considered haute cuisine. Most of the Italian kids went to Our Lady Help of Christians School. I always wondered why the tough Italian kids needed help—they had no problem kicking my ass. And who was this Lady who helped them?

A few days after the pie chart, I bumped into Joey Manzo in the playground. Joey was a year older than me and a great kid athlete, Italian and Catholic. Everyone wanted to be his friend, wanted him to notice them. I told Joey about the pie chart, said Jews are a little religion in the world. I thought he'd thank me for the info.

"Bullshit," he said. "Look around, Jews are the majority. Any moron can see that."

He pointed to the kids in the playground, mostly Jews, some wearing black hats with rims because they were Hasidim. He pointed to the old Jewish men playing chess. He said, "Don't fuck with me, Lowell."

I swore I wasn't fucking with him. I said, just like him, I always thought Jews were the majority, but I checked an encyclopedia, and the Jews are a very small minority. There are way more Christians than Jews.

He put his hand on my shoulder, stared in my eyes.

"Take back what you said, Lowell."

"What?"

"What you said about Jews."

"But it's true. I can show you in the *Encyclopedia Britannica Junior*."

Joey Manzo punched me in the face, got me in a headlock, dragged me to the ground, made me cry until I gave up.

"Don't treat me like a dumb fuck," he said, still holding me down. "Say the truth."

I said the truth. "Judaism is the World's Largest Religion."

Chapter 1

He let me up and gently straightened my clothes, playfully messed my hair. Told me I was a good kid but sometimes too smart for my own good.

I briefly had destroyed Joey Manzo's view of world religions. After a beating, I graciously restored it. Wish he could do that for me.

Chapter 2

Stevie

Stevie said I should hang out his window. He lived on the fifth floor of our apartment house.

I agreed. It was a snow day in Brooklyn, meaning it snowed the night before and they called off school because kids couldn't walk through snowdrifts the half mile or so to P.S. 193 and they needed room for the snowplows in the streets. Stevie and I already had thrown snowballs at each other and pulled each other along E. 18th Street on dinky sleds. And now Stevie, who was eleven—I was eight—said he had a great idea. We should take the elevator up to his apartment, I would hang out his window and we would throw snowballs at people entering the front door of the apartment building five floors below.

I said there was one problem. My parents said I never could go on the roof. The roof was where my mother hung the wash to dry. My mother and I took the elevator to the top floor—the sixth—and then climbed up a flight of stairs and pushed open a huge metal door into the sunlight. That was way before they put up the Verrazzano-Narrows Bridge in 1964. When I helped my mother hang clothes, I could see west across Brooklyn all the way to the waters of the Narrows. It was windy up there, much windier than down below on the street. I would hand my mother the clothespins one by one while she worked, and the clothes on the line would sing *snap* from the wind. My mother and father said it was okay to be on the roof with my mother but never on my own. It was dangerous. I said I understood and promised never to go alone.

The reason my parents told me never to go on the roof was what happened with Stevie one time. He said we could call each other on the telephone, sure, but it would be more fun to use Walkie Talkies. He got two empty orange-juice cans and a very long piece of string, attached an end of the string to one of the cans and the other end to the second can. We took the elevator to Floor 6, walked up the flight of stairs, went onto the roof and hung one can near his window and one by mine. That night we were talking on the walkie-talkies when my father wandered into my bedroom and saw me on the orange can. "What are you doing?" he asked. I said I was talking to Stevie. He came over and felt the string. He asked where the string came from. I said it was hanging from the roof. He asked how it got on the roof. I said I put it up there with Stevie. That got my dad hot. He took off his belt and hit me, but it didn't hurt. He had tears in his eyes. He and my mother said never go on the roof again under any circumstances.

Stevie said sitting outside his window was different from the roof. It was lower for starters. Looking back, I think his living-room window was maybe ninety feet above the street, the distance from home plate to first base. He said I would sit on the window ledge and dangle my feet over the edge of the building, and he would not let me fall. I could take his word for it.

When we entered his apartment, I hoped his mother or his sister Joycie would be there and maybe kill the window idea, but the place was empty and Stevie, whose nickname was The Weasel, said not to worry. I asked why he wouldn't sit on the window ledge, and he said he was too big for me to hold.

Chapter 2

He slid up the bottom pane of the window and all that freezing air rushed into my face. He helped me onto the ledge, and I looked down. I had been to the top of the Empire State Building on a class trip. The people down below the Empire State Building looked like ants. It wasn't like that from Stevie's window. The people in the street still looked like people but they were far away and when I looked at the street in front of our apartment house, I felt dizzy. I said I was scared. Stevie said don't be a baby. He held me tight around the waist and that made me feel better. I looked across the street at the apartment house facing ours, another six-story giant, and I felt I could fly right over there. It would be easy. Then Stevie explained his idea. I would grab snow from the ledge, make snowballs and throw them at the people entering our apartment building from the street. It would be some joke and the people would get a kick out of it. I asked was he sure and he said absolutely.

And that's exactly what I did. People would approach our building, people wearing hats, earmuffs, gloves, galoshes, and as they walked toward the front door, I would let fly a snowball which fell at their feet or behind them. Once I even hit a lady on the shoulder. They would look around wondering where the snowball came from but, with few exceptions, they never looked at me or Stevie. Have you noticed people don't look up that often?

There was plenty of snow and, although my fingers turned red from the cold and began to hurt, I didn't care. I asked Stevie to hold me tighter because when I threw a snowball my tush moved a little on the windowsill. Stevie asked if I was having fun. I said yes. He said I told you so. I asked what happens when we run out of snow at this window. He said the living room has two windows, dummy, and we'll move you to the other one.

My parents said Stevie was a bad influence on me, and I should never be alone with him in his apartment. They asked why doesn't Stevie play with kids his own age? "How should I know?" I said. My father said I was easily suggestible, but I didn't know what that meant. I thought they were wrong about Stevie. I always had a good time with him. Like when we borrowed a shopping bag from my mother—we didn't ask her for it—and collected chestnuts from the big tree in our backyard and threw them at the windows of the fancy private houses on E. 19th Street. Or when we lifted a pack of wooden matches from my kitchen and lit them and tossed them from my first-floor window at kids walking to Hebrew School.

When I would take the elevator to Stevie's apartment, his grandmother would be there and when she saw me, she'd start shrieking in Yiddish. I didn't understand what she was saying and asked Stevie why she always got upset when I showed up. "She says you make me do bad things," he said. "I'm not bad," I said. Stevie said don't worry about her, she's nuts. He shut the bedroom door on the old lady. His little sister Joycie used to hang out in her own room crying. His mother was gone at work most of the time and I never saw a father, although I didn't ask Stevie about it.

One time in the playground across the street, one of the tough Italian kids named Di Gregorio—he might have been twelve—challenged Stevie to a fight. I thought Stevie could beat him up because he was bigger and outweighed the kid, but Stevie said his shoulder hurt. The Italian kid said Stevie was faking it about his shoulder, and Stevie said he would kick his ass except for the shoulder and the Italian kid

Chapter 2

slapped Stevie in the face, a loud smack, and Stevie started to cry and he wouldn't fight. Later another kid challenged Stevie to a fight, but this kid was Jewish and shaped like a pear—his last name was Schenk—and Stevie got him in a headlock and made him give up. Stevie's shoulder didn't look so bad. When we walked back across the street to our apartment house, Stevie said the Italian kid better watch out. And then he said *my damn shoulder*.

There was plenty of snow on the second windowsill. By now I had the hang of it. I would grab snow and make the snowballs real fast, and I'd toss them at people or, for the fun of it, just drop the snowballs in front of them. The surprised looks were a laugh riot. And I would have kept on doing it, except Stevie's doorbell started buzzing. Not just a few buzzes. It was a constant buzz, real annoying. Stevie said, "Who needs this?" He started to turn toward the door, and I felt him loosen his grip on my waist. I shouted don't let go and he pulled me inside. When I stood on the floor, I noticed my legs were shaky like after I'd gone roller skating.

Stevie opened the door and what do you know, it was my mother. "Lowell, come with me now," she said. Her voice was more frozen than the snow, and the look on her face I only had seen once before. At my grandmother's funeral. A serious look like something bad had happened. "What?" I said. "Come with me this instant," she said.

Stevie looked disappointed. I wanted to tell him I'm sorry, but I silently followed my mother. In the elevator she said someone I hit with a snowball told the superintendent's wife I was hanging out Stevie's window, and the superintendent's wife—Anna was her name—had gone running to our apartment.

My mother told me to wait in my bedroom with the door

closed. I heard our front door open, and then I heard my father's voice. He had come home early from work, took the subway from Manhattan. They talked for a while, but I couldn't make out what they said. Then my mother poked her head into my bedroom and told me *come out*.

    We went to the living room. My father sat in his stuffed chair. I stood by the window next to the big DuMont console TV. My father said I had done a very silly thing. He said I could have been killed. He said he and my mother loved me and they had brought me up to be a good boy. He said, "We've put blood, sweat and tears into you." He said he didn't know how I could be so foolish. He reminded me I was not allowed on the roof. I wanted to say Stevie's fifth-floor window was not the roof, but I didn't think it was the right time to make the point.

    My father seemed more sad than angry. He asked, "Do you want me to hit you with my belt again?" I said, "No." My mother didn't exactly cry, but she sighed. My father said, "You're never to play with Stevie again." He asked if I understood that. I said I did. He made me promise never to play with Stevie again. I promised.

    And I kept my promise, I really did, except for the times I played with Stevie, but they never knew.

Chapter 3

Oh, the Pretty Flowers

Mary had the most beautiful breasts. I know this for a fact because when I was eleven, she had the decency to show them to me.

Mary was our housekeeper, a Black woman who lived in downtown Brooklyn, but she had grown up in Newport News, Virginia. Because my mother was teaching all day Monday through Friday, Mary became our substitute mother. Our other mother. This was not unusual in our Flatbush neighborhood. The *shvartze*—forgive me but that was the word—well, the Black housekeeper took care of the middleclass Jewish kids because both parents had jobs to keep up the middleclass life. My Aunt Irene had Vickie, who cleaned her apartment and did the cooking and helped raise my cousins Joel and Ronnie.

Mary rode the subway to Avenue M early in the morning to prepare my father's breakfast before he went to his office near Wall Street, and she spent the rest of the day alone, cleaning, until my brother, sister and I came home from school for lunch, which she prepared, and then took care of us when we came home at the end of the school day. She came to us when I was six years old. My father fired Ella, the cleaning woman before Mary, when neighbors in our apartment house told him she turned tricks in our apartment while my brother, sister and I were at school. Mary cleaned the house and made supper because my mother had no interest in cooking. "If it contains more than two ingredients," my mother proudly announced, "I don't make it."

This was a serious matter for us. My mother worked hard at her teaching at an elementary school, prided herself on being a professional. She ceded the apartment to Mary. Mary worked only a half-day on Thursdays and my mother, unwilling to cook—not knowing how—would say, "Tonight we eat dairy." Which meant frozen strawberries and sour cream. She might make sandwiches with tuna from the can. I don't know how she got away with it.

But one Thursday my mother was unusually ambitious. She heroically attempted a meatloaf, failing, however, to prepare a sauce to pour over the loaf which was as dry and brittle as jerky. It sat on the table like a cadaver. She served us broccoli on the side. Not fresh broccoli. This was frozen broccoli. I'm thinking Birds Eye. When the broccoli reached my father's plate ice still glittered on several stalks. I don't know how this was possible, but I saw ice with my own eyes. My father was legally blind, couldn't read the print in the newspaper and couldn't see the ice. When he finally bit into the broccoli, my sister and I staring and anticipating the crisis moment, his teeth crunched into something solid and cold. He picked up the broccoli with a fork and studied it from an inch away.

"There's ice on this," he declared, astonished.

"Oh no, you're wrong," my mother said. "I cooked it."

That was her mistake. If she had said, "I forgot to turn on the gas," or maybe, "I'm sorry, I must not have cooked it long enough," or, "I suck at cooking"—in other words, if she had openly admitted her mistake and thrown herself on the mercy of the family, my father, a skilled trial attorney, might have let it pass. But she was telling my father, contrary to all physical evidence, he didn't know what he was talking about. He extended the fork across the table

Chapter 3

toward my sister and me as if displaying the murder weapon.

"Look," he said, "ice."

We studied the broccoli. Ice. My father withdrew the evidence, pushed his plate away in disgust.

"She cooks broccoli and there's still ice on it," he said by way of summation. And that pretty much described my mother's culinary abilities, although my mother did get in the last word. As we kids fled the kitchen, I heard her say, "If you don't like the broccoli this way maybe you'd like it as shampoo."

So, Mary stabilized our lives, set a cheerful orderly tone. I imagine Mary regretted her job as an apartment cleaner, an existence with no children of her own. I imagine she told herself, if things had been different, she could have gone to college and been a schoolteacher and made a better wife than my mother for my dad. For starters she could cook—fried chicken and pot pies with leftover turkey from Thanksgiving and ice cream she made herself. Maybe she thought she would have been livelier at sex than my mother, more ready and willing and inventive. These are tricky things to speculate about.

Mary never flirted or acted inappropriately with my dad. She was intelligent and ironic. She could imitate the vegetable man, Mr. Kramer, who parked his old truck with a ratty canvas top on the street and tromped across the lawn of our apartment house to our first-floor kitchen window and sold Mary fruit and vegetables through the window. After rejecting his initial pathetic offerings, string beans and peas dead on arrival, she would hand him cash.

He was from Eastern Europe and pronounced Mary something like Merry, trilling the Rs. And he was gross and dirty and after he left, she would call herself Merry and laugh at Mr. Kramer. She was an American and he wasn't. That's what she thought. We children loved her, and my parents loved her. We loved her until the day she died in 1969 when I was studying in England and my parents didn't tell me she died until after her funeral when it was too late to attend. It felt like a betrayal of Mary, like she merely had been hired help.

Once some capillaries on my father's scrotum bled, and at breakfast, he asked Mary if he should have them cauterized. I never had heard the word cauterized. I don't remember what she told him. But when I came home from school that day, she said to me, imitating his voice, "Should I have them cauterized?" She laughed but it wasn't a happy laugh. My father had stepped across a boundary. Or maybe it wasn't a mere issue of boundaries as in correct manners. It was more serious. My father had marginalized Mary. It was okay to ask her this personal question with the image of an oozing scrotum because she wasn't quite a grownup like my mother or my Aunt Sarah. She inhabited a middle ground between child and adult.

Or maybe my father felt familiar with her the way he'd feel toward a sister. It was hard to know then. It's hard to know now. My father was not a man to come onto a woman or embarrass her. He was crazy about my mother.

Summers we had a bungalow in New Jersey, at what they called a bungalow colony. About forty Jewish families and their kids who went to a day camp there surrounded by woods and brooks. Mary was the only Black person. She slept in the bedroom with us kids. One night she cooked ears of corn and after dinner she called me into the kitchen and said, "Ever smoke a corn-silk cigarette?"

Chapter 3

I never smoked anything, I told her.

"A boy can't grow into a man he hasn't smoked a cornsilk cigarette," she told me. "All the boys back home smoked them."

She gathered the thin threads of corn silk and walked to the back of the bungalow near the clothesline and found a big rock that got plenty of sun and laid the silk on it. About a week later, she handed me a hand-rolled cigarette filled with the silk, now brown and dry.

"Don't tell your mother."

I slid the cigarette into my mouth, and it made me feel grownup, the thin paper and the bits of silk deposited in my mouth and the weight and heft of it. Mary took a box of wooden matches from her apron and struck a match against the box and reached for the end of the cigarette.

"Breathe in gentle," she told me.

I sucked in and the end grew bright, and I felt the hot air in my mouth.

"Don't breathe into your lungs. That comes later. You're a beginner."

She took the cigarette from me and put it into her mouth, and she dragged deep, all the way into her lungs. She closed her eyes. I could smell her sweet sweat. I watched the smoke curling out of her nose, the rest escaping her mouth. She handed the cigarette to me, and I smoked some more, and we smoked the whole corn-silk cigarette down to the end.

We smoked a cigarette once a week, me getting better at it, blowing smoke rings and Mary laughing until one day my mother walked into the backyard. Strode into the backyard, that teacher look on her face. She yanked the cigarette out of my mouth, seized the corn silk from the rock, turned around and walked away. She never spoke to me about it. I don't know if she and Mary spoke about it. Mary was a few years older than my mother and now my mother had treated her like a child. Even I could see that.

Mary remains a mystery to me. I once visited her apartment near the end of her life, although I didn't know how close the end was. She lived in a part of Brooklyn I didn't know. I walked up a flight of stairs. She lived in one room, the furniture Salvation Army. She had a small TV and on her dresser I saw a photo of a young good-looking Black man in an army uniform. The photo was old, from another era. I had no idea who he was. A former boyfriend? A husband? So much I didn't know about Mary although I spent my childhood with her, and she knew everything about me.

I grew up listening to her. I loved listening to her. Her stories. She was the narrative voice of my childhood into my early adulthood. At the end of her workday about five o'clock, I would sit on the closed toilet seat while she applied her makeup at the sink, staring at the mirror on the medicine cabinet. I was looking at her profile. She was thin with a lovely form. Her face was oval with deep beautiful eyes. She used a big round orange sponge which she dipped under the faucet and rubbed into her makeup and then ran across her face. I saw her do this thousands of times.

One day she wore a form-fitting sweater. I don't remember the color. My brother and sister were out. My father wasn't home yet. My mother was in the kitchen. Mary saw me looking at her. I was old enough to admire her figure. She smiled at me. She lifted her sweater in the front, lifted it to her neck. She turned to me. She wasn't wearing a bra.

"What do you think of these?" she said.

I thought they were great, but I didn't say anything. I didn't know what to say. And just like that she lowered her

Chapter 3

sweater, finished her makeup, and went home. I knew something important just took place. But what?

Over the years, I've tried to break down the meaning of what Mary did, although the meaning escapes me still.

Mary was proud of her breasts, which were young-woman breasts although she was in her fifties. Because she loved me, she wanted me to be proud of them too.

Or Mary knew I was approaching adolescence and she wanted to educate me in ways my mother never could.

Or Mary wanted to establish a secret bond between us, something she wouldn't share with my brother or sister.

Or Mary wanted to shock me.

Or Mary was asking, with breasts like these why don't I have a boyfriend? Did she?

Or Mary was saying, I'm not bad for an old broad.

Or Mary proved she trusted me with her life.

Whatever her motives, Mary read me right.

She wasn't being sexual. Nothing like that. It was more serious. I never could tell my parents, never tell anyone what Mary did. It would have been curtains for her, this gift she gave me, this gift between just us. And I never told anyone until now.

Then there was this.

"You see my skin," Mary said one day, she and I alone in the bathroom. She pointed to her arm.

"My skin is black," she said. "But I wasn't supposed to be colored."

This was the 1950s and she used the word *colored*.

"I was supposed to be white like you," she said. "Do you want to know how I became colored?"

I said I did.

She put down her sponge and stared at me.

"Before people are born," she said, "they line up in heaven and wait their turn to come into the world. They are spirits but they have bodies. Do you know what I mean?"

I said I did.

"It was my day to be born and I was standing in line with the other white babies. And I felt so happy. I was way at the back of the line. The sun was shining, and the sky was blue, and I could feel a breeze. Monitors in charge of the lines were telling us life is full of joy. But time dragged on and I wanted to be born. It got to be afternoon and I still had a long way to go, and I was hot and thirsty, and I felt sleepy. Remember I was just a little baby. I wasn't even a baby yet. I saw beautiful flowers along the side of the road. Red and pink and yellow. 'Oh, the pretty flowers,' I said. I walked to the flowers and touched them.

"A monitor told me not to wander away, to stay on the line. I should have listened, but I didn't. The flowers were so beautiful. I smelled them. Without meaning to I walked near the line for the colored people waiting to be born but they weren't colored yet. They were white just like you. A truck drove by and a man on the truck was holding a hose. He sprayed all the people on the colored line black and brown. I was over by the flowers, and I watched him spray them. Because I was there, he sprayed me too. I said, 'Mister, you made a mistake. You sprayed me black, but I'm not supposed to be black. I'm supposed to be on the white line. I'm a white baby.'

"'Sorry, too late,' he said. 'Once you get sprayed colored you're colored.'

"That's how I became colored," Mary said.

I didn't know how to respond. I didn't know how to feel. This was more important than showing me her breasts,

I was sure of that. She put away her sponge and her makeup, grabbed her purse, slipped on a jacket, walked out the front door, walked to the subway, and rode home alone.

Chapter 4

Library Card

They opened a brand-new library on Avenue J in Brooklyn when I was eleven years old. Before that, the library was a second-floor walkup over a candy store where I would buy a Charlotte Russe—sponge cake with custard inside. I would visit the new library, a few blocks from my Hebrew School, and gaze at the brick and iron and oversized windows and smell the books and appreciate the serious quiet of the place. And I would take out books. I remember one series aimed at children my age which specialized in biographies. I read the life of Mozart. Not that I'd ever heard Mozart's music.

One day I walked to the checkout counter of the new library with three books. I took my library card out of my thin wallet which contained no money and handed it to the woman behind the counter. She didn't smile at me, didn't praise me for being a reader. She marked the return date for the books on the card on the inside back cover, marked with that metal gismo that went click and left ink on the card, and as I picked up the books and began to leave, she said, in an angry loud voice, "Next time don't use your father's library card."

I don't remember a grownup being rude to me before. I stared at her, maybe fifty, short gray hair and I said, "This is my library card."

"Right," she said, and she dismissed me.

How did I feel on the two-block walk back to our apartment?

I was shocked and angry and confused. No one had ever questioned my name before.

The woman spoke without knowing the facts. I expected grownups to know the facts, depended on them to know what's what. Instead this woman, a librarian no less, had accused me of being a phony, a fake, of gaming the system, of going behind my father's back, of being a bad son.

Heavy stuff to lay on a kid. A kid named Lowell. I had to live with that name. Three Ls in six letters. The only Lowell I'd ever known in my eleven years was me. I felt weird when I met new kids. *What kind of name is Lowell, anyway?*

I'd learned to deal with that, but never from an adult.

So, sure, I felt all those things on the walk home, the injustice of it all. But I felt something else, and I asked this question. Why would the rude angry lady think I used my father's library card? And I came up with the obvious answer. No grownup in Brooklyn in the 1950s would believe a kid was named Lowell. Lowell was so archaic it had to be from my dad's generation or some generation before his.

You'd think I felt aggrieved at my parents on the walk home from the Avenue J library, aggrieved for putting me in that spot—the Lowell Name Spot. But I didn't feel aggrieved, and this surprised me. I felt proud they had named me Lowell instead of the going names at the time—Howard, Marvin, Ronnie, Eugene. I was Lowell. I was special.

I learned much later how I became Lowell. When I was born my parents first would have given me a Yiddish name. We called it the Jewish name. The Yiddish name came first, before my English name. My parents were the children of immigrants, Jews from Eastern Europe who came to America but never learned to speak English. Growing up, my parents spoke Yiddish in the home with their parents, but they spoke English in the world. Yiddish, based on German and including a mixture of Hebrew and other languages, was the *lingua franca* of Jews from Eastern Europe. They read Yiddish newspapers and Yiddish novels and went to the Yiddish theater. And they kept kosher and were Orthodox Jews. So, of course my Yiddish name came first. My parents were honoring their parents and honoring tradition by giving me a Yiddish name.

For me, they chose Leibel, although they sometimes called me Leibele (pronounced Leibel-a), the diminutive, not that they called me Leibel very often. It was a secret identity, almost a non-identity. My parents chose Leibel because my dad's older brother had died in a fire as a young boy and my father named me after his brother whose name was Leibel. In English they called him Lester, but certainly in the home of my grandparents he was Leibel.

After they named me Leibel, my parents needed an English name with an L, the L to go along with Leibel. They needed an English name because I didn't speak Yiddish and we were not Orthodox and we did not keep a kosher home. And at school and in the playground I could not be Leibel. It would have sounded weird. None of my friends knew me as Leibel. I was a Jew but a secular Jew. Everywhere, including in our apartment, I would be known by my English name, Lowell.

Why a name as rarefied as Lowell? My parents were born in Brooklyn, never moved out of Brooklyn their whole lives. But they had aspirations, chose names to show their upward mobility, to construct a pedigree. My brother's middle name was Merrill. And my sister is Carylann. I got Lowell with its New England patina, and as a reference to those *goyish* very American poets the Lowells—Robert Lowell, James Russell

Lowell and Amy Lowell—a family that could trace its roots to the Mayflower. Lowell was my entrée into the greater American world of names and culture, not that I could trace my roots to the Mayflower. My family was strictly shtetl.

I started Hebrew School when I was eight and I remember my parents sitting down with Rabbi Winograd in the synagogue deciding on a Hebrew name they would call me in the school. The rabbi asked my Yiddish name and when my father said Leibel, the rabbi smiled and said, naturally, my Hebrew name was Aryeh.

Why? Because Leibel means *The Roaring Lion* in Yiddish and Aryeh means *The Lion* in Hebrew. I am the Lion.

And if I had known back then, back when I was eleven, that I was The Lion, I would have stared at the librarian who accused me of lifting my father's library card and roared in her face for her sheer *chutzpah* and rudeness until she peed her pants and timidly begged my forgiveness. And then I would have grabbed my books and stormed out, only to turn back and shout, *Don't be unkind to a kid ever again.* Leibel The Roaring Lion.

Chapter 5

How I Became a Sports Writer

In my first memory I fall into a swimming pool and sit on the bottom relaxed and happy because I am two years old, if that, and don't know about drowning or dying. Then the water crashes over my head and a strong arm yanks me upward through the resisting water and there is the sun and I am laughing and, for some reason, my mom and dad look frightened, and the lifeguard holds me above his head like a trophy. His name is Jerry.

In my next memory my big brother and his friends lock me in a garage on East 18th Street in Brooklyn and it's dark and I can't get out. I can hear my brother and his friends outside laughing. I start to cry.

No one remembers life as a consecutive series of images. Important moments dominate the landscape of our lives like mountains rising above a desert, and one mountain moment for me involved Greenspan and Vazquez. Their memory stays with me even though this happened when I was eleven, give or take. The story has become an archetype in the privacy of my imagination. It was the first sporting event I covered. It defined me and imprinted itself on me.

I spent most days in the Brooklyn playground across the street from our apartment house, played ball with my friends, but also observed the older kids. *Observed* is the operative word. I was a writer in training, didn't know it. But I observed how the older kids acted and wondered about them and remembered details, and one day everyone said Greenspan and Vazquez, two big high-school tough guys, had a serious beef and would fight the next afternoon, would fight in the playground.

The day of the fight, I felt agitated in school. Couldn't concentrate, stared out the window. My teacher asked was anything wrong. I ran to the playground after school and waited around with everyone else. It was all so stylized, like ballet or opera. Greenspan and Vazquez weren't there and then they were there. Greenspan, smaller than Vazquez, approached from one end of the punchball court, Vazquez from the other. They walked toward each other slowly, both wearing pointy French-toed shoes with cleats I heard clicking on the asphalt. They were honoring the rituals of a playground fight. When they came together, they grabbed each other in headlocks—the standard fighting hold in the 1950s—but Vazquez was stronger. He slowly lowered Greenspan to the asphalt as Greenspan's face turned red. Vazquez grabbed Greenspan's hair, banged his head on the ground a few times, Greenspan said I give up and that was it. Ten seconds? They stood up and side by side walked to the men's room in the "park house," an old, smelly, dingy one-story blockhouse, and as they walked each whipped out of his back pocket a black comb and they combed their hair. When they emerged from the men's room, clean and well-groomed, the big kids chose up sides and played one game or another.

I stood there sad. I had rooted for Greenspan, the Jewish guy, and he lost. I never had fought anyone, certainly never banged a head or had my head banged. I observed and played ball. The totality of my existence. I wanted to ask Greenspan how he felt but who was I to interrogate Greenspan?

Why does this stay with me, the anticipation, the

headlock, the submission, the combs, Greenspan's sad face after defeat in front of everyone? Sadness but not resentment. Acceptance of the order of things. Acceptance of Vazquez's superiority.

Is it the danger I remember? Or the definitiveness of Vazquez's victory—Achilles humbling Hector? Or did I relate to one or the other of them?

I have had Greenspan moments in my life, rarely a Vazquez moment. Is that it?

Maybe I don't want to know. But I'm sure of one thing. When I was a sports writer and covered the big fights in Vegas, Greenspan and Vazquez paraded through my mind leading up to the bell. When I sat first row ringside in 1985 and fidgeted awaiting the start of Marvin Hagler vs. Thomas Hearns, I felt the same nerve-wracked tension, the sweaty palms, the thrill of danger, the need for a resolution, the need to be there. I felt the same for 49ers Super Bowls or San Francisco Giants or Oakland A's World Series games, or Golden State Warriors playoff games. I would cover these events, restless, agitated but experiencing the sublime, experiencing awe. Greenspan and Vazquez covered them with me.

When Greenspan and Vazquez had solved their problem, when everything returned to normal, one of the big kids, sixteen or seventeen, someone who probably would end up in jail, said to another kid, "Greenspan got his ass kicked. He's a fucking loser."

"Fucking loser," the other kid agreed.

In the innocence of my young heart I knew those two guys were the real losers, not Greenspan. He had stood up to Vazquez as Thomas Hearns stood up to Marvin Hagler in defeat, a third-round knockout. Greenspan had accepted humiliation in full view, took it, got up, made peace with Vazquez, combed his hair and moved on. There was honor in that and courage, although I couldn't express it at the time. I always have found losing more interesting than victory, believe the way people handle losing reveals their deep-down character.

And then the strangest thing happened. The guy who called Greenspan a fucking loser pointed at Greenspan playing ball with everyone else and said, "He looks fucking emaciated."

"Fucking emaciated," the other loser agreed.

Emaciated?

What did emaciated mean and how did these two morons know?

I fled the playground, sprinted across the street, ran into my apartment, grabbed from the bookcase the big heavy hardback dictionary and looked up the word emaciated.

Lots of italicized words in languages I didn't understand. I was reading about the verb, *emaciate*. Something about it dating from 1646. They could date words? 1: To cause to lose flesh so as to become very thin. 2: to make feeble.

I didn't agree about Greenspan. His color was good. He wasn't feeble. He was in touch with life. I wanted to return to the playground, find the losers and tell them I politely disagreed with their use of emaciated. But they would have said, *Go fuck yourself, kid. Get out of here or we'll kick your emaciated little ass.* So, I shut up.

At least I learned a new word.

Chapter 6

The Vacuum Cleaner Salesman

My father was impressed by the *spiel* from the vacuum cleaner salesman. The man represented Electrolux, the tops in vacuum cleaners at the time, the mid-1950s. The salesman came to our apartment one Saturday morning and set up the vacuum cleaner, which looked like a torpedo with wires and had a long hose in front to suck up *schmutz*—dirt. Unlike today's upright models, it was a cylinder parallel to the floor and moved on wheels behind the salesman like a mechanized schnauzer.

The salesman laid pencil shavings on the carpet—*Oh my*, my mother said—and the Electrolux promptly made the shavings disappear with the most soothing hum. My father was sold on the Electrolux and because he liked the machine, he liked the salesman. In an upsurge of good feeling, he asked, "What is your name, sir?"

To which the salesman replied, "Mr. Schmaltz."

My father ran out of the room. I never had seen him sprint so fast. Along with Mr. Schmaltz we waited, my older brother, my little sister, my mother and me.

"I'll be back in a minute," my mother finally said.

We waited along with Mr. Schmaltz. Waited a long time.

Finally abandoning Mr. Schmaltz in the foyer of our apartment, my brother, sister and I walked into a back bedroom where we could hear our parents. We opened the door. They weren't talking. They were laughing. And they weren't just laughing. They were dying of laughter. My father's face was wheelbarrow red. Tears streamed out his eyes and he was breathing in gasps between snorting paroxysms of laughter. Ditto for my mother.

"What's so funny?" my brother asked.

"His name is Mr. Schmaltz," my father managed to say. "Mr. Schmaltz."

As if that explained anything.

What was so hilarious about the name Schmaltz? I assumed it was a Jewish name. But everyone had Jewish names, many of them severely lacking in euphony. I grew up with kids named Snitkoff, Lipschitz, Aronowsky, Marmelstein, Plotkin and Zitnik. Schmaltz was a walk in the park compared to those.

While Mr. Schmaltz waited, I asked my father to explain.

"His name's Schmaltz," was all he could say and then he laughed like an idiot. He was the kid in school who tries to stop laughing because the teacher's fly is unzipped but the effort to stop makes him laugh even harder. My brother, sister and I started laughing too, although we didn't know what we were laughing at. Something about Schmaltz was funny.

"You have to go out to Mr. Schmaltz," my mother told my father. "You can't just leave the man there."

"I know. I know," my father said. And in good faith he started to leave the room but broke down again.

Poor Mr. Schmaltz.

It became obvious my father couldn't close the deal. My mother, God love her, returned to the hallway and bought the Electrolux, which was a trooper for many years. And then Mr. Schmaltz muttered goodbye and left.

After my father calmed down, we asked about Schmaltz.

"It means chicken fat in Yiddish," my father said. "The man's name is Chicken Fat."

Chapter 6

Somehow chicken fat didn't have the same kick as *schmaltz*. Old World Jews used it as an ingredient in chopped liver or potato latkes or for frying like Crisco. But schmaltz is more than a frying agent. It is a metaphor, as I later learned, a word with many meanings. To call a movie *schmaltzy* is to say it's overly sentimental—laying on the chicken fat too thick. A schmaltzy person is a sentimental person, cries at the sight of a dead sparrow in the street. To *schmaltz it up* is to go for the heartstrings when telling a story. In *The Joys of Yiddish* Leo Rosten gives an example of schmaltz: "The way he delivered that speech, you could cut the schmaltz with a fork."

I know all about schmaltz and schmaltzy now that I'm an old man. I should have known then, but my parents never taught us Yiddish—they wanted us to be Americans, typical of Jews my parents' age. My mother and father spoke Yiddish when they didn't want us to understand or when they were talking about my brother, sister and me. They cut us off from the language and I humbly think the reason most Jews don't speak Yiddish today is because of my parents' generation and the Holocaust. My Yiddish vocabulary is 150 words. Max.

I remember feeling sorry for Mr. Schmaltz, standing alone in the hallway with his state-of-the-art vacuum cleaner. Did he notice something was amiss? Did he hear us laughing at him? Did he feel humiliated?

Oh, cut the schmaltz, what did he care? He made the sale, didn't he?

Chapter 7

The I-Cash Man

It was a sound I didn't understand, something like *ah-caash* over and over, a loud nasal cry coming from the backyard of our apartment house in Brooklyn, loud on a Saturday morning while we relaxed in the apartment, the five of us.

Ahcaash.

"It's the I-Cash Man," my mother said.

"The I-Cash Man?" my father said. He seemed surprised.

What were they talking about?

My mother and father were smiling at the man who had entered the backyard on E. 19th Street and was walking the whole block toward E. 18th Street along an alley in our backyard. My mother threw open her bedroom window and stared at the man. She beckoned to him, and he walked over to the window. We lived on the first floor and my mother was leaning out the window talking to him in Yiddish and nodding her head. She put out her hand to him like a cop stopping traffic, telling him to wait, and turned to my father.

"Should we?" she said.

"Sure," my father said.

She motioned for the man to enter the lobby, told me to open the door for him. I was ten, maybe eleven and this would have been 1955 or 1956. I felt confused. Why was I opening the door for a man in a pork pie hat, dirty pants, a stained white shirt? He wore suspenders, no belt, the suspenders straining against his big belly. He walked on the sides of scuffed shoes, the cuffs of his pants frayed.

My mother met him at the door to our apartment and led him to the master bedroom, where my father, brother and sister waited. My brother and sister were as confused as I was. My mother opened their closet. The man stood there quietly, and I felt sorry for him, a stranger in a strange apartment, there alone at the pleasure of my parents. He waited.

My father took out a blue suit—jacket and pants. He spread the suit on their freshly-made double bed along with a few dress shirts and another pair of slacks. Meanwhile, my mother pulled out some dresses, blouses. a sweater. The I-Cash Man watched.

When my parents were done, all the clothes on their bed in a pile, the man approached and picked up the garments one by one, made clucking sounds of disapproval as he shook his head from side to side like my parents were wasting his time.

Finally, I caught on. This man was a buyer who walked the neighborhood offering cash for clothes—cash for whatever. This was new to me. I imagined my parents had grown up in neighborhoods with I-Cash Men all over the place, dirty-looking, Yiddish-speaking guys patrolling the streets, making deals.

And this delighted my parents because it brought them back to their roots in Brownsville and Williamsburg, the Yiddish-speaking Brooklyn neighborhoods they grew up in, neighborhoods I never had been to and they visited no longer. Or maybe this went further back than that. My dad's folks were from Latvia, my mother's family from Ukraine, Jews on the outskirts of society, Jews trying to make a living from nothing, I-Cash Men staying alive.

The man fingered my father's blue suit, dirt under his fingernails, and said in Yiddish it was worthless—that much

I understood. There was disdain in his voice like my parents were a couple of peasants from beyond the Pale. My father held up the suit and in English told my mother he bought it at some fancy store in downtown Brooklyn I never heard of. Then he turned to the I-Cash Man and, in Yiddish, said these were quality goods and the I-Cash Man should pay attention. The I-Cash Man pointed to a worn patch near the seat of the pants. He threw the suit on the bed like a discard. He grabbed one of my mother's dresses, rubbed the material in an almost sexual way, taking a liberty, I felt. He said something to her in Yiddish, clearly dismissive.

My mother said to my father, "I bought this dress at A&S and paid full price." A&S was short for Abraham and Strauss, a fine store on Fulton Street in downtown Brooklyn where she shopped when she wanted to make a statement. She told the I-Cash Man she bought the dress at A&S. She was speaking Yiddish, but I got the idea. He didn't respond. His silence was a tactic, making her feel insecure about her taste in clothes so he could buy low.

But it was more than that. The I-Cash Man was a reminder of where my parents came from and never wanted to be again. My mother's father, who I vaguely remembered, walked up and down the streets of Williamsburg selling paper bags to merchants. My father's mother lived in Queens with my dad's older sister. My grandmother couldn't read. Her grandchildren—my brother, sister and I—would become a doctor, the head of a preschool, and a Ph.D. from Stanford, but she was illiterate and spoke no English. When my grandmother left her Queens apartment to visit us, my aunt Anna—her daughter—attached a note to her coat with a safety pin. The note gave our address and phone number so, if my grandmother got lost in the confusing subway system, a kind stranger would read the note and direct her to the correct train.

The I-Cash Man reminded my parents of all that and of everyone trying to get an edge, squeeze out a few extra pennies. He played on that. He made them feel they hadn't made it in America. They had moved a few miles from northern Brooklyn south to Flatbush, an up-and-coming Jewish middle-class neighborhood, but they hadn't moved at all, were still the greenhorns who grew up near the delicatessens with knishes and sour pickles and kosher franks, grew up near the small *shuls* where the old religious men prayed, grew up near the stink of the sewers and the garbage on the street and the smell of piss in the public bathrooms. At first, I was excited when the I-Cash Man entered our apartment because he was a character. But now I saw him as an operator, maybe even a cultural blackmailer, and I wanted him to leave.

My parents bickered with the man in Yiddish. This had become war. By saying no or by remaining silent, the I-Cash Man was winning. My parents were losing heart, no longer enjoying the game or him. They touched their clothes, mumbled to each other, and seemed to reach an agreement.

My mother, whose Yiddish was better than my dad's, said something to the man, although I was sure he understood their English but pretended not to. Another tactic. He reached into the left front pocket of his trousers and pulled out a roll of bills. I never had seen so much money. He grabbed greasy bills from the wad and handed them to my father. Then The I-Cash Man roughly picked up the whole pile of clothes, every single item.

"Show the man out," my mother said, ice in her voice.

I walked him to our front door and opened it for him,

Chapter 7

and he walked—actually strode—out of the building. I was happy to get rid of him. When I returned to my parent's bedroom, they were talking English.

"I paid good money for that suit," my dad said, hurt in his voice. "I thought it was worth more."

"*Shah*," (Yiddish for hush) my mother said, trying to calm him. "At least we got something. I couldn't fit into that dress anyway and you never wear those clothes."

Saturday morning was usually the best time in our apartment. But the I-Cash Man had taken the fun out of the day. We went to the kitchen and, as usual, ate lox and bagels and cream cheese and a shiny hard chocolate cake from Ebinger's Bakery down the street, but we were subdued, my dad shaking his head and my mom saying the I-Cash Man was a crook and what the hell did a *schlub* (slob) like him know about good clothes, anyway.

After breakfast, I crossed the street to the playground and stayed there all day, not even going home for lunch, and returned to the apartment at dusk. I never saw the I-Cash Man again and I wonder, are there still I-Cash Men?

Something happened a few weeks later, again in our backyard, again on a Saturday morning. We heard the most beautiful singing and peered out the window. A young man was walking through our backyard from E. 19th Street to E. 18th Street, walking the whole short block, and he sang in Italian. Such singing I never heard before. It must have been opera.

He wore his black hair long with pomade and he was good looking, and certainly Italian, and he sang from the heart as he crossed the backyard. My mother opened her bedroom window, put her hand to her heart and smiled at the handsome singing young man. As he passed our window, she clapped for him, and when he exited the yard, she waved, and he waved back and disappeared. She called to my father, "Mickey, wasn't that beautiful?" It was beautiful, my dad agreed, and he seemed emotional about this man who didn't want anything from anybody except to share the joy of his song.

I thought about him after that, thought about him most of that Saturday, and concluded the Italians are just like us Jews, except they have more fun.

Chapter 8

The Cha-Cha King

I knew I was fucked when Howard King put on what he called his "dancing shoes."

It was 1956 and I was eleven years old and unsophisticated when it came to table manners and wiping my nose and music and dancing. I learned that day people are mysteries and I never can know what they think or how they perceive the world or me, all of us eternal strangers.

Howie had invited me to his house on a Friday afternoon for "a little get-together" with some girls from our elementary school—P.S. 193 on Bedford Avenue in Brooklyn, all of us in the sixth grade. The girls, all Jewish, were Saundy Kaplowsky, Ronnee Katz and the Gabel twins, JoAnn and JoEllen. I thought a get-together meant getting together. The four girls and Howie and I would play spin the bottle or post office, that game the height of sophistication, a girl in a closet sending a message to me and she and I kissing closed-mouthed on chapped lips in the closet. Or if not those games at least chocolate cupcakes and glasses of warm Canada Dry.

We walked the few blocks to his house, a duplex at Avenue I and East 29th Street and climbed the stairs to his second-floor flat. Waiting for us in the living room was his big sister Vita. Or was it Vida? She seemed nice. She showed us around, the kitchen, the parents' bedroom, Howie's bedroom and a sleeping nook for her in the living room alongside a bookcase. No bedroom for her. Primogeniture prevailed in that family.

Howie walked to his bedroom and shut the door. This I noticed and wondered about. Vita or Vida noticed me noticing and said—God, I'll never forget her words—"Howard is putting on his dancing shoes."

He had dancing shoes?

His door burst open and he glided toward the living room like Fred Astaire or Fernando Lamas, wearing a pair of brown loafers with a migraine-inducing shine, a shine that reflected the room and the ceiling. And the loafers had tassels, two on each shoe, the tassels dancing on top of his feet. And he had changed from his school pants into light brown slacks with a herringbone pattern that seemed Continental, although at that time the only idea of Continental I had was that North America was a continent floating somewhere above South America on the schoolroom map next to the blackboard.

And Howie was grinning. He cut quite a figure—was the best-looking boy in the sixth grade and he knew it. And his sister, abetting him—that's how I came to understand it—turned on the record player and inserted a disc over the spindle. There was Perez Prado playing "Cherry Pink and Apple Blossom White" and there were other songs, the words in Spanish. And Howie started whirling around the room like no one I ever saw, like Dancing with the Stars before there ever was Dancing with the Stars.

I stood there gaping in my scuffed Keds, no dancing shoes those, and Vita/Vida said, "Come on, Lowell. This is a dance party."

Now they tell me.

Howie grabbed one of the girls and, holding one arm around her chubby waist, started doing a complicated back-and-forth number with the Perez Prado sound filling the room.

Chapter 8

"That's the cha-cha," Vita/Vida informed me.

The girls Howie danced with knew all the steps and they were whirling around while I stood there like a loser telling myself—with great accuracy—Howie had set me up. I was the foil, the extra one, the uninitiated. There to make Howie look good. Why he chose me, what rivalry he thought we had I didn't know then and I can't ask now.

All the girls knew the steps. They were in the awkward stage like me, all of us wearing big gun-metal braces on our teeth and pink gum-colored bite plates, saliva collecting at the corners of our mouths—all except Howie who wore no braces because he was born perfect. The girls with the braces were dancing with each other and with Howie's sister and with Howie, going one two, one two three. Dipping their knees and sometimes spinning around. And I realized, while I had been learning baseball and stickball and punchball, all the mundane regular Brooklyn boy activities, a whole group of kids had learned dancing. An entire underground subculture secretly developing alongside me, dance covens existing, for all I knew, all over Flatbush Brooklyn, boys and girls sneaking into vacant apartments and cranking up the radio or the hi-fi and practicing the cha-cha and the mambo and God knows what else.

"You don't know how to dance, do you?" Vita/Vida said. Her voice was not an accusation. She was laying her cards on the table.

So, while all the others danced, girls with girls and girls with Howie the sellout, Howie, gorgeous and poised, Howie with golden hair he combed back with pomade, Vita/Vida took me in hand and explained the basics of one two, one two three, and I followed her, the remedial kid, the dope of the group who wanted to run out the door and bound down the steps and flee back to my block where I knew everyone and had mastered the etiquette. I followed her, dancing by the book, dancing by the numbers stiff and embarrassed. The girls didn't even look at me. Why should they? They had Howie. I was jealous of him till the day he died and after.

And while we danced, I heard Vita/Vida utter the words, "breaks."

I stared at her. She said no one could be called a cha-cha expert without knowing the breaks. Oh my God, I never had heard such a specialized word in reference to dancing. Breaks, it turned out, were the extra moves that interrupted the basic one two, one two three action and added spice and tone like an alto-sax solo in a jazz composition. Vita/Vida showed me how to throw one leg to the side while I held her right hand with my left. And sure enough I looked over at Howie and he was breaking all over the place, legs flying to one side and then the other while he deftly kept the beat. A break maniac, a superstar, and me relegated to the older sister, me with the dry mouth, me hating Howie that breakdancing bastard.

I never went to another of Howie's get-togethers although I assume he suckered others into his dance parties, a perennial Pleasure Island (see *Pinocchio*) to unsuspecting adolescent boys who became jackasses while he showed up with his dancing shoes and his sister. But there were odd things about his family. Things he told me. His father, who sold ads for the Yellow Pages, had quite the temper. Howie would sit at the dinner table and if he said something Mr. King didn't like, his father silent, brooding, hulking, would whip his left hand across the table and smack Howie in the puss like Joe Louis flashing his left jab.

Chapter 8

My father never smacked me in the face.

And there was something else Howie told me. One night his mother was changing out of her clothes into her nightgown. She was down to her slip and bra when Howie's dad glanced out the window and saw a man on Nostrand Avenue staring up at Howie's mother.

"Stay there and don't move," Howie's father ordered his mother.

She stood there backlit, silhouetted in the window, stood there as she was told while Howie's dad sneaked out of the apartment and hurried around the corner to Nostrand Avenue where he came upon the happy unsuspecting peeper and beat the shit out of him, punching him in the face several times and leaving him half-dead on the sidewalk. The dad had used the mom as bait. In spite of myself, I felt a certain amount of guilt because I imagined myself on Nostrand Avenue along with the peeper ogling Mrs. King who was quite a dish, and although technically I didn't approve of the man's behavior, I did approve of Mrs. King and I thought Mr. King could have ended the scene simply by lowering the shade, but Howie was proud of what his father did.

After the dance party, Howie always acted superior to me, which he was. A few minutes before his *bar mitzvah* at the Progressive Synagogue on Ocean Avenue, I waited outside while people drove up to the synagogue and he walked down the steps and opened the car doors and kissed his aunts and uncles with a deep-dimpled smile. I never had seen such manners, such poise, and I wondered if someone taught him that stuff or if it came naturally or if he was gaming guests for more bar mitzvah *gelt* (money).

And then a black Caddie drove up and Howie opened

the door and an old gray guy climbed out and Howie put both arms around him and kissed him on the cheek, a loud one, like the guy was his favorite uncle, and the guy spat out real saliva like a bug flew into his mouth and said, "What?" Voice disgusted. He was just some man coming to weekly *Shabbat* services. And Howie's mother ran to the car and said, "Please excuse Howard, he doesn't know his family very well." This rich-looking old Jew was not in the family and Howie didn't know and probably didn't care. Howie looked confused, embarrassed. Because I never would have made that mistake, I felt glad.

He stayed away from me in high school, probably was a dance party maven while I ran track and tried to survive adolescence. He wore designer slacks with cuffs and creases so precise and sharp they could have severed a carotid artery. When he saw me, he would say "Sigaboo." I had no idea what Sigaboo meant although later I understood it was a kind of verbal break, and he went to the University of Pennsylvania, to the Wharton School of Economics, and then I lost him. I lost him in college even though I was an undergraduate in Pennsylvania, not far from him. And I hardly thought of him as I attended graduate school in California. As we grew older, the kids from P.S. 193 and Midwood High School would contact each other, check on lives lived, but no one contacted Howie or knew where he was or what he was doing. It became a common subject. What became of Howie King the Cha-Cha King, the Wharton graduate, Howie who'd been one of us?

Ronnie Salmonson, the greatest punchball player in the neighborhood, visiting me in San Francisco from Long Island where he had been a dentist but now was retired, told me Michael Kramer once saw Howie at a distance on Wall

Street. Or thought he saw him. Michael ran to catch Howie, but Howie vanished like a specter in a Kafka novel. No one else had Howie sightings or even partial Howie sightings. And several years ago, the internet being what it is, I looked up Howard King—I don't know why—and found out he died of an apparent heart attack at age 48. A long time ago. No one could find him because he was dead.

The article, a short one from the *L.A. Times*, said Howie was an entertainment industry lawyer in Los Angeles, said he had "high-profile" clients including Steven Spielberg, Clint Eastwood, Arsenio Hall and Tom Waits. Howie had won a copyright infringement case for Stevie Wonder involving the song "I Just Called to Say I Love You." And he won a case for Tom Waits against Frito-Lay for impersonating his voice in a radio commercial. Howie also represented Walt Disney Pictures, Paramount Pictures, Warner Brothers Records and Capitol Records. He left behind a wife and three kids. And although I didn't miss him—he had not been in my life for more than fifty years—a part of my past had vanished with him without my knowing it. And I felt strange because while he lived in L.A., I lived in the Bay Area and I was a sports columnist at *the San Francisco Chronicle* and people knew who I was and, if Howie visited San Francisco—he must have—and if he picked up the paper, he would have seen my name and I doubt many Lowell Cohns exist writing sports columns, and he could have phoned me.

And I thought, no, he didn't want to phone me. He wanted *not* to phone me. From the day I saw him sitting quietly on the side of the classroom in the second grade, perfect posture, perfect profile, he held himself apart and he wasn't Brooklyn and he wasn't street and he wanted to escape. To fly away. To be other. To be anything but what we were, whatever that was. And I imagined him being lawyer to the stars, a partner in a fancy firm and living life in the fast lane and exiting fast from that life. The *L.A. Times* article didn't say if he had been happy or what he was looking for or who he really was or if he ever visited Brooklyn or what happened to his sister or if he stayed in touch with even one kid from our childhood. Those articles never do.

Guy sure could dance.

Chapter 9
Step Off

In 1956, I became an eleven-year-old tyrant. I was good at it. I'm not saying I was up there with Attila the Hun or Mussolini, real tyrant pros. But I was up there.

It had to do with P.S. 193 and being a good Jewish boy—you don't expect a good Jew to be a tyrant—well, keep reading. To begin with, P.S. 193 means Public School 193, kindergarten through sixth grade when I attended. It's still there on Avenue L and Bedford Avenue in the Flatbush section of Brooklyn, although it's now known as the Gil Hodges School for the famous Brooklyn Dodgers first baseman who lived right down the block.

Every morning before school, Miss McGrath—we called her Mugsy—would blow an ear-piercing whistle like a football coach directing tackling drills, and it meant all the little kids at P.S. 193 had to line up class by class in the concrete schoolyard and stand quietly. The schoolyard was surrounded by a chain link fence like a prison camp. Standing quietly and being quiet almost to the point of self-erasure were considered virtues by the teachers and our parents. We were among the best-behaved school kids in all of New York City—no stealing, no talking back to teachers, no throwing kids out the window. Many of my schoolmates would become doctors, lawyers, scientists, university professors and teachers. The school was almost entirely Jewish. I had one non-Jewish friend, Dennis Natale, an Italian Catholic. Years later when we had our bar mitzvahs, he bought his own *yarmulke* and could chant the prayers in Hebrew. He became a doctor.

Here's how the teachers enforced silence in the classroom. They made us sit at our desks, hands clasped, for long periods and told us not to talk. We didn't learn or read. We just sat there. I thought this request reasonable. As I look back, I imagine one teacher in particular, Miss Riley, must have had a miserable home life and needed peace and quiet at school and we eagerly gave them to her. But sitting with clasped hands was not a passive activity. We wanted to show how eager we were to please her, so we squeezed our hands together until the fingers ached and became red. I was good at this, could feel the tiny delicate bones I was crushing beneath my skin, was proud of my skill and was sure my teacher noticed.

Another teacher, even more noise averse, told us to walk on velvet shoes. Even at age seven I knew this was seriously wacko. She would demonstrate. Although she did not actually wear velvet shoes, she would mince around the classroom on her toes with an index finger pressed against her mouth meaning shush. From time to time, she would whisper so we barely heard her, "Walk on velvet shoes." Then she would order us to try. All thirty of us stood up and began tiptoeing around the room with a finger over our lips. If someone laughed, she made us do it again. Within weeks the entire class for the entire school year walked on velvet shoes, making us resemble ghouls haunting a graveyard.

So, this was the context for lining up in the schoolyard before classes began. The kids in each class stood two-by-two in a long line. If there were thirty kids, there would be fifteen rows of kids standing side by side. Got that? We were not allowed to talk or whisper or move. They allowed us to breathe, but that was begrudging. If a class fulfilled the lining-up requirements of barely appearing alive, it was

Chapter 9

awarded an E-Card, a card with a big red E on it. E meant excellent. If a class received ten E-Cards over a period of time it received one Commendation Card, a valuable commodity in our hermetically sealed little world. The class with the most Commendation Cards at the end of the school year got to leave its classroom and watch a movie in the auditorium which didn't then, but now sports a painted portrait of Gil Hodges grinning at all the quiet good P.S. 193 children.

Maybe you're thinking ahead and see the looming dilemma. Some classes never got E-Cards. Why? Because of bad behavior. Maybe some fifth-grade joker made a wisecrack saying this Commendation Card business was bullshit or started to jiggle in line just because he was ten years old and felt like jiggling. Or maybe Peter Goldstein smacked Bonnie Stone on the back of the head out of boredom. And Bonnie turned around and left-hooked him in the rib cage and he started to cry and the kids on their line began a rigorous debate about who was morally culpable, Peter or Bonnie. There had to be a way to police this retrograde behavior.

And there was. Some sixth graders were designated "Monitors," and it was their job to patrol the lineup like SS Troopers terrorizing all those Jewish kids. They would walk between class lines searching for behavior infractions, even minor ones, and if they found a miscreant, they would yell for everyone to hear, "Step off."

"Step off" were the most frightening two words of our childhood because stepping off meant publicly leaving our class line, being singled out, extracted from the herd while everyone else thought, "Thank God it's not me." The Monitor would march the poor sucker to the handball wall about twenty feet away. This had happened to me in the second grade. I did something or other and a sixth-grade Monitor loomed over me like Godzilla eye-balling Bambi. He said step off and forced me, weak-kneed, needing to pee, to the handball wall, a chipped, fading-brown wood structure. Already I was crying, snot dripping from my nose.

"Stand there," the Monitor said.

Stand there meant standing in front of the handball wall and facing the entire student body and all the teachers. Everyone stared at me. I imagined there were clucking sounds of disapproval. Standing in front of the handball wall was like being assigned to the stocks in Colonial America. Criminals back then were insulted, kicked, spat upon, even tickled. Citizens threw rotten food at them, sometimes rocks. Nothing like that happened at P.S. 193, but I was a social outcast, a pariah. I could have worn a scarlet letter. Not an "A", but an "S" for stepped off. I pictured the principal phoning my mother and saying, "See to your son, Mrs. Cohn. Today he got stepped off."

In the previous paragraph I mentioned the principal. I need to fill out his character. He wasn't your typical elementary school petty dictator overseeing his personal prison camp. He was way more.

His name was Mr. Galant and when he burst up the stairs to the stage of the auditorium on Assembly Day and stood behind the lectern, he would raise his hands and the children, kindergarten through sixth grade, stood and chanted, "Good morning, Mr. Galant." Like he was a cult leader. Then we were allowed to sit down.

What followed was exceptional. Mr. Galant was obsessed with Elvis Presley. Why, I don't know. Later in life, after I became a journalist, I might have asked him. He was probably dead by then. But after the kids monotonously said "Good morning, Mr. Galant," he would launch into a frothing monologue about the dangers of Elvis. Mr. Galant did this on a regular basis.

He criticized Elvis's grammar in "Hound Dog," although Elvis did not write that terrific song. Jerry Lieber and Mike Stoller did. And it's a fact—you can look it up—Big Mama Thornton recorded it four years before Elvis, but Mr. Galant didn't mention Big Mama, probably because he never heard of her. He was appalled by Elvis' use of double negatives, as in, "Well, you ain't never caught a rabbit/And you ain't no friend of mine."

Me, I was not confused by "ain't no" and I considered the use of ain't—clearly informal English but catchy—creative on the part of the Elvis, Lieber, Stoller trio. The words took me to the South, a place I never had been, and made me smell the collard greens and the grits even though Lieber from Baltimore and Stoller from Long Island were Jews like me.

For Mr. Galant, the bad grammar was a sure sign civilization was going to hell. Forget that Lieber and Stoller are in the Songwriters Hall of Fame and the Rock and Roll Hall of Fame. They were a bad model for upward-striving children like us.

There was more. After Mr. Galant ranted about the use of dialect—I guess you didn't pass the Mr. Galant Test, Huck Finn—well after that, Mr. Galant got down to business. He would walk to the front of the stage, and start gyrating his hips like Elvis. He said he was making fun of Elvis. And it was educational to see a man in his sixties gyrating and bopping in a navy-blue suit. Even as a child, I understood something was seriously wrong with Mr. Galant, although I didn't know what.

Now, I think he was jealous of Elvis. Maybe he wasn't

getting enough at home, or in a convoluted way wanted to be Elvis, women swooning at his feet. But I know this. Once, when Mr. Galant was doing the Elvis on stage, I glanced at Mrs. Schwartz, who taught the smart six-grade class, and her face was gray, and she was shaking her head. She must have thought, "My principal is a mad man." But what could she do? He was her boss and he had important friends at the Board of Ed. Otherwise, how did he become principal of P.S. 193, a plum assignment, a sinecure verging on early retirement?

When Mr. Galant wasn't obsessing over Elvis, he launched into diatribes against crinoline skirts. He wanted them banned, although half the girls in the auditorium were wearing them. He would pound his little fists and yell, "Degradation! Degradation!"

It was Mr. Galant who allowed the step-off system.

While he relaxed in his office fantasizing about "Hound Dog" and, perhaps, staring out the window at the stylish homes on Avenue L, and thanking God he had a school full of Jews, Gestapo Monitors were stepping off kids at an alarming rate and the handball wall became a ghetto of sniveling, crying, wailing children—a wall of shame.

I knew school wasn't supposed to be fun, but I had no idea it would be a penal colony. So, one day, it was in the fifth grade, I promised myself I would become a Monitor in the sixth grade, my final year at P.S. 193. I would be the hunter, not the hunted.

A hunter I became. After Mugsy McGrath blew her whistle, her eyes popping out of her head from the sheer exhale of it, I patrolled the class lines searching for the closet whisperers, the slouchers, the criers, the gigglers, the note passers, the coughers, the sneezers and, of course, the weak.

Chapter 9

I searched for anyone who wasn't standing absolutely still and stiff-backed. I searched for my enemies.

And I would shout in my prepubescent voice, STEP OFF!!!!!!!!!!!

It felt freaking great. What an electric charge to see the misbehaver feign ignorance.

Who me?
Yes, you.
What did I do?
You know what you did.

Such delicious power. And then to repeat the words step off, but this time in the quiet, stern voice of authority, and to see the poor sap hesitantly exit the safety of the lineup and follow me to the handball wall while everyone looked on, teachers included, to join the ranks of the humbled, the lowly, the meek, the submissive, the ashamed, the bowed down. And I was not one of them. I had made them them. P.S. 193 allowed me to do it. Encouraged me. Rewarded me.

Until the sixth grade my parents fought with me every morning because I was habitually late for school. I hated school. I hadn't finished my homework and I was sprinting through math problems in my bedroom. I wasn't dressed. I didn't have time for breakfast let alone a shower, my mother practically dragging me through the door for the five-block walk to P.S. 193.

But not in the sixth grade. I was Johnny on the spot. Finished my homework the night before, laid out my clothes the previous night, had plenty of time for scrambled eggs and toast and jam. Arrived first in the schoolyard. On the prowl.

One cold morning, I rounded a class line, lower grade. Third grade, in fact. I snuck up from behind so they couldn't see me, spotted a girl with a ponytail, dirty blond hair, whispering, giggling, enjoying herself. Flagrant violation of all that was moral and righteous. I sprinted over to her, stared in her eyes, ready for the ceremony of sin and absolution. Oh my God. My sister. I loved my sister. Her name is Carylann and I still love her. She and I are all who remain from our five-member family. As kids, we shared the same bedroom, a bookcase separating us for privacy, and at night, we went to bed the same time and raced to see who fell asleep first and she always won, breathing peacefully and happily while I lay there wondering how anyone could be so innocent and well-adjusted, although I didn't have those words then.

And now she was in my crosshairs. Her eyes were pleading. I imagined my parents at dinner that night. "Why did you step off your sister? Why did you make her cry?" I imagined begging her forgiveness. At that moment, I became a better person.

I looked past my sister to the little girl next to her and stepped her off.

Chapter 10

Farbissener

One thing you could say about Mrs. Samson, she owned a car. A 1958 state-of-the-art Buick Roadmaster, sleek black with chrome trimming, always immaculately clean and shined.

We all admired her car, my friends and I. When we played pickup games in the street the car was right there, the best car on East 18th Street. But that was the problem. The car was so there, parked along the curb on the lefthand side. We couldn't miss it with footballs—*you run to the sewer, cut left and I'll throw it to you.* Or with rubber balls if we were playing stickball. The thereness of Mrs. Samson's Buick was not a problem in itself. We were respectful and, at first at least, tried not to hit the doors or mirrors. The problem was Mrs. Samson.

Mrs. Samson was the nut on East 18th Street. Or the lunatic. Or the crazy lady. Take your pick.

Here's the thing about growing up in New York in the 1950s. There was a crazy person on every block. The crazy person was as standard as fire hydrants and streetlights, often an overworked, bedraggled housewife hanging the wash with clothespins and shouting at the street, shouting at life in general. The crazy people made things interesting. I became so accustomed to crazy people nothing about human behavior surprised me after the age of twelve.

We had two crazies on our block. In addition to Mrs. Samson, who I'll get back to in a moment—there was Mr. Grumps. That was our name for him. We'd walk past the old guy's house, and he'd yell at us. The sidewalk was his, he'd shout, and we better get lost or else. Naturally, we walked by his house as often as possible just to get a rise out of him. I imagine the poor guy suffered from Alzheimer's, but who knew about Alzheimer's back then?

There was one other crazy person in our neighborhood, a grown man. Wait, that's not fair. He wasn't crazy. He was fully grown but mentally he was a child. Even I understood that. In the playground he would take out his penis and his mother would scream at him and slap him and make him put it away. The kids made fun of him. I always wondered if the mother could protect her son better. What did I know?

Then there were the subway nuts—call them mixed nuts. One time I was riding the subway to Manhattan when a man burst into the train at the Prospect Park Station in Brooklyn. "I'm going to the moon," he announced to everyone in the car. "I've been there before."

He looked around the car at the people who averted their eyes, buried their faces in the *New York Daily News*.

"Don't you believe me?" he asked one poor woman who stared at him amazed. "I'm going to the moon. I've been there before."

Have a good trip, I whispered to myself.

And there were other characters on the subway. I won't call them nuts. Colorful characters. The guy with the accordion who played like mad in the fast-swaying car, somehow keeping his balance with nothing to hold onto. He'd play songs between stops, the uncomfortable passengers trying to look the other way, and then he'd move through the car where some softhearted folks dropped coins into his cup.

Or the tap dancer. He'd bust into the car wearing tap-dance shoes and he'd dance up a storm accompanied by a

Chapter 10

boombox turned up to blast-off level. You could hear his shoes clicking on the floor. After a dance outburst, he'd roam the car, hand outstretched for money.

Which brings me back to Mrs. Samson and her car. When we played ball in the street—me, the Wolfert brothers, Ronnie Rappaport, Jackie Weber—she would rush out of her house shrieking we'd hurt her car, a vehicle so beautiful my wife, the Californian, would call it *cherry*, meaning brand new, never used, or for a car with high mileage in mint condition. Mrs. Samson wore a housecoat that ended near the knees, and we could see her bony shins and varicose veins. She wore thin white slippers turned gray. Her long gray unwashed hair went all over the place. Her voice was shrill.

"Get away," she'd yell. "You'll ruin my car."

Then she'd stand guard in the street, protecting the car. If a ball came near the car, she'd yell, *"Oy vey,* my car."

My mother told me, "Don't talk to Mrs. Samson. She's *psychosatummel.*" As far as I know pshychosatummel was my mother's made-up word. In Yiddish *tummel* means noisy, disordered. My mom meant Mrs. Samson was psychologically disordered.

To describe Mrs. Samson, I prefer the Yiddish word *farbissener.* It means a bitter person, and Mrs. Samson certainly was bitter. About what I have no idea. I never saw a husband. Was that it?

I'll tell you what I did see. A driveway and a garage. Mrs. Samson had a long wide well-paved driveway leading to a double-car garage. She easily could have stored the Roadmaster in the driveway or garage and it would have been safe from kids playing ball in the street. But she never parked the car in the driveway or garage. She left it at the curb, exposed, unsafe.

Before long, we'd hit her car with a ball on purpose, nothing hard, just enough to get her going. Oh, one time we broke a mirror. The idea was to get her out of the house, onto the street. The pure drama of it. Mrs. Samson with her Medusa hair, Mrs. Samson running around like a hockey goalie protecting the beautiful Buick from all manner of balls.

It occurred to me Mrs. Samson devoted her life to her car. I couldn't understand this. She made her car vulnerable so she could protect it. If I had been sophisticated, a grownup, I would have walked over to Mrs. Samson and said in a polite gentle voice, "Mrs. Samson, what do you get out of leaving your car in the street? What do you get out of going crazy every time we play ball? What is the payoff for you?"

But I didn't know about such things then. What I did know, I could hit her windshield with a short pass to the flat. And I did. Happily. Poor addled farbissener.

Chapter 11

Sex on the Go

We wanted to see female breasts. We wanted to see vaginas, although we used the crudest terms for those parts of the female anatomy. We were twelve and hungry with zero experience and zero opportunity, and that took us to Coney Island, specifically to the Tornado Roller Coaster.

The Tornado was not the best roller coaster in Coney Island. Everyone knew that. The Cyclone was the best. On the Cyclone you felt your Nathan's hotdog and root beer rising in your gorge as the roller coaster climbed slowly and haltingly up the first hill and you wondered if this wooden antique of a structure would blow apart under you, and then you'd reach the top and the roller coaster just waited there, and then it moved, moved downward and the world sprang to warp speed and the scream rushed out of your mouth and you'd feel that lightness in your testicles as you plunged down that first hill, eighty-five horrifying feet at sixty miles an hour.

That was the Cyclone, what they call The Big Momma of Coney Island.

But, as we rode the few stops on the Brighton Line subway train from the Avenue M station in Brooklyn south toward Coney Island we weren't thinking Cyclone. We were thinking Tornado, an underachiever by roller-coaster standards. It had no death-defying first hill. It had no death-defying anything.

The Tornado with its wooden track and steel structure

was built in 1926, predating the Cyclone by one year. Arson burned most of it down in 1977 and the poor dear got demolished a year later.

But this is 1957 and I'm on the Tornado with my friends, frantically awaiting the first hill. Not for the thrill of plummeting down—there is no such thrill—but for the moment of hesitation when the roller coaster briefly stands there at the poised point between up and down. And then I look left over my shoulder. And my friends look left. We look down at a distant rooftop. We get a fleeting glimpse, a second, maybe two seconds of the rooftop far below the first hill of the Tornado.

What do we see on the rooftop far below the first hill of the Tornado?

Naked women. That's what we see. We see freaking naked women on a rooftop far below the first hill of the Tornado.

Why do we see naked women on a rooftop far below the first hill of the Tornado?

Because the rooftop has a *mikvah*.

What is a mikvah?

A mikvah is a ritual bath religious Jewish women take at the end of their period. There are other reasons for a mikvah, but the end of the menstrual cycle gives you the idea. My mother was not religious and, as far as I know, never attended a bathhouse for a mikvah.

What do we observe when we see naked women on a rooftop far below the first hill of the Tornado?

What we don't see are babes with young perky breasts and silk-smooth skin and bitable asses and flowing hair and that lazy sexual look we'd come to love. We don't see actress Suzanne Pleshette who, according to my Aunt Sarah, grew up in her apartment building in Brooklyn. Suzanne Pleshette is a babe. A Jewish babe. But she is not at the mikvah in Coney Island.

What we see are middle-aged Jewish women immersed in water or waddling around the rooftop wrapping towels around their heads or folding towels around their waists. If we're lucky we catch a glimpse of fat tummies, bloated thighs, sagging boobs. We see the darkness you know where. This is what we see for the instant the Tornado is suspended between rising and falling. Screams of joy rush out of our mouths and we're punching each other and slapping the metal safety railing over our laps and we're yelling, "You see those giant tits? Are they great or what?"

And then the Tornado moves and performs its ritual fall, and the women vanish, and the Tornado ride isn't ever exciting. Except when it's over, we pay for another ride. And another. And another.

Chapter 12

A Fast-Moving Car

I was the only person on Earth who could fly. I knew that for certain. And flying was delicious. I was flying above Avenue L in Brooklyn, flying towards Bedford Avenue. I felt free and I was flapping my arms and they worked like wings, just like wings, and I was swooping and diving and roaring to the sky. True, the world looked different. Long streaks of finger painting, mostly grays and blacks, although a deep red color, almost purple, intruded on my flying and I heard a screech, but I didn't care. I was a twelve-year-old who could fly.

Then I turned over in my bed and pulled up the covers, but the bed was hard and cold. I opened my eyes. I lay on the sidewalk outside my old elementary school, P.S. 193, which I hadn't attended for a year because I was in junior high school, and I saw people standing over me. Someone had covered me with a blanket. My big brother Robert, home from college, was kneeling over me and holding my hand and looking scared.

"Can you move your legs?" he asked.

Why would Robert ask that?

Panicked, I tried to move my legs. They moved.

"Robert, what happened?"

"You were hit by a car."

That explained the flying. I started to cry.

A woman took a makeup mirror from her purse. "Do you want to see your face?" she asked. I said yes. She moved the mirror to my face. I looked. It was a smear of blood,

blood all over my eyes, blood on my nose and cheeks. A blood painting. My face didn't look like me, it was red and swollen, like someone had hit it with a baseball bat. I wondered why the lady, who now was smiling, had shown me my face. Was she some kind of nut? I started crying even harder. *Will I ever look like me again? Will I be a freak for life?* It would take months for the cuts and abrasions to heal, and my friends called me Scarface.

I cried until the ambulance arrived. They put me in the ambulance. Robert rode with me, said my parents would meet us at Kings County Hospital. Robert, who would grow up to be a doctor, asked if I had a headache. I said I had a hell of a headache. Robert said I had a concussion.

In the hospital my parents tried to cheer me up, but they spoke in whispers. My mother, a New York City teacher, said the principal of P.S. 193 had phoned her. She worked at a different school, but she knew him. Teachers were a small community. The principal had told her, "Eve, it will be a miracle if he lives."

"He's an idiot," my mother said to my father. She hissed the S in *he's*, the S pure hatred and disgust.

My mother saw I would live. My father wore a fedora. Men wore fedoras in those days—this would have been 1957—and he looked serious and official. Later, I learned the crash had been my fault. It was the first day of spring break and in a hurry to play softball with my friends, I sped through a red light on my Schwinn. The driver of the deep red car was okay. I felt guilty. I still feel guilty.

While my parents hovered and the nurses took my vitals, doctors rushed a man to the adjoining bed in the Emergency Room. I heard the man ask why he was there.

The doctor said, "Sir, you've lost part of your leg."

The man groaned a deep wretched sound I never heard before.

"How much of my leg have I lost?" the man asked.

"From an area just below your kneecap," the doctor said.

"Oh my God," the man said.

I saw the bloody jagged stump. I stared. The world returned to gray again and my headache got worse. A nurse noticed my horror, grabbed the curtain near my bed and pulled it around me. I was inside the curtain with my parents, but I heard the man crying.

That man will never be the same, I told myself. *What must it feel like never to be the same and to know it?*

I ask myself: what is this story about—my car accident or the man with the severed leg?

Chapter 13

Bar Mitzvah Season

It was bar mitzvah season in my Jewish neighborhood, the Midwood section of Flatbush Brooklyn. All my friends and I were turning thirteen and there were bar mitzvahs galore every weekend, kids having to divvy up Saturday bar mitzvah dates so there wouldn't be conflicts, so friends wouldn't have to choose which bar mitzvah to attend. The year was 1958.

The morning of my bar mitzvah was warm for November. My father, mother, sister, brother and I walked two blocks to the synagogue, me wearing my new bar mitzvah suit, a herringbone affair. I was wondering if I would be a man when the service ended. You turn thirteen and say the prayers, you're a man taking responsibility for your life, committed to living the Jewish tradition. The bar mitzvah celebrates this coming of age, but I didn't feel like a man. I was five feet tall, weighed about a hundred pounds without a sniff of puberty. I had a habit of wiping my nose with my right hand.

Once in the synagogue, my father, brother and I walked to the front of the room while my mother, sister and Aunt Sarah sat in the back behind a curtain. This was an Orthodox shul and women stayed hidden. My mother didn't complain.

Let's leave the women sitting patiently behind the curtain for a moment while I tell you about David Aronowsky's bar mitzvah. It was bar mitzvah season for David, too, and his bar mitzvah was the *piece de resistance* of bar mitzvahs. Like me David was a shrimp and weighed as much as a giant prawn, but there was one difference. His father had dough and liked to flash it around.

Mr. Aronowsky owned some business or other and he drove flashy cars—lots of chrome and big grilles and fins and electric windows that flowed up and down with the touch of a button. In David's basement in a house the father had custom built on an oversized lot across the street from Madison High School which David eventually would attend, they had installed a soda fountain where we could make ice cream sodas and milk shakes. The soda fountain was a monument to materialism, but it was also, I think, a way to make David popular. There was a state-of-the-art hi-fi system in the basement on which the dad played Redd Foxx records. David and I secretly listened to the records because Redd Foxx was bawdy.

David told me the plans for his bar mitzvah. He would have a regular bar mitzvah service on a regular Saturday at the East Midwood Jewish Center, a famous Conservative synagogue with Renaissance Revival architecture. They filmed the interior synagogue scenes for *The Marvelous Mrs. Maisel* at the East Midwood, a block from my family's apartment. A week or two after the bar mitzvah, David's father would rent a bus and transport family (*mishpocheh*) and friends to Lakewood, New Jersey, where he'd take over an entire hotel and put on the biggest, fattest spread anyone this side of the Catskills had ever seen. That put David in a power position. Weeks leading up to the Lakewood extravaganza David would routinely disinvite friends to the Lakewood trip for the slightest provocation. If someone didn't choose him first for a game of punchball, disinvited. If someone said something snotty, disinvited. And sometimes friends would get disinvited for no reason at all.

Chapter 13

During school lunches the primary topic of conversation was whom David had disinvited that day. Everyone wanted a piece of Lakewood and if you got disinvited—thank goodness I never did—you'd have to kiss David's ass until he reinvited you. Which he always did. At Lakewood we mostly hung around the indoor swimming pool which had the humidity of Miami and at night we ran around the hotel halls giggling hysterically like the children we were.

All of which means David's bar mitzvah was for show. They all were for show, mine included. Our parents were first-generation Americans, offspring of pushcart peddlers and tailors and people who slaved in sweatshops. Lavish bar mitzvahs proved my parents' generation had arrived. The after-party for my bar mitzvah took place in a huge ballroom with giant chandeliers at the Hotel St. George in fancyshmancy Brooklyn Heights. I don't think my parents understood the irony of having a bar mitzvah reception at the St. George where my parents mostly schmoozed with other parents and business associates, and we kids were spectators. It was my big day, but I felt like a supporting character. The presents I received were mostly cash in special bar mitzvah envelopes and my parents put all that money into my college fund.

The reception for Howie King's bar mitzvah took place in his living room where waiters in uniforms dished out the catered food. Howie's parents gave each boy a set of gold cufflinks, put the cufflinks at our place settings, a nice touch. I heard one kid say to another, "This is better than what Mrs. Cohn gives us for bar mitzvah presents." It was true. My mom got a deal on those traveling kits for toiletries you fit in a suitcase. They were imitation leather and looked cheap and she gave them to everyone. I never thought about the cheapo traveling kits until that moment, and then I didn't think about them long because when I looked back at my plate the cufflinks were gone. I searched the table, then on my hands and knees looked under the table. No cufflinks. I told Mrs. King about my cufflinks and she ordered all the waiters to empty their pockets, which they grimly did with a sense of moral outrage. No cufflinks turned up but to this day I'm sure a *gonif* (thief) waiter grabbed mine.

Let's return to my bar mitzvah—I think my mother, sister and Aunt Sarah have waited long enough behind the curtain. My synagogue was much smaller than The East Midwood. It was called the Ocean Avenue Synagogue although it was two blocks from Ocean Avenue. My parents probably sent me to Hebrew School there because they got a deal on tuition just as my mom got a deal on traveling kits.

It was a strange shul when you consider the family that ran the synagogue lived there. I never fully understood this. The synagogue was a converted single-family home, the bottom floor consisting of the house of prayer and a small classroom where I attended lessons with boys named Pinchuk, Plotkin and Pinsky. The Klayman family, which had the franchise on the synagogue, lived on the upper floors, a private space none of the students ever visited.

Rabbi Klayman was a good-natured yarmulke-wearing man who taught the upper-grade classes in the Hebrew School. He had a day job as a teacher at Morris High School in the Bronx. When I was twelve or thirteen, I asked Rabbi Klayman if he wore a yarmulke at Morris High and he said no, which bothered me.

Rabbi Klayman was not devoted to teaching the way teachers are. Instead of drilling down on prayer or Jewish history or Talmud, he challenged our pre-bar-mitzvah class to a game. Holding a stopwatch, he would shout GO! Each of us in turn had to recite the Shema Yisrael as fast as possible, just slamming through the Hebrew words.

The Shema is the most important prayer for Jews, who are supposed to recite it twice a day. It captures the monotheistic essence of Judaism and begins with the dramatic call: *Hear, O Israel, The Lord our God, the Lord is One.* Kenny Marshall held the land-speed record for the Shema, reciting the entire 245-word prayer in one breath, although at the end his face was purple, and I thought he'd fall down in a fit and start twitching and they'd have to insert a No. 2 pencil between his upper and lower teeth so he wouldn't bite off his tongue. Rabbi Klayman said Kenny did a good job.

Rabbi Klayman's wife, Mrs. Klayman, taught the beginner classes. She didn't like me because I acted bored because I was bored. She never told us what the Hebrew words meant and, although I could read Hebrew right to left in that foreign alphabet, I could not understand the words. Mrs. Klayman—and many Hebrew teachers of her generation—taught us, smart, eager-to-learn boys, to be Jewish parakeets reciting meaningless sounds.

One time Mrs. Klayman told our class she had walked past a Chinese restaurant. The door to its basement, the door through which deliveries arrived was open and Mrs. Klayman smelled the Chinese food. She said the stink made her nauseous. She told us never to eat at Chinese restaurants. I liked Chinese food and privately thought she had a prejudice although I did not have the word *prejudice* at that time.

The Klaymans had several children, I think. I'm sure there was a son my age named Earl. Being named Lowell,

I'm in no position to judge an Earl. On the other hand, I wasn't the son of a rabbi and Hebrew teacher. Earl?

In describing the Klayman family, I've left out the Big Kahuna. He was Rabbi Winograd, father of Mrs. Klayman and the big-deal rabbi at the Ocean Avenue Synagogue. We rarely saw him during the day. In his absence he was a presence. I imagined him on some upper floor of the private quarters discussing Torah with God himself.

Late in the afternoon Rabbi Winograd would descend from the ethereal realm to conduct afternoon prayers, and that created a problem. To perform a proper service, he needed a *minyan*, a quorum containing at least ten worshippers at least thirteen years old. In our case, it had to be ten men — remember my mother, sister and Aunt Sarah relegated to life behind the curtain. We were an Orthodox synagogue and there weren't many Orthodox Jews in our neighborhood — most were Conservative or Reform — and it was difficult for Rabbi Winograd to round up ten live ones, usually old men with tobacco-stained beards. Before he could start services, the rabbi would send the worshippers into the street like a press gang to buttonhole strangers for a minyan.

During Saturday services, worshippers would drink the *kiddush* wine as a benediction and later when people were leaving the synagogue, I observed Rabbi Winograd drinking the leftover wine glass by glass. He must have enjoyed the rest of each Saturday.

And that brings me to my bar mitzvah service. One moment sticks with me more than sixty years later. My father was called to the *bimah* (podium) to perform a Torah blessing. This walking to the Torah and saying the prayer is called an *Aliyah* (going up) and it is a great honor. My father

Chapter 13

was to recite the first Aliyah—there are seven. But my dad was legally blind and could not read the words. Someone kindly printed in extra-large type a transliteration of the Hebrew and my father, slowly, haltingly got through the prayer. I felt proud of him and loved him then and love him now.

Because we were an Orthodox synagogue, I chanted my Haftarah with my back to the congregation. The Haftarah is a selection from *Prophets* I learned to sing according to an ancient melody, but no one at the synagogue told me that I was reading from *Prophets*, why I was reading from *Prophets*, what my selection said or why it meant something special to Jews or to me, the bar mitzvah boy. At the most important moment of my young life, I was a spiritual blank.

Rabbi Klayman, the younger rabbi, told me when to start and when to stop at various stages of the service, and I sailed along singing this foreign tongue which made no sense to me. When I was done, he said I did a good job, although I twice had lost my place.

And then it was time for old Rabbi Winograd to address the congregation, the men in the front of the room, the women behind the curtain, and my twenty or so friends there for my bar mitzvah. I expected Rabbi Winograd to discuss my Haftarah portion, explain its significance to a modern audience. Or maybe talk about our ineffable God and the gifts the Almighty has bestowed on us. Or maybe the Holocaust. This was 1958 and the Holocaust was present in the minds of every person there. Or the land of Israel, and how Jews were creating a country in the desert. But Rabbi Winograd didn't go to any of those places. He talked about crime in Brooklyn.

Crime was bothering him. Especially crime against

young people—children like my friends and me. The rabbi, who came from Eastern Europe, spoke in a heavy accent. Yiddish obviously was his first language, English his second or maybe third. In a voice filled with grief and moral condemnation, he said children in Brooklyn were being *kidnipped*.

I thought I heard the guy wrong. Or maybe it was like reading a book and there's a typo the proofreader missed. It happens. So instead of kidnapped it came out *kidnipped*. The rabbi, a man of learning, merely misspoke one vowel. Chuck him a break.

He kept going on about injustice toward children and he was doing well. And then he said it again. *Kidnipped*. This was no verbal typo. The man thought kidnapped was *kidnipped*.

Let me be clear. He pronounced kidnapped k-i-d-n-I-p-p-e-d.

He referred to the kidnappers as *kidnippers*.

There was more. He inserted a high nasal "Y" after the K and before the "I," so it sounded like *kyidnipped* and *kyidnippers*.

I sat there frozen. It was the day I became a man, and the exalted rabbi was slaughtering the word kidnapped. I hoped no one else noticed. Except, my friend Stuie Kucker, seated near me, started giggling. And so did Peter Goldstein and Danny Gover and Glenn May. Even Dennis Natale laughed, and he was Italian Catholic. All my friends were laid out with laughs and snorts. Oy vey.

My poor father pretended to cough to cover up his laughing. From behind the curtain, I could hear snickers and outright guffaws from the women. Rabbi Winograd didn't hear the laughter or ignored it because he kept going, really laying into the word *kidnipped*.

This was the revered rabbi? Thirteen-year-old me wanted to *plotz*.

Finally, thank God, Rabbi Winograd ran out of steam, wrapped up his sermon and we all piled out of the synagogue and headed for the reception at the Hotel St. George.

Within a year of my bar mitzvah, I forgot how to read Hebrew. Between Rabbi Klayman with his Shema race and Mrs. Klayman never translating the words and Rabbi Winograd murdering English, they stole my heritage from me. That was the worst *kidnipping* of all.

Chapter 14

The Never-Ending Importance of the Bunny Hop

My cousin Alison Bernstein died June 30, 2016. She was the daughter of my mother's younger sister, Beverly, and I was older than Alison by a year-and-a-half. She was extraordinary. After she graduated from Vassar in 1969, Vassar made her a trustee of the college at age twenty-two. At the time, her dad, my Uncle Bob, told a reporter writing an article on the young Vassar trustee, "It's okay with me as long as I don't have to pay for a building."

She was a vice president at the Ford Foundation where she worked 1983 through 2010, and she was a dean at Princeton and Rutgers. And merely keeping up with her took my breath away. A few weeks before she died of cancer, I flew to New York from California to be with her. Just be with her. I ordered a jumbo pizza for dinner on a Friday night—Alison couldn't cook or eat—and over the weekend we watched nonstop episodes of "Law and Order," Alison in bed, me lying next to her, holding her hand, eating the pizza.

In September 2016, the Ford Foundation hosted a ceremony for Alison in their big auditorium, an homage to her extraordinary life, the room packed with people who loved her, many of them famous. I was one of the speakers along with Gloria Steinem and Anna Deavere Smith and others. This is what I said.

I'm Alison's cousin Lowell Cohn and I want to tell you how she led the bunny hop at my bar mitzvah reception.

That was November 1958 at the Hotel St. George in Brooklyn. She was eleven.

The bar mitzvah itself took place at a synagogue on Avenue J in Flatbush Brooklyn. Then we all jumped in cars for the drive north to the St. George in Brooklyn Heights. We would have driven right past the apartment house Alison lived in her first few years. You might think of her as Alison from Roslyn, Long Island, or Upper Brookville or the Upper West Side or the Hamptons, all places she lived. But she first lived on Avenue H in Brooklyn right near the Long Island Railroad tracks.

At my bar mitzvah reception the usual things happened. I got introduced along with my parents and brother and sister. They cut a cake. Said a prayer. Those kinds of things. I know all this because I have an old, grainy eight-millimeter film of the bar mitzvah which I've watched several times the past few weeks to see Alison then.

In the film, I see Alison walk to the middle of the large ballroom. Obviously, music has started but the film has no sound. One thing is absolutely clear. It's bunny hop time.

Alison starts dancing with the biggest smile on her young face. My little sister Carylann is right behind Alison, holding onto Alison's waist. They dance. Alison is wearing a ponytail which bobs up and down with every step she takes. She's in a white dress with a black velvet vest. It looks Tyrolean. She dances. She and Carylann grin.

For a while it's just the two of them. Then the women in the room attach themselves to the line. They are up for it. They are laughing. They are mostly New York City school teachers because my mother and Alison's mother and our Aunt Sarah—all sisters—were New York City school teachers. Salt of the Earth. And they are dancing behind Alison.

Chapter 14

I want to describe the bunny hop so you won't confuse it with the hokey pokey. Let's get this straight because Alison would settle for nothing less.

Everyone forms a conga line. Everyone dances holding onto the hips of the person in front. They tap the floor two times with their right foot, then with their left foot, then they hop forwards, backwards, and finally three hops forward. And on and on.

Now, I come to the important part. The first person in the line guides the group around the floor. Meaning she has great responsibility, has to show daring and good judgment and the right dance moves. And above all else leadership.

Alison.

Classic Alison.

The pure joy of it, Alison.

When I look at the video, I think, "Of course, Alison would be the leader. Even then. It came naturally to her, and everyone knew it and followed. Happily."

So, Alison and my sister and the women are dancing. Alison leads them around the room, snakes around the room. Avoids tables. Going strong. Having a blast.

And then the men jump onto the line, the men so reserved in those years. But that day at the Hotel St. George in 1958 the line grows as the men join in and tap their feet and hop. They are teachers, principals, some lawyers and doctors and businessmen in those serious gray suits from the serious 1950s, the men with serious gray faces not used to laughing or being silly or being led. The men throw off their gray exteriors and get into it behind Alison. The whole room dancing now.

It's like Alison is leading the entire New York City Board of Education. And everyone is smiling because Alison is good at this and, in case you haven't done it lately, the bunny hop is fun.

Leading up to my bar mitzvah I had spent a weekend at Alison's house on Carriage Lane in Long Island. That weekend she told me what syncopation means. She told me the universe ends somewhere out there in space. We sat in her attic where her dad, Bob Bernstein, wrote Superman comics. On his typewriter you could see dialog between Clark Kent and Lois Lane and Jimmy Olsen, not to mention Perry White shouting, "Great Caesar's ghost!"

Alison and I sat in the attic trying to imagine what was on the other side of the universe until we both got headaches and felt nauseous, and her mom—my Aunt Beverly—gave us two aspirins apiece and told us not to think of silly things.

This episode, naturally, was years before I was teaching a creative writing class in the evenings at a community college in Oakland, California. And Alison was visiting me and wanted to attend the class because she was interested in education of any kind and at any level and wanted to see what went on at a community college in California.

I was teaching the short story "A Couple of Hamburgers" by James Thurber, as I recall, and Alison, who was sitting quietly on the side of the room, sighed or groaned and shot me a look. She disagreed with something I had said. The students noticed. I tried to shut her up. Not a chance.

"Let's hear from the cousin," the students shouted in unison. And then they said it again. "Let's hear from the cousin."

Alison, the cousin, took over the class. Brilliantly. And I would have felt like a hamburger or a giant meatball or an entire meatloaf except she deftly and sweetly handed back the class to me as only Alison could. On the way out of the room that night she said, "Real education took place there tonight, Lowell. It wouldn't be any better at Columbia or Stanford."

I was impressed. I had no idea. Every time I met that class after that, the students would say, "Where's the cousin?" as if that was her name. The Cousin. I tried to explain The Cousin lives in New York, but they didn't want to hear about it.

But I come back to the video of my bar mitzvah in 1958 and Alison leading a horde of dancing people, leading with gusto and style and joy. And the dance ends and Alison dances still, dances all by herself, can't stop, dances across the floor, dances out of the frame. Dances into eternity.

And I think, "Dance, Alison. Dance for everyone in that video. Dance for everyone in this room right now, the people who know you and love you. Dance for all of us. Dance your beautiful heart out."

Chapter 15

The Price of a Pea Coat

Do you remember pea coats?

In Brooklyn in 1961 when I was fifteen, pea coats were the rage with their dark blue heavy wool and their dual sets of buttons and their large collars and the coat resting at mid-thigh, all of which suggested a pseudo-nautical theme and made the wearer—me—look like an extra in *Mutiny on the Bounty*. I wanted a pea coat because, although the orthodontist had, thank God, wrenched the braces off my teeth a few years earlier, I was still an undersized dweeb. Everyone else wore pea coats and I wanted one, too, so I could belong. Whatever belong meant.

My parents bought me one. It cost about fifty dollars, a big number in 1961. They understood my need and indulged me, although there wasn't much money in our little apartment, and my brother and sister also needed clothes and weren't begging for pea coats.

When I wore my pea coat, I was engulfed by the heavy fabric, and I looked good—that's what I thought—and I felt confident. Self-contained. Not that I'd ever been on a ship, or even in a canoe. We lived a few subway stops from Coney Island and the Atlantic Ocean, which amounted to something, I guess. Later I would write my doctoral thesis on Joseph Conrad with all his sea storms and loony sailors, so maybe this coat was foreshadowing. Or maybe I'm blowing smoke.

In high school, I was not a joiner. Midwood High School had an annual Sing. Talented kids created songs and skits and presented them in the big auditorium on Sing Night, but I never joined Sing or went to Sing or cared about Sing. I'm sure Sing didn't care about me. I didn't join the Literary Club or the newspaper—it rejected me—or the Spanish Club. But I joined one group. I joined the track team.

Track you wonder. I liked running and it was simple, something just about everyone can do, and it doesn't involve studying the isosceles triangle. I was reasonably fast for a five-foot-seven, hundred-thirty-pound kid who had skipped the eighth grade and was now a high-school junior, a tadpole still in the larval stage.

On the day in question, I grabbed my track bag which contained my shorts and Midwood T-shirt and sneakers and a book of irregular Spanish verbs I was memorizing for a test, and I put on my pea coat.

"You're not wearing *that* coat?" my mother said.

"What's the big deal?" I said. "I wear it all the time."

My mother shook her head and wished me luck in the track meet.

In the winter it was too cold to run outdoors, so on Saturday afternoons I took the subway to an armory way north in Manhattan in a neighborhood I barely knew, the armory a big solid stark building with a large floor on which they'd laid down a wooden track, and in which, upon entering, you were assaulted by the smell, the overwhelming essence of oil of wintergreen which wasn't so much a smell as a medium we walked through and ran through and breathed. It was a world of spearmint leaves, those little candies we bought in the movie theater along with Necco wafers. But now the whole world was wintergreen, an ointment which

Chapter 15

came in tubes with various names, an ointment you spread on your thighs to get them hot to increase the blood flow so you could run fast, your legs pounding on the floor-board track, and fans from all the New York high schools—parochial schools included—smacking the floor and walls, cheering on their teammates.

Of course, the first time I eagerly applied oil of wintergreen, I accidentally smeared it on my scrotum—who knew?—and levitated from the searing-cold-searing-hot spasm that shot through you know where. Oh my God. And there were Black runners. I never had seen so many Black people. They came from Boys High and Wingate and Erasmus and spoke an accent I couldn't penetrate and, God, they could run. High school track in New York City was a straightforward enterprise. You ran fast, you won. You ran slow, you lost. Period.

I mostly lost. Which means I was a novice. The system was elegant in its brutal simplicity. If you won a medal, you were considered an "open" runner and thereafter had to compete against other open runners. Before you won a medal—if you ever did—you were a novice runner. Winning your first medal was called breaking your novice. Do you spy the sexual subtext?

On this day, I would break my novice. That's what I believed. Our coach was a man named Eisenberg, a congenital yeller with a red face that turned deep scarlet when he shouted. I once heard him confide to our team manager, "We have nothing on this track team," meaning my friends and I were little Jewish losers. Not exactly a great motivator that Eisenberg. He coached the Midwood football team and barely bothered with us.

Eisenberg entered us in the mile relay, each member of

our team running a quarter mile, which is a bitch. It's longer than a sprint but you have to sprint anyway, and at the end, your lungs burn and your thighs quiver. My best friend Stuie and I were part of the relay team. I ran the first lap because I had a fast start, and I liked the one-on-one competition only the first runner experiences. Everyone else begins with a lead or starts from behind after receiving the baton. I was a loner and still am and liked being on my own reacting fast-twitch to the gun.

Eisenberg always had us run the relay, not individual sprints, because he reasoned, if we won medals, we could break four novices at once. And we were good, mostly because we had perfected the hand-offs one to the other, that was Lowell Cohn to Stuie Kucker to Joel Cohen to Paul Cohen, a relay team of Jews. Give us a few more and we could have formed a minyan right there in the wintergreen armory.

We were assigned the first heat. When the gun cracked that day, I took the lead, the world all lights and smears, nothing in focus, no sounds, except my breathing and running. I ran cautiously at first because I was afraid of the distance, of dying at the end—not literally—but as I ran no one challenged me and I felt myself pulling away from the others. This was new. And then I took a risk, the biggest risk of my young life. I began to run as fast as I could. To hell with caution. My whole life had been cautious. I risked running out of breath, doubling over from fatigue, as I sprinted twice around that tiny two-hundred-twenty-yard indoor track, half the size of a regulation outdoor track. I ran. I forgot about the invasion of puberty which haunted me, my acne, my crummy posture, my adolescent body odor, the onset of my tribal big nose. I ran toward something. Or maybe I ran away from something. I ran.

Chapter 15

I handed Stuie the baton in first place—I could swear Stuie smiled at me—and he increased our lead, and by the time the two Cohens had run we lapped one team and came in first in our heat. One coach from another school, who'd heard Stuie and me worrying about living through the sheer effort of surviving four-hundred-forty yards, said, "You guys were great. I don't know why you were shitting pickles."

There were many other heats in the novice mile relay that day, and we kept track of the winners' times. We slowly fell from first place to second to third and finished fourth out of all those teams. Fourth place made us proud, except they awarded only three medals, and we were out in the cold. But Stuie, an optimist—he still is—said forget not winning a medal. Soon we'd be competing in the Brooklyn Champs, a meet with fewer competitors and, according to Stuie, we'd win easy. "They give out medals as big as Clark Gable's ears," he said. Not that I ever got near Clark's ears. I never broke my novice in high school.

Now we were on the subway traveling home after the meet. It was late because Stuie and I, who lived across the street from each other, stayed to see the finals in the open 100-yard dash and 220-yard dash, and to hear the loud cheering that vibrated our eardrums, and to wonder what it felt like to be sprint heroes like high-school legends Paul Anthony and Mel Posey.

There were three of us on the train car, a subway line we didn't know, Stuie and I and Hameroff, a boy with a man's body. Hameroff and I had attended the same Hebrew School and I knew him in the way you know people who live lives parallel to yours. He passed through my life at that time and then I never saw him again. I liked Hameroff, although he was goofy in ways I couldn't understand. He was fast enough to be an open runner, but something always went wrong. He crashed into other runners around the 220 turn and fell down or ran onto the infield, an instant disqualification, and when he talked, he mumbled. I never asked for clarification because I had issues of my own.

Hameroff, Stuie and I were sitting on two rattan benches on the subway train, the rattan the color of old straw. Hameroff was next to the window, Stuie next to him, and I sat opposite facing them. The car was overheated—in those days the New York subway was either too hot or too cold. I took off my pea coat and laid it gently in my lap and listened to the metal wheels grind the tracks and I read the names of stations foreign to me.

Stuie and I were quiet, basking in the afterglow of coming in fourth among fifty or so teams, but Hameroff seemed annoyed. He had run a sprint and, although he should have won, he didn't even place. He grabbed the pea coat from my lap. He inspected the coat. With his right hand he shoved the coat out the partially-open window of the speeding subway train and held it there.

"Lowell, I'm holding your coat out the window," he said.

I had noticed.

"Give me back my coat," I said. I tried to be calm.

"What, you don't trust me?" he said, grinning.

"I want my coat back."

"Do something about it," he said.

Fat chance. He outweighed me by eighty pounds. As his hand stuck out the window, coat attached, I wondered why he took my coat. Maybe he was pissed he was still a novice like Stuie and me. Or maybe he was jealous I had such an elegant garment. Or maybe holding pea coats out subway windows with the express train going fast is something *schmucky* adolescent boys do.

He held the coat out the window a long time. My mouth was dry. I felt he was holding me out the window. I felt myself knocking against the outside of the train in the underground wind rush, traveling faster on those gleaming tracks than I'd run on the armory track.

I waited patiently for him to hand over the coat, and I would thank him, and we would laugh—although I'd hate him for life. And then his face went from healthy pink to death white. His mouth opened and I saw deep inside. Edvard Munch's *The Scream*.

"What?" I shouted.

He pulled his right hand from the open window and showed me. Bare fingers. No coat.

"It fell out of my hand," he said.

Fell out of his hand. Onto the tracks.

Then he said this. "I can't buy you a new coat. My mother is sick, and we don't have money." His voice pissed. At me.

Let me get this straight. Because I had failed to retrieve my coat by either strangling him or sticking a switchblade between his ribs, I was the villain of the piece who'd put his mother and whole family at the poor-house door.

Stuie looked at me and the look said this guy is fucking crazy. Stuie said, "Let's get off at the next station and tell the guy in the booth what happened." Stuie and I got up to leave. Hameroff sat there.

"You're not coming with us?" I asked.

"I have to go home," he said, not meeting our eyes.

I hated him for his stupidity and carelessness and indifference and for losing the pea coat, the one thing that me made me special, that made me me. Stuie and I exited the train, Stuie leading me, a zombie. It was one of the kindest things anyone ever did for me. We walked to the man in the booth, the man behind an iron grill and told him I lost my coat out the train window. He didn't say a word, gave me a look like who needs this shit. And then he said the most unexpected thing.

"I'll get a track walker on it."

A track walker? Did you know people like that exist? People who walk the New York subway tracks to pick up detritus dropped out windows or off station platforms—wallets and umbrellas and briefcases and, yes, pea coats. I imagined an entire species inhabiting the subterranean subway world. Remember *Superman and the Mole Men*?

Stuie said, "You should call your parents, tell them what happened."

How was I going to explain this one?

My mother answered. "Where are you?"

I said I was at a subway station in Manhattan.

"Why are you calling so late?"

I told her my coat fell onto the tracks, but someone was looking for it. I'd be home when I could.

"I'll put your father on the phone," she said. I hung up, short-circuiting his verbal avalanche. I knew what he'd say. That was a lot of money out the window—literally. I would pay for this, not sure how.

We waited two hours, Stuie and I, killing time on the deserted platform, mostly-empty trains pulling in and out of the station that smelled of damp and rats and peanuts. Now I'd have to wear some threadbare rag they bought me in junior high.

And then it happened. Way down the tracks, we saw a

Chapter 15

man slowly walking, a coat under his arm. The pea coat. He was an old Black man. He looked tired, weary of performing tasks like this. He climbed the stairs at the end of the station and approached us. He never spoke to Stuie and me, just handed the coat to the man in the booth, and then he vanished. Had I been older, had I understood the world, I would have stopped the old tired man and slipped him a twenty. If I had a twenty.

The man in the booth explained the jacket had flown to downtown Manhattan and landed on the side of the tracks, not on the tracks where a train would have shredded it. The man in the booth said the walker walked all the way to Greenwich Village for the coat, more than a mile. The man in the booth said I was lucky.

I slid my arms into the coat, enjoying the feel of it, the feel of me, and we boarded a train and rode to Avenue M, our local stop. I said good night to Stuie and inserted the key in the lock to our apartment. It was after 2 in the morning, but my mother and father were up waiting. My little sister, Carylann, was there, an impartial observer.

You've heard of the wrath of Achilles. He had nothing on the wrath of Emanuel (Mickey) Cohn, my father, who was pacing our foyer like someone waiting for, you guessed it, a train.

"You act like this? Is this how we brought you up?" my father shouted as I shut the apartment door. "You should be ashamed."

I didn't answer.

"Do you know what that coat cost us?"

I told him I knew.

"Do you think money grows on trees?

I said money doesn't grow on trees.

"Maybe running track isn't for you, young man. If you give it up, you'll study harder and get into a good college."

That again.

I was breathless with guilt, why I don't know, and I felt worse when this thought crossed my mind. If we had left the armory early, hadn't waited for the open sprint finals and if Hameroff had dropped my coat out the window at, say, 5 p.m. and if the track walker found the coat and gave it to the man who gave it to me at, say, 7 p.m., I wouldn't have been late, wouldn't have needed to phone my parents, wouldn't have needed to explain. Home free.

But no. First, a moron loses my coat out the train window late at night and now my dad is breaking my chops for what the moron did and when I try to explain it wasn't my fault, he angrily waves his arm. It is like a casting out.

What motivated my dad, a sweet, loving man? He always fretted about money. He was a lawyer but legally blind and sometimes didn't have cases, and when he didn't our apartment lived under a cloud.

He and my mother were children of the Great Depression and grew up hating money—the lack of it. Every day could see them on the street, their couches and end tables and plates and bowls there for everyone to gawk at. They bought the cheapest canned salmon at the grocery. Canned salmon?

They didn't buy clothes at a store. They bought clothes from Danny's Hideaway. What was Danny's Hideaway? It was a guy named Danny who sat in a beach chair in his driveway on a residential street in Brooklyn. You walked up to Danny and if you knew what to say—like gaining entrance to a speakeasy during Prohibition—he got up, lumbered to the garage door, and pulled it open. Inside were rows and rows of *shlocky* clothes that smelled old. I once asked Danny where he got his clothes. He eyeballed me and said, "Don't ask no questions, kid." I couldn't tell if his answer was an evasion or a threat. And there were my mother and dad fingering the old-lady's housecoats and faux-leather handbags and suit jackets held over from a previous generation. Cash only for Danny.

That was my parents' mindset. But they didn't buy the pea coat from Danny. They paid full price at an Army Navy store and that investment frightened them and they expected me to respect it.

Or maybe what I just wrote is a bullshit overinterpretation. Maybe my father was pissed at Hameroff—who wouldn't be?—but Hameroff wasn't there, and I was the stand-in.

"Let me see the coat," he said.

He yanked it from my hands and put it to his eyes, which barely saw. My mother took it gently from him, told my father, "Shah. No rips. Just some dirt I can wipe off with a damp rag."

She was right. The coat, my coat, had survived. My dad later told me he'd sent money to the track walker, I don't know how. God bless my dad.

All these years later—more than sixty—I wonder was that just another useless, dreary, annoying high-school Saturday night, a scrap of life you remember briefly and toss in the ash can of experience like millions of scraps that lead nowhere and mean nothing? Or did I, on that night with Stuie and Hameroff and the track walker and my father, on that night did I finally break my novice?

Chapter 16

Death Knell for Old MacDonald

There was the undeniable fact of a farm less than a block from my apartment house in Brooklyn, the farm there for decades before I was born, the farm there until the 1960s, the farm right in the middle of all that city life, a relic from another time, the farm in a neighborhood of Jews, most who worked with their brains not their hands.

An old high battered wood fence surrounded the farm which fit neatly into half a city block. The farmhouse, mostly hidden by the fence, was a faded white with bare wood showing through the paint, and there was a weathervane on the roof with a sad-eyed rooster casing out the neighborhood. I never saw the farmer until that one day, but I could peek through gaps in the fence and see chickens and roosters and neat rows of vegetables. I guess you'd call them crops. The street alongside the farm was a dirt road, more like an alley than a road. I always wondered about a dirt road in the middle of all that Brooklyn asphalt.

Turns out Brooklyn used to be agricultural. According to a book called *Cabbages and Kings County* (Brooklyn is Kings County), Brooklyn was a major U.S. agricultural producer in the nineteenth century. And the neighborhood of Flatbush, where I lived, was choice farmland. Of course, all that ended when Brooklyn became part of New York City in 1898, when housing developments moved south toward Coney Island and the Atlantic Ocean. My parents grew up in Northern Brooklyn, my father in Brownsville, my mother in Williamsburg, and moved south to Flatbush and never left. Flatbush surely smelled better when it was agricultural, no odor steaming out of the sewers, no piss and garbage on the sidewalk.

Before I write the sad thing that happened, I need to write about nihilism in my neighborhood, nihilism among the teenagers and young adults. All boys and young men. We knew in high school—maybe before—which kids would make it and who would fall to the side. I played games with my friends in the playground but at night I did homework for honors classes and many of my friends weren't in honors classes and most of them didn't do homework. I knew someday I would get out. They never would. And they were angry. Maybe because they knew it, too.

One time they threw water on two old men playing chess on a stone table in the playground. Did it just to do it. At least it was only water.

One time they beat up a new kid in the playground because he had a duck's ass haircut.

Another time, two guys were walking down Avenue M. Oak said they were *faggots*. We called this one guy Oak, more flora than fauna, I guess. He was older than us and was said to work in the post office although he had plenty of time on his hands. How he decided the two guys were gay I don't know. I had no idea if they were. They wore fresh-pressed jeans and looked neat and that could have been it. Oak hated them on sight.

"No faggots walk down my street," he shouted at them.

Avenue M had become his street.

He picked up a wooden crate in front of a grocery store and ran toward the two unsuspecting guys intending to beat them with the crate while his friends followed him shouting.

Chapter 16

Straight out of *Lord of the Flies*. The strangers didn't know what was happening, probably had never encountered such atavistic behavior. They started to run, but Oak caught up to them and swung the crate near his head like someone wielding a baseball bat. He miscalculated and, on the backswing, hit himself above the eye with a nail from the crate.

"My eye! My eye!" he screamed, and he dropped the crate while his blood gushed onto the street and his friends ministered to him and said they'd attend to the faggots later, the two guys having fled, thank God.

I stared at Oak and felt an upsurge of hatred and whispered to myself, "Fuck you, moron."

Another time, they went after Hal. Hal was in his late thirties or early forties—age was so hard for me to determine as a teenager—and he performed dips and handstands on the parallel bars in the playground with his torso bare, and his arms and chest molded with muscles, and he had a Doberman named Otto Boy—he would sing out in a loud authoritative voice, "Come here, Otto Boy," and Otto Boy loved him and minded him—and Hal was well-mannered and self-possessed and sophisticated and seemed happy, on top of life, and I wondered why he lived in our neighborhood which, at that time anyway, was a distant province, far from the action of the City. He was a Greenwich Village sort of person.

One weeknight about seven o'clock, I was buying a newspaper for my parents at the newsstand on the street underneath the Avenue M subway station when Hal emerged in a crowd of people from the station room. He wore a suit and tie and a grownup fedora, the kind men wore in those days, and he was obviously returning from

Manhattan where he worked. I never had seen him this way and I was impressed.

A woman was with him, younger than Hal, a beautiful light-skinned African-American wearing a light-weight summer dress. The nihilists were milling near the station. They often milled. They had no fixed place to be. One of them, about twenty, with a fucked-up nickname like Stinky or Pudgy or Fatty, something like that, was high on some drug. He noticed Hal with the woman and announced, "Hal got himself a n***** bitch." Hal was white.

I felt wounded for Hal, wounded for me, and I wondered what I'd do if some lowlife said that to me. Hal never hesitated. He walked over to Stinky Pudgy Fatty, grabbed his shirt with both hands, lifted him off the pavement until they were eye to eye and spat in his face. Nothing is more demeaning than someone spitting in your face. Hal threw Stinky Pudgy Fatty to the curb, walked back to the woman, took her by the elbow and led her away. The nihilists never said a word, did not shout at Hal or pursue him down the street. If they went after Hal, he would have killed them.

What they did to the farmer was worse.

One summer night—maybe 1961, I'm guessing—I spotted flames from my window. I hurried out of the apartment and ran down the street toward the fire. No fire trucks had arrived yet. The farmer's fences were ablaze and so was his house, roaring red and yellow flames reaching to the sky. I felt the heat. I imagined his animals in danger and his crops burning. Things were burning fast and thoroughly, and the wood was crackling like a campfire, the sound loud, a sound I never forgot. The farmer emerged onto the street. He was old and skinny, and his face was leather and, although he was in his sixties, he wore old, soil-stained jeans with a leather belt and scarred boots. He wore no hat. He might have been one of the Oklahoma Joads. He looked Western, not Brooklyn. The fire highlighted his grieving face, and I saw he was crying. Life-stricken. This was the end of his farm, the end of an era in our neighborhood and he was discarded—later, someone would build an apartment house on his vacant lot, and when I visit now the apartment house looks old and faded.

The nihilists, like jackals, loitered in the shadows. They laughed at the farmer. *Snickered* is a better word. I'm sure they lit the fire. But why? I didn't understand then and I don't understand now. As I watched them, an entirely new thought entered my mind.

I need to get out of here.

I could not have explained it then, but it had something to do with Flatbush being a small town in a big city, Flatbush being parochial, Flatbush—Mom and Dad, please forgive me—holding me back. From what I had no idea.

Chapter 17

Christ Descending

My father sat on the twin bed staring at me. My dorm room. My first day at Lafayette College, Easton, Pennsylvania. Fall 1962. My father, who had been jolly earlier in the day as he, my mother and I took a walking tour of the beautiful campus, now was dead serious, and my mother, for some reason, had disappeared.

"I want to talk to you," my father said.

My dad was a lawyer, and he gave me The Lawyer Look, a combination of aggression and skepticism. Searching for the weak spot. Getting at the real truth. The Look was how he stared at a hostile witness in court. He never had looked at me with The Look before this.

"Your mother and I expect you to do well here, otherwise we'll pull you out and send you to Brooklyn College."

My father meant I was at Lafayette College on a trial basis. I was in the academic courtroom, and he was the prosecuting attorney, the judge and the jury. This wasn't merely a warning to do well. It was a doom statement. Brooklyn College is the local college in our neighborhood, part of the City of New York university system, and it is right next to my high school, Midwood. Looking at Midwood you'd think it's a section of Brooklyn College, the buildings all stuck together on Bedford Avenue. So, if I got crummy grades at Lafayette, my father would pass sentence, yank me from Lafayette and I'd go back to high school, live at home, sleep in my twin bed, have dinner with my parents, never grow up, never get out.

"Do you understand me?" my father said.

I said I understood him. I also understood this was a setup, a plan he and my mother had cooked up. As he delivered his decree, my mother probably was waiting in the hallway nervously squeezing her purse which she called a pocketbook. I knew she agreed one hundred percent with my dad.

To them, there was something suspect about me. About my character. In high school, I earned a 92 average, was in the honor society, and won a state scholarship if I were to attend a New York State college. I wasn't a grades loser—although we didn't use the word grades. We said marks. But my parents didn't approve of my friends—the tough Italian kids, some of whom would go to jail. My parents thought I was up to shady behavior—and they were right. I used to play poker for nickels and dimes and quarters. I said *fuck* a lot. I snuck onto the BMT subway train headed for Manhattan without paying. But I didn't smoke or drink or cheat on tests, and I never stole anything or threw a kid off the Marine Parkway Bridge or told a teacher to drop dead. My parents had a vision of me, I believe, wiling away my time at Lafayette gambling, getting laid (fat chance), falling behind on my reading assignments and being an embarrassment to them in the neighborhood and at our temple.

Such a heavy load for a sixteen-year-old kid. There was more. My parents were first-generation Jewish people of a certain era. Because Jews got screwed left and right in business, at prestigious universities, at fancy country clubs, my parents believed in a meritocracy. Do well in school is the key to success. The *goyim* (non-Jews) couldn't hold us back if we kicked their ass in the classroom. My parents bought into this equation: good grades equal a good life. Obviously, this is bullshit, but in the innocence of their hearts, my parents believed it. They had to.

Lafayette was an all-men's college my parents picked for me—not knowing women in college set me back years. I was Flounder in *Animal House*. My parents also picked Yale and Colgate, but those two places rejected me. As a freshman at Lafayette, I had to walk around campus wearing a beanie and if an upper classman told me, "Doff it, frosh," I submissively took off my beanie for him. Lafayette required two years compulsory Reserved Officers Training Corps (ROTC), a pain in the ass. I had no choice in the matter.

Lafayette also introduced me to pork chops. Bear with me a moment. At home in Brooklyn, we ate ham sandwiches and bacon. No problem eating this *traif*, non-kosher, unclean food. But my parents drew the line at pork chops. A pork chop never stood a chance of landing at our kitchen table. Why my parents made this distinction between bacon and pork chops I have no idea.

As a freshman at Lafayette, I ate in a school dining room, ate what they served, and one night they served pork chops for dinner. I stood on the line holding my tray watching the server dole out the chops. I felt queasy. What would my parents say, not to mention my rabbi? Now it was my turn. I allowed the server to place a pork chop on my tray. I stared at the chop. It was sin incarnate. I walked to a table carefully carrying the chop as if it was a stick of dynamite. I sat down.

Would I eat this non-kosher food? I decided no way. But then it occurred to me I was hungry, and I wouldn't eat until the next morning when I'd load up on bacon and eggs. I took a deep breath like someone about to do a somersault off the high diving board. I picked up my knife and fork and cut into the chop. I placed the piece of forbidden meat in my mouth—God forgive me. And the damn thing tasted good. No other way to say it. The sucker tasted good. No messenger of God struck me dead or turned me into a pillar of salt. I ate the pork chop and would eat many pork chops before I graduated. I majored in pork chops.

Okay, back to my first day in college. As my dad eyeballed me in my dorm room, I thought about my brother. To be honest, I probably didn't think about my brother at this precise moment. Maybe I thought about him later that day. I mean, it would be quite a lengthy thought interlude on my part while my dad did a heavy-breathing number in my dorm room. But I want this scene to work so I'm bringing in my brother Robert now.

My brother was four-and-a-half years older than me and was born an adult. He was brilliant and mature and by the age of twelve he was my parents' equal. They never would have laid the we'll-pull-you-out-and-send-you-to-Brooklyn-College routine on him. I never heard them yell at Robert or correct him, not like my father shouting at me, "God damn it, Lowell!"

But there was one incident, still puzzling to me. My brother was attending Yale Medical School and dating another med student named Amy who was from the Midwest and wasn't Jewish. The non-Jewish part gave my mother a nervous stomach. "My son's going with a *shiksa*?" she'd say and wring her hands and belch from nerves.

Then came the explosion. I was peacefully lying in bed one Sunday morning, awakened by my dad yelling to someone on the wall-extension phone in the kitchen.

My father: I don't give a God damn if it's art. Take it down.

My father: Did you hear what I told you? Take it down God damn it.

Chapter 17

My father: It's a sin for a Jewish boy to put that on his wall.

My father: Do you promise to take it down?

My father: Good. I don't want to see that the next time we visit you in New Haven.

My father slammed down the phone.

"Who was dad yelling at?" I asked my mother.

"Robert," she managed to say.

Yelling at Robert, the saint? "Why?"

My mother pointed at my dad. He said, still fuming, my brother had put a print of a painting on his dorm-room wall. The painting was called *Christ Descending* or something like that. I never got that straight, although I checked Google and read in 1435 a Flemish artist van der Weyden painted *The Descent from the Cross* showing poor Jesus after he died and what looks like his mother fainting in the foreground. Maybe this was the deadly print my dad flipped over.

I don't know why Robert put up the print. I don't know why he told my parents. This was Robert's one rebellion in life, and he couldn't pull it off. He informed on himself.

But let's get back to my dad in my dorm room, giving me The Lawyer Look business. After he unloaded on me, my mom magically opened the door and slid into the room. Perfect timing. I wanted to puke. I hadn't stepped into a single classroom, and I already hated college. They told me to walk them to the bus stop, my father cheerful now, telling me college would be a great experience, make the most of it.

Sure, when my motivation was stark terror. I did well at Lafayette, graduated seventh in my class, was Phi Beta Kappa. My mom was pissed I paid for the smallest Phi Beta Kappa key—she liked wearing the key in public and preferred the Tyrannosaurus-Rex size. I won a fellowship at

Lafayette which paid for my first year of graduate school in Stanford's Department of English. But to perform well at Lafayette, I took easy courses for easy grades, not courses I loved or could learn from. I was a grubber for good grades. This was the lesson I learned from my father and mother.

Because the school was Presbyterian—I have no idea what distinguishes Presbyterians from, say, Methodists, Lutherans or Episcopalians—we were required to take religion courses, among my favorite classes in college. This meant Christian religion, not Jewish. For example, we learned about the holy trinity, a concept new to me. The professor would explain there's one God, but he comes in three forms. For me, this was a mind-bender. I never grasped the concept, although I admit the parting of the Red Sea and the burning bush are a bit of a stretch. But to a Jewish kid like me they had nothing on the father, son and the holy ghost. The whole time the prof talked about the three-in-one-concept I kept thinking about those Ronco ads on TV where if you bought the boning knife you also got the cleaver and slicer and dicer. Presbyterians out there please forgive me. I knew not what I did.

One of our religion profs was a Christian existential. He tried to explain leaps of faith to us and several times in each class would say—I swear this is true—"Ride that faith concept down." Rabbi Klayman on Avenue J in Brooklyn never said, "Ride that faith concept down." I didn't know how to ride a faith concept down. Every time the prof said it, I had visions of Slim Pickens at the end of *Dr. Strangelove* riding that atomic bomb and waving his cowboy hat.

We had required chapel once a week, a new one for a Jewish kid. I expected them to convert us—or at least try. But it was nothing like that. The first time I filtered into

Chapter 17

Colton Chapel I imagined seeing Christ in agony on the cross and the room smelling of incense and there would be a priest—I mean, minister—mumbling some incomprehensible language. Esperanto?

It was nothing like that. The minister, a kindly old man, didn't talk much about God or Presbyterianism, preached mostly about being a good person and living a good life. That was okay by me. Colton Chapel, designed by the architects of New York City's public library, wasn't so different from synagogues I knew, maybe a little more austere. The polished wood and smell of old prayer books felt familiar, even normal. I never felt in danger of not being a Jew.

We had an enrollment of twenty percent Jews from New York, New Jersey, Philadelphia and Connecticut. I got along with the Presbyterians and other Christians but was not allowed to join or have lunch at most of their fraternities. Four fraternities, give or take, accepted Jews.

The fraternity system flourished at Lafayette, meaning after the freshman year, most guys lived in frats. I did not join Pi Lambda Phi, the Jewish fraternity, because I grew up in a Jewish ghetto and wanted something different from Flatbush, my neighborhood and Brooklyn College. I didn't want to live with all those striving sweating pre-med and pre-law grinders, people who already had their lives planned out for them. Some Pi Lambs who went to high school with me said I was a sellout.

I joined Alpha Chi Rho, a half-Jewish loser house. It had writers, actors, engineering students, mixed nuts and misfits like me. A few brothers specialized in lighting farts with matches. The first semester of my sophomore year, The Crow House, as we were called, had among the worst grade-point averages on campus. Even I didn't do well, and I heard from my dad about that in a loud phone conversation.

The national committee of Alpha Chi Rho sent a dean from a local college, a Crow alum, to read us the riot act. His name was Dean Sloka. He was a big man about sixty who slouched into our house wearing a flea-market tie and a dark suit with so many shiny spots I almost went full migraine just glancing at him. He looked like a tent preacher. He sat in the middle of our living room in a stuffed chair with his big worn black briefcase that could have carried a small bomb. He unlatched the briefcase clasps, gunshots in the room.

He read out loud our pathetic cumulative grade-point average, sarcasm mixed with disgust. We were not true Crow men, he said. Brother by brother he went over our grades from the previous semester, how he got the grades I don't know. This was public shaming. Do Presbyterians public shame?

The whole time Dean Sloka made us feel like shit, my friend Robert Greenberg stayed in the backyard. I saw him through the window and what Greenie was doing was playing basketball by himself. Jumpers. Layups. The occasional hook shot. Behind-the-back dribbles. The works. He did not care about Dean Sloka. He did not care about the national committee. He did not care about many things. I wished I had Greenie's guts, but I was brought up to be a good boy.

Lafayette was strict. Get caught cheating you got thrown out no questions asked. When we took exams in bluebooks, we had to use blue or black ink. On one English midterm, Greenie wrote in green ink. When he got back the bluebook Greenie noticed that Willie Watt, head of the English Department, had written, "If your name were Blueberg would you write in blue ink?"

Because Greenie played hoops that Saturday morning, he missed the greatest moment in Alpha Chi Rho history.

While Dean Sloka slammed our grades from his chair in the middle of the living room, Artie Gray, our house president, stood several feet away framed in the high wide opening between the living room and the dining room. Artie Gray was studying Dean Sloka. Artie, a fifth-year student going for a master's in engineering, was a tough guy from The Bronx. A tough Jew. He was not mean or cutting but no one messed with him. Had that don't-fuck-with-me aura.

Artie was the guy leaning against the bar in a movie western waiting for an insult so he could one-gulp his shot of whiskey, slam down the glass, quick-draw his six-shooter and kill the bragging loudmouth. Dean Sloka gave Artie his chance.

When Dean Sloka finished, when we thought thank God the bore finally would leave, he said, "Do something for me, men. I want all of you to fall to your knees and accept Christ into your lives." He fell to his knees, hands clasped before his heart in prayer, expecting us to fall with him in hopes the deity would descend through the living-room ceiling. We stared at each other clueless. I already had accepted pork chops into my life, but would my mom and dad want me to accept Christ into my life from this lunatic if it meant improving my grade-point average and getting into a good grad school or maybe even law school? It would be like them giving the A-okay to *Christ Descending*.

I never had to resolve that dilemma. From behind me I heard Artie Gray shout at Dean Sloka, "Who the hell do you think you are? You come in here saying all that shit about our grades, and we take it and now you want us to accept Christ into our lives. Half the guys in this room are Jewish. Get out of here."

Dean Sloka stared at Artie in shock, about to rebut him, assert his God-given dominion over underperforming undergraduates, then thought better of it. Maybe he considered Jew Boys irredeemable heathens. Or maybe he was afraid Artie would punch his lights out. Red-faced, breathing hard, Dean Sloka shoved his papers—our grades—into his briefcase, snapped shut the clasps with a bang and dragged his sermonizing ass out of there. Never in my life had I heard a college student talk to a dean—an authority figure—like that. I loved Artie Gray for it.

That day my education began.

Chapter 18

Subway Token

For me it started after my sophomore year of college when I was eighteen, home in Brooklyn in the summer of 1964, a hot sweaty summer. I'm talking about a glimmer of self-awareness. One night we sat at the kitchen table eating dinner off plates on the slick oil cloth, my father, my mother, my sister and I. Suddenly, from out of nowhere, my father said to me, "To get along with you, Lowell, I have to bend like a pretzel." He meant one of those twisty pretzels that loops around on itself.

I didn't know what he was talking about. From my point of view, I was an angel. And then I thought—for the first time in my life—maybe my point of view wasn't the only point of view. Maybe my father saw me differently from how I saw myself. Maybe everyone saw me differently. Maybe I was being a dick without knowing I was a dick. Clearly, I had upset my dad, given him a hard time, although I didn't know how. And that made me think deeply about myself. But it didn't make me change.

A few weeks later, we repeated the scene, but worse. After dinner at the kitchen table my dad asked if I'd give him a subway token. Just that. A subway token.

He asked me because I had a bunch of tokens, those little coins with a groove in the middle you'd slide into a subway turnstile to enter the station. That summer I was working in the Bronx at John Hancock Life Insurance Company as a temporary clerk, and I had tokens and my father knew that. I rode the subway from Brooklyn to the Bronx five days a week, more than an hour each way, sometimes standing up. I liked the job, partly because I was leaving it in September to be a junior in college and wouldn't have to think about insurance policies, and partly because the people in the office were interesting.

One man, a few years older than me with a wife and kids, took me aside one day. He had something to tell me. I could see he was serious. I could see he'd sought me out, just me. He said he was riding home on the bus the other night when a profound thought occurred to him. I nodded my head, encouraged him. People always liked to tell me things and here was another example. It's why I became a journalist. I was proud of my listening ability and considered myself sensitive to other people's needs. He said he was on the bus as night descended and he looked up and saw lights in all the apartments he passed.

"And you know what I thought?" he asked.

"What did you think?" I said, ready to hear something profound.

"I thought hundreds of people are getting laid in those apartments right now, and I'm missing out, and that's why I play around on my wife."

Oh.

So, my father knew I had subway tokens. He wasn't doing well in his law business, and he had lost an important client and money was scarce and he was worried.

"May I have a token?" he said.

"If you pay me fifteen cents," I said

A token cost fifteen cents in 1964.

My father was a yeller and when he yelled you could hear him on the next block. But he didn't yell this time. "When you ask me for a token," he said in the softest saddest voice, "I don't charge you."

And then I really saw myself as he saw me. Saw myself in his pale-blue, almost-blind eyes. Rude. Petty. Insensitive. Cruel. Young. Stupid. I saw his utter disappointment in me, imagined him thinking, *This is my son? This is whom I raised? This is what he amounts to?*

I wanted to throw up. I handed over the token but didn't apologize. And he didn't say anything. Not thank you, because I didn't deserve thank you. And I feel the shame of that scene to this day when I am just three years younger than my dad when he died. And I say, *I'm sorry, Dad. I am so very sorry.*

Chapter 19

Twenty-Year-Old Virgin

Dionne Warwick had just told a drunk heckler to shut the hell up. She was singing "Walk on By" and he kept interrupting, and she stepped out of character and gave him the business and thousands of people cheered. This was the summer of 1966, and she was giving an outdoor concert in Central Park and I was with a woman I'll call Helen.

But I'm getting ahead of myself.

I had just graduated from college and was a month away from flying to California to attend graduate school at Stanford, and at dinner in our tiny Brooklyn apartment my dad casually asked what I was doing that night. I said I was going to a concert.

"Who with?" he said.

"Helen," I said.

"She's the girl you met working at John Hancock Life Insurance in the Bronx."

"That's the one."

"Isn't she colored?"

He was staring hard at me.

"So, what," I said, beginning to feel edgy.

"You're playing with fire," my father said.

"You've got it all wrong," I said. "We're just friends."

"I hope so," he said. "I don't care how smart you are. It doesn't impress me that you're going to Stanford because you know nothing about the world."

I had no reply, so I didn't say anything.

"You listen to me," he said. "It's okay you're going to the concert and I'm sure she's a nice girl, but when the concert ends, I want you to come straight home. Get on the subway and come home. Do you understand me?"

I said I did.

"You get her pregnant it could ruin your life."

I thought my dad was way out of line, but I didn't say it.

After Dionne told the moron to shut the hell up, she got on with her singing, sang a long time. I felt grown up being in Manhattan after spending four years at Lafayette, a tiny all-men's college in Easton, Pennsylvania, where I never learned about women.

We had "mixers"—dances—with nearby women's colleges like Cedar Crest and Beaver. I swear it was named Beaver, not that I got any. Sometimes I would kiss girls, especially when I took them back to their dorms where they had an 11 p.m. curfew. Lafayette guys, me included, frantically smooched them on the dorm steps, getting that extra bit of tongue. But intercourse? Not a chance. So, yes, I felt grown up with Helen, a year or two older than me, a New Yorker who knew the city better than I did, who wore her hair in a small Afro and was a looker. I knew she was a looker because guys kept looking at her. I had a girlfriend in New Jersey named Doris and I liked Doris a lot, but I didn't tell her about Dionne and Helen. What was to tell?

When we had worked at John Hancock, Helen and I sometimes would eat lunch together at a place down the street where she introduced me to cheeseburgers. I never ate a cheeseburger because Jews don't eat meat with milk products, and although I wasn't kosher, a cheeseburger seemed weird to me. But I instantly liked cheeseburgers and still do, which makes me a fallen Jew, I guess.

Chapter 19

Helen didn't go to college, but she was a reader, read James Baldwin, Ralph Ellison, Booker T. Washington and Lorraine Hansberry, none of whom I had read, although, as an English major, I was up on Milton's *Paradise Lost*, which Helen had no interest in. When I told her about Milton's Satan, she looked at me funny. If I said something she didn't like, or I thought she didn't like, she would say, "That was very white of you." Or she would call me Jew Boy. I never knew if she was serious.

The reason I was with her, she had phoned me after almost a year and proposed the concert, which I leapt at. When the concert ended and all those people started leaving, heading for subways, Helen said to me, "You're coming to the apartment, right?"

What I wanted to say: "I'd love to visit your apartment, but my dad said I have to come home immediately."

What I imagined Helen would say: "Are you a baby?"

What I really said after Helen asked if I'd visit her apartment: "Sure."

Why did I say sure? Even though I was frightened of my father, never disobeyed him on anything important, I didn't want Helen to think me a wimp.

She led me to a subway line I never had taken, and we started traveling north toward Harlem, I think, but I was lost by then. The train was crowded, and we were standing together, holding onto one of those vertical poles, when I heard loud voices. Some young Black men across the car were yelling, "Get yourself a n*****, bitch."

Get yourself a n*****, bitch?

What was that about?

They kept yelling it. They were yelling at Helen and me. That's when my sphincter tightened and sweat poured down my back. I looked around the subway car headed for Harlem or who knows where and realized I was the only white person there.

Helen, who seemed unimpressed by the young Black men said, "You're scared, aren't you?"

"Are you kidding?" I said, wanting to pee my pants, thinking I should have gone home right after the concert like my father told me, thinking these guys are going to kill me. When our stop came, Helen took me by the hand and led me onto the platform. No one tried to knife me, but someone from the train yelled fuck you. This anger was all new to me, and I wanted to say, "You've got it all wrong. Helen and I are just friends who once worked together in the Bronx and she taught me all about cheeseburgers and she says that was very white of you and if you knew me, you'd really like me." But Helen was dragging me away and I didn't have the guts to speak up anyway.

We climbed a long flight of stairs into the warm New York summer night onto a street I never heard of and walked the few blocks to her apartment house. "When a Man Loves a Woman" by Percy Sledge was blasting from someone's open window. The AM stations were playing Percy Sledge that summer. We took the elevator up to her floor, the elevator smelling of years of sweat and piss. She put the key in the lock, and we entered a typically tiny New York apartment with a kitchenette, a small living room and a smaller bedroom. She went to the fridge, pulled out a bottle of chilled white wine and opened it. I never had wine before except that kosher dreck on Jewish holidays.

She poured the wine, and it smelled good. She sat on the couch and patted the cushion next to her like I was a puppy,

Chapter 19

and she was expecting me to sit next to her. Which I did. After we drank a few sips, she did something unexpected.

"You've got to see this," she said.

She went to a window and pulled up the venetian blind.

"Come over here," she said. "Look out the window."

I looked out the window. Across the street was a guy in his apartment staring at Helen. Through his open window I could see he was jerking off. He was grinning.

"He does it all the time," Helen said.

"Is it for everyone, or just for you?" I asked.

"Just for me. He waits till I pull up the blinds."

"Why don't you call the cops?" I asked.

"It's his word against mine and I don't take him seriously."

She lowered the blind and went back to the couch while I thought this evening has been an all-timer, first the n*****-bitch guys, and now The Jerk Off King.

After a while, Helen put her glass on the coffee table and said, "I'm going to slip into something more comfortable."

She really said that, a line I'd heard in a thousand B movies. I knew what this meant. At least, I thought I knew. I was a twenty-year-old virgin with the emotional age of a fourteen-year-old. I waited for her to emerge from the bedroom when I'd say I must be running along. I could hear my father shouting, "Get the hell out of there, you don't want to be a father right now, and you don't want a colored baby." My dad was a product of a Jewish culture that would not accept Helen and me at that time. And I was ready to leave, but when Helen came back, she was wearing a white T-shirt just about covering her tush and I could see her nipples pushing against the cotton. Oh my God, I had been living a Single-A existence and this was The Show.

Sorry, Dad, but I'm staying.

Helen sat next to me, and she had a womanly smell. When she spoke, I could feel her breath on my ear.

"You're kind of cute," she said.

This was news to me.

She placed my hand on her breast. She placed my hand on her privates—she wasn't wearing panties.

I'm going to call a timeout here, call for a break in the action before I proceed. Think of this as the seventh-inning stretch. What I've wondered for more than half a century is why Helen wanted me that night that moment in that apartment. Was it to do with my being white? Was she bringing me along—an act of kindness? Was it something else? I wish I could ask Helen, but I never saw her after that evening.

Back to the play-by-play.

Helen said, "Don't worry I'll be gentle with you."

She opened my fly, and I slid off my pants. Without foreplay—who knew from foreplay?—I laid myself on top of her. "It's finally going to happen," I thought, and just like that I ejaculated all over her thighs and on top of her vagina. I was a rookie.

Years later when I was still a schmuck and counted the number of women I slept with—bulletin: young men do that—I didn't know how to count her. Certainly, we didn't have intercourse, but we almost did. Did I count her as a half? But I stopped counting long ago, not that the final number was high, and anyway I have more to tell because the evening wasn't over yet.

Helen wet a washcloth, cleaned herself, then cleaned me. She told me not to feel bad, which made me feel a little better.

"Stay the night," she said.

Chapter 19

I said sure I would stay the night. I was thinking I'd get a do-over. But first, I told her, I had to phone my dad, tell him I wouldn't be home until morning. She said I definitely should phone my dad. I thought I heard sarcasm in her voice.

I dialed our number and my father answered groggy—it was two in the morning.

"I'm sleeping at Helen's tonight," I said.

"The hell you are," he said. "Walk to the subway and come home immediately."

I returned the phone to the cradle. "My dad said I have to go home," I told Helen.

She wrote me off for life. I knew that.

I walked the dark streets to the subway stop foreign to me. I stood on the deserted platform a long time, lonely, frightened. I wondered if I got Helen pregnant without entering her. I would call my friend Stuie and ask if I could get a girl pregnant by coming on her thighs and outside her vagina.

I silently apologized to Helen. I wanted to fly to California right then, not in a month, to get the hell out of New York, finally to grow up although that would take years. And then the strangest thought entered my mind. I was secretly grateful my father told me to come home even though at any point I could have said, "I'm a college graduate. I'm a man and I'm staying out tonight."

But I wasn't up to staying with Helen, and I knew it. I wasn't up to anything about that night. For all the wrong reasons, my dad rescued me.

Chapter 20

On Reading Aldous Huxley

I was fifteen, a junior in high school when I learned to hate Aldous Huxley. It wasn't his fault, poor guy. My older brother Robert was on spring break from medical school and one Saturday afternoon in 1961 I could hear him and my parents talking in strained voices in the kitchen of our Brooklyn apartment which usually meant they were worried about me and my future. I was in a back bedroom watching a boxing match on TV, my idea of sophistication, but I had not performed well on the PSAT, and they weren't sure I could get into a good college and be a success in life.

A few minutes later, Robert walked into the bedroom, shut off the TV as one fighter took a right flush on the jaw and went down. Robert said I wasn't an intellectual. I would have considered this the highest praise except he was frowning. Robert was an intellectual. He was born that way. When all other teenage boys were outside playing ball, he hung around our bedroom listening to long-playing records on our tiny record player—Mozart's *Requiem*, Tchaikovsky's *Pathetique* and the score from the movie *Victory at Sea*.

He had a world-class collection of socks in the top drawer of his dresser. I'd walk into the room, and he'd stare at me with a lascivious grin like someone selling porn and, opening the drawer, he'd say, "You want to see my socks?" He'd show me the argyles which were basically plaids and then the lisles, much thinner and smoother. I'd never heard the words "argyle" or "lisle." He'd explain lisle is the finest cotton money can buy, especially Egyptian lisle of which he was a connoisseur. The intricate designs on the lisle socks, he said, are called clocks.

Robert said I should read more. The word "more" didn't apply, as I hardly read anything, not seeing the need. I was sprawled on a bed. I didn't say a word. Reading was a major theme in our Jewish family. We would improve ourselves by reading. When I was little and told my mother, "I'm bored," she would say "Go read a book." She didn't say, "Change the spark plugs in the car," something a goyish kid might know about. I didn't know from spark plugs, plus we didn't own a car. We took the subway everywhere.

"What authors do you like?" Robert asked. His voice a challenge.

I started thinking fast. I didn't actually like any authors or know any authors, but I didn't want to seem a dope. A year before, I got assigned Aldous Huxley's *Brave New World*. It was the sophomore-year novel, the kiss of death for any book. *Julius Caesar* had been the ninth-grade play. Good God, I can't stand *Julius Caesar* to this day with its lean and hungry look. The surest way to ruin a book or play or any worthwhile piece of literature is to assign it to an entire class—a thousand uninterested souls in my case.

"Come on, there must be some author you like," Robert said, irritated.

I once had read a book about a girl who did it for a Charlotte Russe, but I didn't think Robert had that kind of literature in mind and, besides, I couldn't remember the writer's name. So, I blurted out Aldous Huxley, a complete lie but an answer. A glow spread across Robert's earnest face. And then he walked out of the room. I was pleased with myself for having good taste in authors.

Chapter 20

Later when I wandered into the kitchen, I noticed my brother wasn't around.

"Where's Robert?"

"He ran to the City on an errand," my father said.

The City being Manhattan. Brooklyn being not-the-City. Robert took the Brighton Line to the City. Hmm.

A few hours later, he returned carrying a huge wrinkled brown paper bag. The bag was loaded. With books. He must have gone to Strand Book Store in the Village or someplace like that. He turned the bag over and dumped a bunch of paperbacks on my bed.

"You told me you like Huxley," he announced. Proud of himself.

All the books were Huxley. Total Huxley. No need for *Brave New World*. I had that one covered. But there was the horrifying reality of *Crome Yellow, Mortal Coils, Antic Hay, Point Counter Point, Eyeless in Gaza, Ape and Essence* and more. I admit memory can be deceptive—this was more than sixty years ago—but there must have been ten books, a pound apiece. I had ten pounds of Huxley weighing down my bed.

"Start reading one today and then we'll talk," Robert said like he was the parent. It was clear he was trying to save me.

I read a few pages of *Crome Yellow*, but I didn't know what Huxley was talking about. Or care. And I gave up. Every day Robert would walk into the bedroom cheerfully. "How's the Huxley going?" he'd say in a chipper voice like a camp counselor announcing volleyball in five minutes. I never replied. "Do you want to discuss Huxley?" he'd ask. I kept putting him off until he finally went back to medical school, and we never spoke about it again, although the books sat in my Brooklyn bookcase years after I moved to California, big, unread, yellowing, accusing.

I got my revenge on Robert, although "revenge" is too strong. I loved my older brother, who died a few years ago from cancer. Each year on my birthday, he sent me a check for 150 dollars. He still took care of me, the best big brother even though I was grown up. But I got my revenge, anyway.

In the 1960s a speed-reading craze seized certain social strata of New York. Maybe it was nationwide. My brother went for it. People wanted to read books faster, get through them in no time at all. In reading, speed became a virtue. I had a high-school English teacher who told us description in novels was a waste of time. She skipped all description, she said. Even though I was no reader, this sounded wrong to me and, years later reading *Huckleberry Finn*, I wondered if she would have skipped this description.

> "Sometimes on the water you could see a spark or two—on a raft or a scow, you know; and maybe you could hear a fiddle or a song coming over from one of them crafts. It's lovely to live on a raft. We had the sky up there, all speckled with stars, and we used to lay on our backs and look up at them, and discuss about whether they was made or only just happened."

If my teacher had skipped that, she would have missed Huck's simple juxtaposition between life on the river and life on land. But she would have missed more. The language. The words. All those liquid Esses. Reading them, you want to dive in, duck under the water and swim free. You'd hold your breath and come up, your senses sharp. The descriptive words create the river.

My brother took the Evelyn Wood Reading Dynamics course. Remember that one? Not long ago, I went online to

Chapter 20

learn about Reading Dynamics. It said you can double your reading speed and still have "astounding comprehension." You can "learn to read as fast as you can flip the page." It said U.S. presidents in addition to a million successful people have used Evelyn Wood. And I'm sure many smart eager readers have benefited from Evelyn Wood Reading Dynamics.

Robert started with books that had wide margins, the text as narrow as a newspaper column. And he'd move his hand down the page—wiggle his hand really—as he read the print. Eventually he graduated to wider text, still wiggling. As far as I understand it, the purpose of that technique is to keep your eyes moving, to read phrases and chunks of words so you don't bog down on every word—as if reading every word is proof you're a moron. Writers write every word. They don't write word chunks.

I would ride to Manhattan with him on the subway and he'd wiggle-read and I would have thought he looked insane except there always were other people reading like that, a train full of wigglers. And I would think, "What's the fucking hurry? Why is reading faster reading better? Is this a reading race?" Evidently the SAT was because I never finished it. I couldn't read fast enough, and the proctor would say, "Time's up, pencils down." And there'd be all those circles I hadn't filled in, and I'd weakly lay down my Number 2 pencil knowing I was screwed.

When I started reading for real—not the Huxley bullshit—I always read slowly. Saying each word in my mind. Might as well have read out loud because I moved my lips. Still do. In love with the sounds. In love with Dickens sounds and Jane Austen sounds and Joseph Conrad sounds and P.G. Wodehouse sounds and Vladimir Nabokov sounds and Ralph Ellison sounds and Elmore Leonard sounds and Toni Morrison sounds. All great sound-makers. And I realized the meaning of books is the sounds as much as the themes we talked about in English classes and all that author's-intention stuff. Themes, I decided, are 40-watt bulbs in a large dark room of mystery, lighting one small corner.

Several years after the Huxley horror scene, I lived with my brother in his Philadelphia apartment for part of a summer. He was a doctor at Children's Hospital at the University of Pennsylvania, and I was a graduate student in the English Department at Stanford. I had finished my first year in Palo Alto, but before I could begin my second year, I had to take the Qualifying Exam, a three-day whopper, as I recall, covering all English and American Literature.

If I passed the exam, I qualified and could move on in the Ph.D. program. If I flopped, Stanford would give me a master's degree along with a kiss-off. It was like trying out for the Yankees in spring training. If you didn't make the big-league squad, they'd send you to the minors or cut you altogether. Stanford had printed out a reading list of the minimum stuff all my classmates and I should know about. Things I never heard of. The Venerable Bead. John Lyly's *Euphues*. And things I had heard of but never read like *Gulliver's Travels*. The Lilliputians, in case you forgot, named Gulliver Quinbus Flestrin. Knowing Quinbus Flestrin got you one point on the multiple-choice section of the Qualifying Exam.

I lived with Robert so I could use the library at Penn to study for the Qualifying Exam and to spend time with him. Every day I would walk to the Penn library and read and read and I'd have lunch by myself in a cafeteria on campus. And Robert and I would meet for dinner at his place.

Chapter 20

We were reading quietly one night in his apartment. I was trudging through a novel on the Qualifying Exam list, *A Passage to India* by E.M. Forster—try speed reading that baby. Robert was flipping pages of some book, wiggling his hand. Every few seconds, he'd turn the page with a loud violent snap, and start wiggling his hand again.

"You call that reading," I said.

Robert looked offended.

"I can absorb the essence of the book this way," he told me.

"What's the essence?" I asked.

"Well, in a novel I can absorb the basics of the plot and the characters without getting bogged down in extraneous details. Speed-reading really is a useful tool."

"It is?"

"I once read *The Stranger* by Camus in ten minutes," he said. "You heard of *The Stranger*, right?"

I said I heard of *The Stranger*. I said I even read it. I said *The Stranger* is short, about 150 pages. Even so, ten minutes seemed a stretch. Robert could see I didn't believe him.

"I absorbed the essence of the book," he said. "Ask me any question about it." He sat there waiting.

I told Robert I'd give him an easy one. "Tell me about the end of the novel, the scene where the prison chaplain comes to the jail cell."

Robert looked stunned. "You're shitting me," he said.

"I'm serious."

"There's no prison chaplain in *The Stranger*." Pissed now.

"Yes, there is. He's in the climactic scene."

I grabbed the book from his shelf and showed him. How the prison chaplain walks into the cell of the condemned narrator, Meursault, and the chaplain says Meursault should believe in God to give his life meaning, to receive forgiveness for his sin of murder, and Meursault says he refuses to waste his remaining time on Earth thinking about God, and when the chaplain persists Meursault grabs him by the collar. In a rage.

Robert was quiet after that, rethinking speed reading. And I felt vindicated. It's impossible to be as poised as you'd like at key moments of your life, and I sure wasn't then. But if I had been poised, I would have tapped Robert playfully on the shoulder and suggested, in the kindest possible voice, he speed read the novels of Aldous Huxley. Our mother had a shitload of them gathering dust in the apartment in Brooklyn.

Chapter 21

The Dip Master

Dip changed my life. I'm talking about onion dip, cheese dip, spinach dip, you name the dip.

It was my second year at Stanford as a graduate student in the English Department circa 1968. How I ended up at Stanford was a hoot. In my senior year at Lafayette College, I caught a bad cold, so bad I couldn't go home for winter break, not at first. I lay in the infirmary, the only student still on campus, taking antibiotics and watching TV. When they finally released me, and my cousin Alison drove me home to Brooklyn, my mother said, "When you apply to graduate school, send an application to Stanford. It's warm in California and you won't catch so many colds. You catch too many colds."

I'd never heard of Stanford, although I didn't tell that to my mother. I assumed Stanford was in Los Angeles. Imagine my surprise.

The first day I drove onto the Stanford campus and cruised along Palm Drive and was struck by Stanford's exotic beauty, I said to my dad, "Does the Earth actually look like this?" Brooklyn sure didn't.

Okay, back to my life-defining experience with dip. I had just completed a seminar on the novelists Joseph Conrad, Henry James and Ford Madox Ford taught by Tom Moser, the head of the English Department at the time. Stanford had a tradition. At the end of the quarter, the instructor invited the class home for a party. It was to celebrate the work we had done, to celebrate us. As a graduate student, I taught Freshman English, and the department allotted all the teaching assistants money for our own parties. When I threw a party at my apartment, one of my students brought his girlfriend who drank too much and vomited into my kitchen sink.

So, this party tradition existed, and Tom Moser threw his for our seminar of eight students at his place on campus. He told us there would be dinner. When I met his wife I chatted nervously, overwhelmed by being in the department head's house and meeting her. And then, Mrs. Moser, in the most sophisticated voice, said to us, "Go over and try the dip." She was pointing at the dining-room table which, I noticed, had stuff resembling food on it.

I had no idea what she was talking about. I never had heard the word *dip* applied to food. I had heard of *to dip* as in dipping Jeannie Lieberman at the end of a slow dance; *taking a dip* in a swimming pool; *dip* as in the chewing tobacco baseball players stuff in their cheeks; dipstick; and, of course, dipshit. But dip, as an edible, never.

I was from south Brooklyn, a culinary wasteland, plus my mother didn't cook. It's possible people all over Manhattan and even in Brooklyn Heights were eating dip to their hearts' content and washing down the stuff with Perrier. But my family never got that memo.

Here's some food I never heard of until I moved to the Bay Area: avocados, guacamole, hash-browns, Arrabbiata sauce, Caesar salad, anchovies, Indian of any kind, sushi (raw fish, are you kidding me?), artichokes, penne pasta, camembert (Couldn't even pronounce it. Velveeta was our cheese of choice.), tri-tip, fresh English peas, fresh anything, New York Steak (How in the world did we not have New

York Steak in New York?), fried calamari (As in squid, oh my God!), kale, romaine lettuce (Were there others besides iceberg?), balsamic vinegar, carbonara sauce, chicken fricken' mole. Never tasted a craft beer or pinot noir or cabernet sauvignon (The Concord grape was the limit of our sophistication.), escargot (Holy mackerel!) and amuse-bouche (Give me a break.).

Now there was dip.

I hung back when Mrs. Moser proudly announced the dip. I felt like an émigré from a shtetl in nineteenth century Latvia learning American ways. The other students knowingly hustled to the buffet, grabbed tiny plates and tiny napkins and tiny forks. Everything appropriate for a team of munchkins. My colleagues had been undergraduates at schools like Harvard, Yale and Princeton and knew the deal. (Was the Ivy League Ground Zero for dip?) I eyeballed the table, saw carrots, celery, all raw — was this even hygienic? — and elegant bowls with colorful gooey stuff. Clearly, I was the only Jew in the room. What was the etiquette here? And where was the real chow?

I sprinted to the back of the line, affecting politeness, trying to scope out the scene. "Oh, go ahead of me. It would be my pleasure." My classmates took crackers and veggies and loaded up on the goo. The goo was the dip, that much I understood. And it wasn't just any old goo. It was Stanford English Department goo. My classmates took polite small bites of the veggie-goo combo. They seemed to like it. I imitated them and smiled as I nibbled and sucked, and as my hunger increased.

This was eating? When I'd have dinner at my Aunt Irene's apartment in Brooklyn, she served brisket and stuffed cabbage and potato latkes and green beans smothered in hot butter. When the meal was over, they had to wheel me out.

Like the other Henry James scholars, I sat in a chair and daintily ate this rabbit food from the plate I nervously balanced on my lap. And wouldn't the great Henry James have been a prime dip devotee? I wiped my mouth with the pint-sized appetizers napkin—no way would I get dip stuck on my upper lip like a Coney Island greenhorn.

I looked around the room. I was doing as well as everyone else. No one pointed at me and shouted, "Dip fraud!" And I felt great. I had passed a test as momentous as my doctoral orals. I had no doubt about that.

As she approached me with more pint-sized carrots, her face glowing like she was delivering a platter of Triple Whoppers with Cheese, I called out to Mrs. Moser like the veteran I had become, "Hey, Mrs. M, kudos on the dip."

Chapter 22

Carl and the Jewish Huckleberry Finn

When I was in my second year in Stanford's graduate English program, 1968, another Ph.D. student, a woman, told me Carl Maves, a year ahead of us, was light in the ass. I didn't know what she was talking about. I formed a mental picture of someone shoving a hose up Carl's tush and forcing helium up his rectum and Carl floating away. Lighter than air.

I was inexperienced, had gone to college at sixteen, an all men's college and, although statistically, there had to be gay men at Lafayette College (the word then was homosexual), I knew little about sex, hetero, homo, you name it. Sometimes when I was a kid my mother would say about one man or another, "Is he a *feygele*?" I kind of knew what she meant, or thought I did. The Yiddish word feygele is associated with the German *vogel*, which means bird. And I thought she meant the man in question was like a little bird, kind of effeminate. I had no idea she meant homosexual. My Flatbush upbringing had left me innocent—or was it ignorant?—and I was entirely unprepared to decode a phrase like light in the ass.

I was only twenty-two at the time with an emotional age embedded in adolescence and, sure, I understood Carl was different, but I liked the difference. He spoke in exaggerated tones, making everything dramatic. And when we went for beer at the Oasis, the favorite Stanford hangout (now defunct), he stared at handsome guys. It meant nothing to me.

One night at the beer joint, Carl announced out of the

blue, "You know I'm gay." He might have called himself faggot or queer. He liked those nouns.

I sputtered meaningless syllables, then said, sure, I knew, although I didn't. I was thinking fast. Would he make a move on me? He never did. Would people think less of me if I were friends with him? Who the hell cared? He was from Los Angeles and hadn't met anyone like me—a Brooklyn Jew—and he found me exotic, found Brooklyn, my little patch of Earth, exotic, and he called me the Jewish Huckleberry Finn for my naivete.

Everyone knew he was the smartest in our graduate program—one hell of a program filled with brainy people who took my breath away. It's how they spoke and what they'd read and what they knew and how they took apart a text. Carl was better than everyone. He was not a great abstract thinker. Our fellow Stanford student Bill Gairdner, who became a well-known Canadian political essayist and philosopher, was a superior abstract thinker to Carl. Certainly, to me.

Bill could read *Robinson Crusoe* and give an existential analysis of the book with a little Karl Marx thrown in. Bill loved to go to the next level. Carl stayed with the text, the words on the page, the people in the book.

We would go for beer and Carl would talk about Isabel Archer as if she were at the table with us pouring ketchup on a double cheeseburger. And there with us would be Gilbert Osmond and Madame Merle, the principal characters from *The Portrait of a Lady,* and Carl could look at each person—to him they were real—and understand where each was coming from, what they needed, and he could get into each point of view without judging the point of view and explain what each wanted from the other, how each manipulated the other, and Carl's voice would soar above the jukebox and the laughing and yelling and he'd rise in his chair and wave his arms. And although Carl had zero insight into real people, was in some ways a child, I loved the gift of his insights about fictional people and the pleasure of his introducing me to Isabel Archer, God love her. Carl wrote his dissertation on Henry James. He would have been called a Jamesian. I was a Conradian. We had the same thesis adviser, Ian Watt, who loved Carl's work and didn't so much love mine.

Carl published his dissertation as a book, *Sensuous Pessimism: Italy in the Work of Henry James*. He became assistant professor at Dartmouth, where he'd been an undergraduate. But he left Dartmouth, then an all-men's school, because the gay life wasn't what he wanted, too much sneaking around—this was the 1970s. And then he went to Southern Methodist in Texas. But left there too, because he could more easily be openly gay in the San Francisco Bay Area. Ian Watt washed his hands of Carl because Carl kept giving up teaching positions, making Ian look bad. I can't blame Ian and I don't think Carl blamed him.

And Carl came back to Palo Alto where I was a struggling freelance writer. Now he also was a struggling freelancer. We would sit at the same table in his neat little sun-drenched apartment and write. And then we'd go over each other's prose and make suggestions and write the stuff a second time. We learned to write together, each believing in the other.

When I couldn't come up with an idea for an article or a story I would panic, and Carl would say, "Calm down. You can't go looking for an idea. An idea looks for you."

"What do you mean?"

"An idea is like a fawn," Carl said. "It's standing in a meadow, and you see its beauty and you want to touch it and you walk toward it, but the fawn runs away. It's frightened. But if you stand still the fawn may come to you and you can pet it and touch its nose. It's the same with an idea. If you rush toward the idea, it runs away. You must let it come to you."

And Carl was right. Ideas have approached me in the most unusual places. The shower. In bed after the afternoon nap. On a walk. Shopping at Safeway. I am forever on the lookout for fawns.

Carl was writing a memoir about his cat named Prince. He called the memoir *Someday My Prince Will Come* and it was brilliant.

The first chapter begins with the lines: *Because it wasn't, I swear, my idea to begin with—it's not too strong to say that that cat went out of his way to seduce me. Soon after moving in I woke one morning around 11 (my usual hour) when everybody else was away at work, and found him crouched outside my door, waiting.*

At the very end, after Prince has died, Carl writes, imagining Prince communicating from the beyond: *And as he turns his head to look at me he meows. Or, as he often did in life, merely opens his mouth and pantomimes the sound. He knows I'll understand anyway: I'm off for a while to do cat things, he's saying, but I'll be back. And he always was.*

Carl gives Prince various names, so creative:

Besides being Prettyman, he was my fat white cat-man or Faman, Wyman and Caman; his opulent indolence made him my Pasha Pig; instead of Othello's "Farewell the plumed war" he was "Hello the plumed tail," he was Sugarman and Angelkitten, Kittenperson and Puppetmouth, Flowerface and Velvetface.

As I read Carl's cat love story, I felt Carl was as good as

Chapter 22

Vladimir Nabokov. Nabokov, so brilliant in *Lolita*, would have been challenged to write about a cat as Carl did. Carl and I both worked as freelance critics at the *Palo Alto Times*. I wrote film and drama. He wrote drama, music, books. He could write about anything.

I almost never asked Carl about his other life, his gay life which I imagined he engaged in every night. I was afraid to say the wrong thing mostly because I didn't know what the wrong thing was. I didn't know what went on, didn't want to know. Once he said he needed surgery on his tush. This was news to me. I asked what he needed surgery for. He said, "You don't want to know."

Which brings me to the time I had a rash on my penis. I was a young man catching up for lost time and I was sexually active. I was thinking about going to the doctor—this could be something serious. But I thought I'd ask Carl's opinion about the rash. He was way more experienced than I. I once casually asked how many sexual partners he'd had in his life—we were in our thirties then.

"How many do you think?" he asked.

I didn't want to offend him, so I came up with a high number. "One hundred?"

Carl laughed in my face. "Five hundred at the very least," he said.

Five freaking hundred? To reach five hundred I'd have to live several lifetimes. So, I was at his apartment, and we had finished writing and editing and I mentioned my rash and asked his opinion.

"Let me look," he said.

Let him look? He was gay. What would he do?

He saw my hesitation.

"Don't worry, Lowell. Your virtue will remain intact."

I laughed nervously and I showed him, and he told me he'd had that rash a million times and it would go away, and it did.

He said we should take a drive to Santa Cruz, see the ocean, walk the boardwalk, smell the salt air. It might have been 1973 and I would have been twenty-eight, Carl thirty-three. I drove. We spent time and had lunch and as it grew dark, I said we should head home. When we got to San Jose, he said there was a gay bar he wanted to show me. I hadn't expected this. I never had been to a gay bar and was afraid. This involved special etiquette on my part. I could have said, *No*. It's what I wanted to say — Hell no, are you kidding me? But that wouldn't have been fair. I didn't want to offend Carl. He'd asked me to see his life, his life as it was. He was offering a gift and a dare, and I said yes although my mouth had gone dry. We drove to the bar and ordered beers and sat at a table. Guys were dancing with each other. I'd never been in a place where men danced with each other, slow danced. It was all very polite. Someone walked to our table and asked Carl to dance and they danced. For the next half hour guys asked Carl to dance but no one asked me.

I didn't want anyone to ask me, but I was ticked off no one found me interesting — or was it attractive? Finally, Carl said, "Let's get out of here." As I pulled away from the parking lot, I said, "Carl, I couldn't help noticing no one asked me to dance."

"Well, Lowell," he said, "when you sit with your forehead on the table and your hands covering the back of your head people tend to get the message."

Oh.

Carl fell in love with San Francisco 49ers quarterback Joe Montana. I wonder how Joe would feel about this. Would he be flattered? All over his apartment Carl had placed photos of Joe on his walls, most of the photos cut from the newspaper. Joe was Carl's heartthrob. Once at a party at my house, Carl drank too much and started crying. Someone asked why and Carl said, "I love Joe Montana so much."

One time, Carl wandered into the sports department at the *San Francisco Chronicle* where I was a sports columnist. He wrote freelance book reviews for the *Chronicle* and was in the building and wanted to say hello. We walked to the center of the sports department, Carl flamingly effeminate, Carl raising his voice with enthusiasm, the two of us laughing. After he left, one of the people from sports approached me. "Who was that *fellow?*" he asked. He pronounced fellow in a mincing, lilting way, meaning Carl was a faggot and had no business in the heterosexual fortress of sports, meaning I had breached the fortress by allowing Carl in, meaning I, by implication, was suspect, me hanging around with queers. "He's my dear friend," I told my sports colleague, and he looked at me with disgust, or was it hatred. And I thought *Carl is worth so much more than you, you piece of shit.*

Here's an example of why I loved Carl, aside from his brilliance and his loyalty and his friendship wanting nothing in return. After I married and moved away from Palo Alto to Oakland—a forty-minute drive—I would visit Carl one Tuesday each month and we'd spend the afternoon together. He no longer had a car and I did.

We were sitting around his living room one Tuesday afternoon and I mentioned I never understood William Butler Yeats. Some people in the know think Yeats was the best poet in English in the twentieth century.

"Why don't you get him?" Carl asked, and I said I had

trouble with his language, so many things to look up like *perne in a gyre.*

And I didn't understand the last line of "Among School Children," *How can we know the dancer from the dance?*

I said it gave me a headache thinking about the dancer and the dance, trying to untangle them. Or wasn't I supposed to untangle them? Reading the poem, which I had to do in graduate school, I always wondered where did the dancer-dance idea come from anyway? It suddenly appeared at the end of the poem. I blamed myself for being obtuse, certainly didn't blame Yeats for his poem. I admitted to Carl I was a prose-fiction guy. I liked stories. Poems were hard.

In his most dramatic voice, almost operatic, Carl sang out, "You've read the wrong Yeats poems. You've never read "The Circus Animals' Desertion."

Well, actually, I had read it, but I probably sped through it like someone rushing for the 5 p.m. special from Grand Central Station to Connecticut. Carl stood up, walked to his bookcase, the book spines in neat rows, and pulled out his collected Yeats.

"You must hear 'The Circus Animals' Desertion,'" Carl said. Emphasis on *must.*

He opened the book and found the poem and before he read, he spread his legs in a masculine way like Gary Cooper getting ready to draw on the Miller Brothers in *High Noon.* And he read, his voice rolling on the beautiful rhythms, his voice rising appassionato, finally his eyes closing from sheer pleasure because he knew the poem by heart.

> Winter and summer till old age began
> My circus animals were all on show,

Chapter 22

> Those stilted boys, that burnished chariot,
> Lion and woman and the Lord knows what.

I listened as Carl read, read for me and I studied him. Carl in love with reading the words out loud. Carl short like me and his hair still red although we both were in our fifties now. And I thought the poem was something about a circus, and the animals were the poet's talents, his young talents and his young ideas, his life force. And all these were deserting him as they were deserting Carl and me.

And as Carl read, I heard Yeats remembering poems and plays he wrote in his youth and Yeats feeling he no longer had the energy to do this. How age was breaking him down. As it breaks everyone down. And Yeats ends with:

> Now, that my ladder's gone,
> I must lie down where all the ladders start
> In the foul rag-and-bone shop of the heart.

And I felt what Yeats meant. He was writing about where all creativity begins and finally ends, and we are left with mere debris, the unlovely debris of life, but we keep trying. We start again. And when Carl was done, he opened his eyes, his eyes wet, and he stared at me. And I thought *What a gift Carl just gave me. On the entire Planet Earth, on all the continents, no one else just did what Carl did, read to a friend "The Circus Animals' Desertion," read the poem in his living room for the pure love of it.* And I loved him for it.

A few weeks later Carl phoned me and said he didn't feel well. He said he wasn't worried because he had a good doctor, but could I drive to his place. He needed the company. So, I made the forty-minute drive and when he opened the door, my heart caved in. Carl was orange. Not a little orange. He glowed.

"It's something about my pancreas," he said. "I think I have pancreatic cancer."

He looked thin and weak, and I asked if he'd been eating. He said he had no food because he was orange and didn't want people to see him in the market. I drove to a supermarket and bought food in cans, things easy to prepare—soups, chili, stews—and my hands shook on the shopping cart and tears ran down my cheeks and snot dripped from my nose, and I drove back to his house and stocked his shelves and heated up soup, but he didn't eat it.

Who will bring me soup?

Carl was dying and I was leaving soon for the Sydney Olympics in Australia. This was the year 2000. The day I left I drove to Stanford Hospital where Carl lay in bed. Still orange. A doctor checked on him and when the doctor left, I followed him.

"How much longer does Carl have to live?" I asked, afraid of hearing the answer. God I was afraid.

"Not more than a few days," the doctor said.

I walked back to Carl.

"You were talking about how long I have to live," he said. It sounded like an accusation.

"We were."

"What did the doctor say?"

"The doctor said you easily will live several weeks, probably a few more months."

"Thank God," Carl said. "I thought he told you I only have a few more days."

"You must have heard wrong," I said.

Is this how I will feel at the end?

Chapter 22

He fell asleep. I held his hand. I cried. I left and drove home and packed for the Olympics and drove to San Francisco Airport for a midnight flight. I met my friend Ann Killion, then a sports columnist at the *San Jose Mercury News*, also flying to Sydney. She wanted to talk, but I was unresponsive, and she gave a look like I was rude and walked away for a coffee.

When I arrived in Sydney fourteen hours later my wife emailed me and said Carl had died. She wrote that Carl's friends were having him cremated but would wait for me to spread his ashes.

I was in Sydney several weeks and when I returned, I met three of Carl's friends, all gay, at a house in Redwood City, just north of Palo Alto. The house's owner, Gary, had planted beautiful fruit trees in his yard, and each of us took a handful of Carl and spread his ashes under a tree. I was honored to be included with Carl's gay friends. Then we walked into the house, the four of us, and chatted about Carl until one of them took out a joint and lit it. He began to pass the joint and, as I calculated the joint's circuit, it would reach me last. I knew at least one of Carl's friends was HIV positive. Maybe one or both of the others also was HIV positive. Still not yet clear how the disease was transmitted, no way would I put that joint to my lips. I was trying to figure out what to say, how not to be offensive in turning down the joint. When the third man took a hit, he passed the joint back to the one who had lit it. He'd bypassed me.

So how did he know I wouldn't smoke their joint? How did he know to spare me the embarrassment and the moral dilemma? Maybe I had my hands covering the back of my head again. Carl could explain it. Carl would forgive me.

Coda

I am the one who remains. I am the memory holder. I am seventy-nine years old. I remember Carl, long dead now, and my parents and my brother Robert and Aunt Sarah and my cousin Alison and Mary and The Prof (see Chapter 24) and my dear friend from Stanford Bill Gairdner (see Chapter 26) and my most brilliant student Lucinda Ryan and Paula Satlow (she appears later in these pages) and my wife, Dawn. And so many more. I am the bearer of these memories, responsible for these lives all gone. So many have left me, the people who populated my days, the people who made me who I am. I honor them. I say *kaddish*.

Chapter 23

Kindergarten Baby

*K*indergarten baby, stick your head in gravy, wash it off with bubblegum and send it to the navy.

- Children's taunting rhyme.

When I was a child my parents told me everything would be okay, would always be okay. I was a special child and could achieve whatever I wanted, and everyone loved me.

The love part, of course, was true. My mother and father hugged me every day and said, "We love you, Lowelly." My Aunt Sarah, widowed early, was at our apartment all the time and she said she loved me. Suche (pronounced Suchee, real name Sarah,) the woman who lived in the apartment to our right, made me coffee with extra sugar starting when I was five, and said she loved me. Mary, our housekeeper, loved and protected me.

I was a loved, coddled, adored child. This was a Jewish thing—correct me if I'm wrong—I was a Jewish boy surrounded by love. I learned early on I was the prince. The metaphor for my childhood was me falling down scraping my knee and my mother frantically shouting, "Get the Mercurochrome." Then as she lathered it on, she said, "This will sting but it's good for you." And then she hugged me to her bosom. Mercurochrome is now banned in the United States because it contains mercury. Who knew then?

The result of all this mothering was obvious. I became

the classic kindergarten baby and remained a kindergarten baby into my thirties. On the first day of school at P.S. 193 I wept, shrieked and begged to be taken home, wanting to sit in front of the television and eat Cheerios with Mary and Suche taking care of me. This crying on Day One lasted from kindergarten into the second grade when I was seven.

There was more to being a kindergarten baby than being babied. From birth, I knew one immutable fact. The world was a kind and benign place crying out to comfort Lowell Cohn. And then I met Ian Watt.

He was Chair of Stanford's English Department when I was a graduate student there and he directed my dissertation on Joseph Conrad—I finished my Ph.D. in 1972. He was an academic genius. Wrote *The Rise of the Novel*, an astonishing work of scholarship explaining how the novel rose as a brand-new literary form in eighteenth century England. And he was among the best Joseph Conrad scholars in the world. I felt honored when he agreed to be my thesis adviser and knew he would guide me to a stellar academic career, me lecturing to thrilled Ivy League undergraduates about the mysteries of *Heart of Darkness* and *The Secret Sharer*, a story that still baffles me.

Ian Watt was British and in World War II joined the army at twenty-two and was captured by the Japanese in Singapore and was a prisoner of war almost four years and helped build the Burma Railway across Thailand and the Bridge on the River Kwai—yes, that bridge—and, afterward, he taught at Berkeley before Stanford and he chain-smoked Player's Navy Cut cigarettes and he was tanned and large-boned and handsome and manly and his face was wrinkled like old leather and he laughed on the inhale and he kept a linen handkerchief sticking out of his left shirt cuff and he grew up near Dover, a coast town in the southeast of England where his father taught French at the Dover County School for Boys which Ian attended, and Ian's schoolmates called Ian's dad "Froggy Watt," and that embarrassed Ian whose middle name was Pierre.

He was not a kind man. I was not used to not-kind-men. My Uncle Irving was kind and bought me ice cream sodas. Ian was polite and witty with a hyper-verbal British style—it was like being with Kingsley Amis or how I imagined being with Kingsley Amis would be. But he was cold and formal in a distinctly British way and almost never made suggestions that would help me write my dissertation, was scathing when he talked about my writing, making comments in the margins of my chapters in handwriting so microscopic I almost needed a magnifying glass to read them. And when I tried to defend a point, I had no chance against him. He would inhale wearily and say, "Yes, but." The "but" was the killer, the signal he would knock me out. And he would begin his rebuttal with the word "well," which he pronounced "Welllllllllllll," stepping hard on the "ell" and drawing it out several seconds in a high-nasal range. At the sound of his well I wanted to faint.

He was smarter than I was and where I saw one possibility, he saw five. When I would write something and he would say yes but and well and I would say, stupidly, *you know what I mean*, he would give me that arch Cambridge stare and say, correctly, he only knew the meaning of what I wrote not what I thought I meant, and that I had to be precise with words. Sometimes he crushed me, a wrecking ball when a feather duster would have worked better, and he could see I felt crushed. But he didn't care.

My parents and Aunt Sarah and Suche and Mary

protected me. Ian expected me to protect myself. He was writing his magnum opus on Conrad (*Conrad in the Nineteenth Century*) and although I was not in his league as a critic, he remained *shtum* about his ideas because he didn't want my competition or thought I would steal from him. Who knows? Years later, after I became a fairly-well-known sports columnist in San Francisco, he invited me to dinner at his house on the Stanford campus—Ian would be teaching a class that night but drank Leoville las Cases as a warmup. Joking, I said to him, "You drove me to journalism." He shot back, "You did it to yourself." As if journalism is something to be ashamed of. As if English Literary Criticism is the world according to God. As if I had failed him.

But this story takes place long before that night at his house, takes place in the summer of 1969 when I was a twenty-three-year-old graduate student and despite his arctic manner, I believed Ian really cared for me.

The story starts with a man named Tony Tanner, also British, who was a visiting professor at Stanford. Tanner was eighteen years younger than Ian and he was brilliant and a beautiful writer. I wasn't then capable of comparing them—nor am I now. I knew Tanner had become a specialist in American Literature, helped make American Literature a serious topic for English scholars, starting with his breakthrough study, *The Reign of Wonder*. He also wrote on Conrad, a significant fact for this narrative. Ian and Tony Tanner were writing on Conrad contemporaneously and Tanner was in the younger generation of critics. In the world of academics that can lead to fireworks. And I got caught in the middle.

The first time I met Tanner was early in the 1969 summer quarter. Ian and his wife, Ruth, held a cocktail party at their

Chapter 23

house to welcome visiting faculty and faculty from the English Department in general. It was where professors acted like they got along with each other and drank a lot. Ian asked me to drive Tanner from campus to Ian's house. I guess Tanner didn't own a car—he was at Stanford only for the summer and most likely rented a place on campus. I picked him up and his wife, Marcia. Very pretty, very talkative.

"You're the graduate student," she said in the car.

"Huh?" I said.

"There's always one who drives visiting faculty to parties like this one and you've been designated."

I told her I was the one.

"You're working with Ian, right?"

I said she was right. I felt proud to work with Ian on Conrad. Singled out. Preferred. Tony didn't say anything.

As we drove to Ian's party, Tanner stared out the window. The party was loud. Lots of mixed drinks and the clinking of ice cubes. I hung around the outside deck, hung around not talking to anyone. I was the only student there and no one cared about me. It grew late and I walked into the house and Ian's wife, Ruth, asked what I was still doing there.

"I'm waiting for Tony and Marcia Tanner so I can drive them back to campus."

"Oh, they got a ride home hours ago," Ruth said.

Funny feeling when you are invisible. I didn't exist for Tony and Marcia, who would get divorced. In Tanner's obituary—he died in 1998 after a life plagued by alcoholism and depression—someone wrote their marriage was "dissolved." I drove home from the party calling myself schmuck.

I didn't know how Ian felt about Tanner. He once told me Tanner tacked a photo of the Beatles on the wall of his Stanford office. Ian thought that was cool, a word he never would use. Which told me Ian wasn't cool and Tanner probably wasn't either, a photo of the Beatles at that time being—what?—obvious, predictable, a cliché. Maybe I'm being unkind.

Ian didn't speak to me about Tanner until the one time I'm getting to, that conversation being at the end of this story, or at the beginning. Endings and beginnings get mixed up with each other. I knew how Ian felt about other professors in the English Department. Knew firsthand. I would walk through the halls with him—feeling I was special, although now I reject that feeling. He would greet Professor X as they passed, greet Professor X warmly, Professor X thrilled to be noticed by Ian. And when Professor X was out of earshot, Ian would whisper to me, "His scholarship is so weak." He told *me* that, me a graduate student who knew Professor X and had taken classes from him. I witnessed scenes like this a dozen times.

In the early 1970s at the Modern Language Association convention in New York, a job market for aspiring professors and a place for professors to hobnob, Ian asked me to walk with him to a nearby hotel where NYU had rented a suite and was hosting a cocktail party. Ian seemed uninterested in the party, but Leon Edel, a well-known Henry James scholar, had invited him, although they were rivals in the inner circle of James critics. Ian felt an obligation to show up.

So, we walked to the NYU suite on a winter night, walked through the crunching snow. Someone opened the door for us and when Ian entered, Edel, who had been sitting in a chair, shot to his feet, propelled with admiration and gratitude that Ian had done this for him. The man's face was red with joy, and he pumped Ian's hand and Ian laughed, drawing in air and making a croaking sound and being gracious in his distant way. Edel fetched me a drink, thinking I was important because I was Ian's pupil. After a suitable interval, Ian said we had to leave and Edel escorted us to the door. After we walked down the hallway and boarded the elevator and Edel couldn't hear us, Ian looked at me and said, "Dreary little man."

Wow!

This hurt me, although I didn't understand why. My father was not an intellectual like Ian, didn't know *Lord Jim* from The Hardy Boys, but he wouldn't have called a colleague dreary little man in my company. He taught me to behave like a gentleman. I thought Ian was brilliant but maybe not so wise. There is a difference between intelligence and wisdom, although it took me years to learn that.

Ian was a bad teacher, had no interest in teaching, cared only for writing his own books. He led small seminars in the eighteenth century English novel, and Conrad, and Henry James. Graduate students competed like hell to get into his seminar. Eight made it. The class was scheduled to meet two afternoons a week but on the first day, Ian would announce he was condensing the two meetings into one long one and, instead of on campus, we would meet one night a week at his house high in Los Altos Hills.

I felt honored to learn in Ian's home. I was fascinated by him then and I still am although he's been gone many years. He would drink gin and tonic while he taught the seminar, and he would smoke his Player's. He never actually taught Conrad, although I took several Conrad seminars with him.

He would bullshit about anything but the books. Once when we were discussing *The Secret Sharer*, he went off on a time he had picked up a criminal in his car—he was sure the man was a criminal—and had given him a lift just as the narrator of the story picks up a criminal. This did not help me understand *The Secret Sharer*.

Years later, I came to understand Ian's method. He was not a sharer, secret or otherwise. He had ideas about Conrad, but he refused to disclose them. They were his property for books and articles he was writing. He was intellectually stingy. So, his teaching mission was *not* to teach, merely to give the impression of teaching.

At the end of the summer of 1969, I was in Ian's office on the first floor of the English Department, and this is the climax of my story. I had written a chapter of my dissertation on Conrad's novel *Under Western Eyes*. We worked quietly in his office, Ian deciphering his tiny hieroglyphic script for me, mostly criticism. When we were done, I got ready to say goodbye. I was leaving in a few days to study at the British Museum for a year. "I'll write to you from London," I said.

"Don't rush off," Ian said, unusually cordial.

The building was quiet, most people on summer break. Ian walked me to the hallway and pointed to the staircase leading up to the second floor.

"You know Tony Tanner's office is at the top of these stairs?" he said.

Ian and Tony Tanner, the visiting professor, were fierce Conrad competitors but friendly, I assumed.

"He's in there right now," Ian said, pointing to Tony's office.

I didn't see how this related to me.

"Your ideas about *Under Western Eyes* directly contradict Tony's," Ian said. "Did you know that?"

Chapter 23

I knew but wasn't confident.

"Go upstairs," Ian said. "Tell Tony you disagree with him."

I wanted to say, "You're shitting me, Ian," but I said, "I don't feel comfortable doing that."

"Why?"

"It wouldn't be polite."

"Oh, politeness has nothing to do with it."

I didn't move.

"You're so naïve, Lowell," Ian said. "The academy is all about the free exchange of ideas. You owe it to Tony to tell him."

Owe it?

When I still didn't move, Ian said, "Tony will welcome the discussion. Trust me."

Based on "trust me,"—I trusted Ian—I trudged up the stairs, every step an agony. I knocked on the office door and heard a weak, "Yes." I walked in and saw Tanner behind his desk, his face red as a tomato. He was wearing shorts and sandals with socks. Ascot around his throat. He looked gift-wrapped. The windows were open, but it was a hot August day and there was no air conditioning, and the office was a steam bath.

Tanner stared at me. He didn't remember me from when I drove him. I didn't know how to begin.

"I wrote an essay on *Under Western Eyes*," I said.

Tanner didn't respond.

"And, well, what I wrote is different from what you wrote. It takes issue with you. I mean not frontally. More indirectly. I don't actually mention you."

"Look, I have all these final papers to grade before I leave town." Tanner pointed to a stack of papers on his desk.

"I know," I said, swallowing hard. "But this won't take long. My thesis directly contradicts yours. I thought you'd like to know."

Thought you'd like to know.

Tony eyeballed me as if I were a lunatic escaped from Atascadero State Hospital for the mentally ill. A lone chair sat across from his desk. Tony didn't invite me to sit but I sat down anyway. He sighed in a distinctly British way. He wanted me to leave but was too polite to throw me out of his office. I explained my thesis in a halting fumbling way. I had no business disputing *Under Western Eyes* with Tony Tanner. We both knew that.

As I tried to explain my point, he fumbled through the stack of essays. Then he carefully straightened the pile. He didn't look at me. I wasn't sure he even was listening, but I kept going because there seemed no alternative even though the exercise was futile and by now, I was almost whispering. I kept going because Ian had told me to—I could feel him urging me on. I knew Ian had my best interest at heart like my parents and Aunt Sarah and Suche. It never occurred to me to say, "Look, Tony, this is total bullshit, and you know it and I know it."

When I was done—thank God—Tanner looked at me his eyes dead, nothing behind them. He stood up, a signal to get lost. "Very interesting, fascinating," he mumbled, as he walked to the door and opened it, and stood to the side so I could slither out. I wandered into the hallway not knowing what to think. I felt a dagger of anger, but against whom?

I started walking down the stairs, walking slowly, taking one careful step at a time, feeling I might fall down the entire flight. I smelled the varnish on the wooden banisters. As I reached the halfway point, I noticed Ian standing outside his office where I'd left him. I was surprised he had waited. He looked up at me.

"How did it go with Tony?" he asked, as I continued down.

I said not so well.

"Hmm," he said.

I kept walking down the stairs. I reached the bottom. Ian and I were facing each other.

"How did he react?"

"React?"

"When you told him you disagree, how did he react? I want to know how he reacted."

"He didn't like it," I said.

"He didn't like it," Ian repeated. This seemed to please him. "What did he say? Tell me what he said."

"He didn't say anything. He listened to me and then asked me to leave. I don't think he appreciated what I did. He seemed uncomfortable."

Ian took his time. "What you did was good for Tony," he finally said.

Good for Tony?

Ian laughed. All I got from him was, "Well, never mind."

"Never mind?" I said.

"You told him. That's what matters."

Over-heated, stressed-out Tony Tanner sure didn't think it mattered. Why did Ian send me up there?

Ian happily wafted into his office and shut the door behind him. I walked into the large broad Stanford quad as a cooling late-afternoon breeze swept in from the west. The air smelled clean. I made my way into Memorial Church next door to the English Department. I often went there to think things over. It is the most opulent building on campus, a dead ringer for cathedrals in Europe.

I sat alone in the deserted church, everything still, and told myself something strange had just happened. In the limitations of my unformed intellect, I vaguely understood Ian had shown me something I needed to learn about the world and its indifference—hostility?—to me the loved one, something about things being more complicated than I imagined, about people having motives which eluded me.

I wearily leaned back in the pew of the glorious cathedral and stared at the golden altar, an offering to God and the pursuit of higher learning.

Chapter 24

My Catholic Jewish Father

I am the kind of man who has loved older men although most have disappointed me. A young man needs a mentor who is not his father to help him navigate life.

What I just wrote is my axiom for this story. A writer is entitled to his axiom. My older man was chairman of the French and Italian Department at Stanford years ago when I went there for graduate school, and we became friends even though he was twenty-three years older than me and I didn't study French or Italian. We both ran track. He was the fastest runner in the world for men fifty and over and I was just a runner. So, I was always running to keep up with him. That is my central metaphor for this story and now you know my axiom and my metaphor.

He was French and his first name was Alphonse and his last name was not easy for an English speaker—Juilland—so I called him Prof. When I was young and not fully formed, he taught me how to be a man. He told me about the French existentialist philosopher Jean-Paul Sartre whom he admired within limits, told me Sartre stressed a world of free choice. "Even if a man is captured by the enemy," The Prof told me as a way of explaining Sartre, "and the enemy tortures him, this man makes a free choice when to capitulate and give the torturers the information they want."

I said I didn't understand.

"It's simple," he said, making it sound simple. "There is no absolute point at which the prisoner must give up. He chooses the moment. I am not saying it's a good choice, but it's his choice. He can sit there and say to himself, 'Not this moment,' and then he can say, 'Not this moment,' and then he says, 'This moment.'"

The Prof always could defeat me in an argument. He could take my facts and use them against me, but he did it gently, teaching me, bringing me along. When I was still a student at Stanford, I made a careless comment, said God's existence made no sense, said this with arrogant certainty. We were playing pinball at the time. The Prof hit his ball which sailed into the Gorgon's castle, and I heard bells and whistles and The Prof scored triple points and won a free game.

"How do you know God doesn't exist?" he asked.

"His existence can't be proved."

The Prof, who may have believed in God, smiled kindly. I felt a strangling in my throat.

"So, you'd say it's a leap of faith to believe in God," he said.

"Yes, yes, right," I said. "That's exactly it. A leap of faith."

"My dear, Lowell," he said, "it's the same leap of faith *not* to believe in God. Surely you see that."

"It is?"

"Well, obviously. These are not issues of reason or science. You can't prove God exists, but you also can't prove God does not exist. Each position is a leap of faith."

Oh.

The Prof held my hand while I wrote my dissertation. He was the opposite of my thesis adviser Ian Watt (see previous chapter), who was as distant as Zeus. The Prof told me, "Directing a Ph.D. dissertation is ninety percent psychological handholding. He held my hand—psychologically—when I would meet him after a session with Ian Watt, my confidence shattered. He would say, "Let's grab a beer," and we'd drink beer and eat chips and he cheered me up.

My dad once said to me, "I know The Prof is your father on the West Coast. I'm not jealous. I'm glad you have him." My dad wasn't competitive, didn't mind my other father was a French Catholic who showed me the world. My dad was a loving man and I needed someone else like him.

The Prof thought about fundamental questions: how do we lead a meaningful life? what is loyalty? what is the true nature of touching a woman?

That last question always has stayed with me. "When a man caresses a woman's derriere," he said one day, "is it to give her a feeling of pleasure or to give himself the feeling of pleasure?"

I said I never had thought about that.

"It's important," he told me. "The world is divided between men who give themselves pleasure and men who give a woman pleasure. Be a man who gives a woman pleasure, Lowell."

This, I never had discussed with my father. I mean can you imagine me buttonholing him at the kitchen table in our apartment and saying, "Dad, how do you give a woman pleasure?" It would have been a *shonda* (a shame, a disgrace, an embarrassment). Out of the question.

And it was The Prof who made me a sports writer—gave me a start in life.

I was in my late twenties, and we had been running at San Jose State and on the way back I said, "I need a career." I had graduated Stanford but never worked at a fulltime job, and my parents were sending me money and worrying I would be a bum.

"I don't have the slightest idea what to do," I told The Prof.

"What makes you catch fire?" he asked.

Catch fire still sounds so French to me.

"Well, I like writing and I like sports," I said."

He smiled the wisdom smile. "My dear Lowell, let me remind you there is a thing called sports writing."

There it was. I could be a sports writer. But to be a sports writer I needed a topic. I said I wanted to write about him. He graciously agreed. I wrote a piece called "The Existential Sprinter" and sold it to the Sunday magazine of the *San Francisco Examiner*. So, The Prof was the catalyst for my career and the subject of my first article.

After years of freelancing, I became a sports columnist at the *San Francisco Chronicle*. At first, I was controversial in the way young men can be, frontal, rude sometimes belligerent. "I'm printing a letter about you from some Stanford professor," the sports editor casually told me. I didn't think much about it but when I opened the paper Saturday morning, I read a letter that said Lowell Cohn is a good columnist, but he needs to learn wisdom. It was signed by The Prof and gave his title and the name of his endowed chair, and I understood I had let him down. I never asked him about the letter because among other things he taught me subtlety.

I worked fifteen years at the *Chronicle* but didn't like it there. I told The Prof, "They are making me unhappy," and he said, "My dear, Lowell, you have complicity. You know who they are, but you stay. You choose to stay."

So, I left.

The Prof was 5-9, bald and had a gray beard and lively blue eyes and women loved him even though he was married to an elegant Romanian woman he had met at the Sorbonne. Some men, especially older men, need to be taken care of by women. Not The Prof. He made a woman feel like a woman. He pulled out chairs and praised necklaces and earrings in his French accent and wore a suit jacket with a handkerchief folded into the breast pocket and kissed a hand. He was the only hand kisser I've known, and women love a hand kisser if the man has style and is older and especially if he is French.

One time he met me in San Francisco on a Wednesday night—we tried to meet one night a month after I had married and moved from Palo Alto to Oakland. The Prof always said, "Never miss an opportunity to celebrate." He didn't mean celebrate a particular event. He meant celebrate the sheer joy of life. So, we celebrated one night each month.

I picked him up at the Southern Pacific station and we drove to an Italian place near Union Street where we ordered spaghetti carbonara and drank Ruffino Chianti Riserva Ducale and he called the waitress my dear and she loved it and he smoked his pipe—you were allowed to smoke a pipe in a restaurant in those days—and afterward we were feeling expansive and lightheaded and it was a beautiful San Francisco night and we walked along Union Street talking about boxing. That's one thing I liked about The Prof. I could go to him for an explanation of Hegel or Sartre but, like me, he knew every important boxer from every era and had seen many of them in person. The Prof made no distinction between high and low culture. Everything interested him.

So, we were walking along Union Street after dinner, and he slid his right arm around my shoulder. As I say, he was French, and I imagine French men have been sliding arms around each other's shoulders in gestures of masculine *bonhomie* for centuries. But I wasn't French, and I wasn't used to that.

My God, I thought, people will take one look at us and think old guy and young male lover. But I didn't want to offend him. I had a dilemma, just the kind I could discuss with The Prof. I thought about shrugging off his arm and decided, wrong move. And then I told myself the hell with that, embrace the arm around the shoulder, love it. Half of San Francisco is gay, and no one will give a shit.

I was feeling good about The Prof's arm when a man with worried eyes rushed up to us. He mumbled something about leaving his wallet at home and needing a few bucks for gas. He held out a gallon gas can. The Prof slid his hand off my shoulder, shoved it deep into his pocket, whipped out his wallet and handed the man a fiver.

"How could you do that, Prof?" I said after the man scurried away. "It was a scam."

"Of course it was, but, my dear Lowell, he went to the trouble of getting the gas can. I paid for his creativity."

Being friends with The Prof meant I had to accept certain mysteries. Take his experience during World War II. He almost never spoke about the war. I felt, without his warning me, the topic was off limits. Occasionally, he would bring it up—as he brought up other painful topics—out of the blue. We were driving toward the Pacific Ocean over the hills from Palo Alto, and into this pastoral scene he inserted, for no reason I understood, the information that, yes, he had been part of the French Resistance and got caught by the Germans who locked him in a prisoner-of-war camp. He escaped with a friend, he said, but as they ran his friend took a bullet and The Prof picked him up and carried him on his back until he could carry him no longer. "I put him down," The Prof told me in a voice of grief. "As I ran away, I heard one shot."

CHAPTER 24 179

A friend told me something he'd heard—I don't know from whom. The Prof had divulged information to the Nazis when he was a prisoner after they threatened to chop off his testicles. Which brings me back to Sartre and a man freely choosing the moment to capitulate under torture. Was The Prof trying to tell me something about his life?

I also don't know why he never had kids. I assumed his wife could not conceive or The Prof was not fertile, and I left it at that, but one day The Prof interrupted a conversation we were having and—I'll never forget how he put it—"Do you know why we never had children, Lowell? The maturity wasn't there."

I heard the word maturity and peered through that word as though staring through a window. He meant he and his wife were fixed on their careers—The Prof on becoming a world-renowned structural linguist, she on teaching Romance Languages—and that allowed no room for kids and also explained where I fit in, a surrogate son, along with William Gairdner, a Canadian decathlete and Stanford Ph.D. in English. The Prof knew I wouldn't ask questions. He counted on that.

I'm ashamed of something that happened a few years before The Prof died. We had gone to a Stanford bar called Rossotti's to play pinball and drink beer on the old wooden tables in the outdoor beer garden. He told me about an item he read in the paper, how parents in some city objected to gay teachers teaching their kids. The Prof was a philosophical conservative, admired William Buckley, Ronald Reagan and Edmund Burke and worried America was becoming a socialist state. He objected to the government's gaining undue influence over people's lives. I never thought about things like that.

"Parents are entitled to have the teachers they want," he said.

I couldn't help thinking of Carl.

"What about gay teachers, don't they have rights too?"

"The parents have their own rights," The Prof replied.

We weren't getting anywhere until he uttered the crucial sentence. "Parents can reject a gay model if they don't want one."

"What is a gay model?" I asked. I kept my voice calm, but I was lining him up for the knockout punch.

The mid-afternoon sun was boring into The Prof's face. I noticed he was sweating, sweat beads on his bald pate and sweat suddenly pouring onto his mustache and beard, and I knew I had him. Over the years he always defeated me by making me commit myself first. Now he had made his move and I wielded gay model like a hammer.

"Some men act effeminate but aren't gay," I said. "Some men are masculine but they're homosexuals. You can't know by looking. What do you mean by gay model?"

He didn't speak. His face turned red and he looked away. I finally had beaten him. I wanted to win. Then I stared at him, and his posture was bad, and I said to myself, "Fuck this, just fuck it." I led him out of the sun and said Muhammad Ali could have knocked out Joe Louis and we laughed, and the tension floated away.

I promised myself never to beat The Prof again. I needed a world in which The Prof could defeat me, even when I thought he was wrong.

When The Prof was a teenager, his uncle phoned him and said his dad was ill. He told The Prof to meet him at the train station for the trip to the hospital. While they stood somberly on the platform, The Prof saw his uncle reach into his jacket pocket and pull out a tie. The tie was black. The uncle handed The Prof the black tie and turned away and The Prof knew his father was dead. He died of a brain hemorrhage.

In June 2000 my wife and I came home from vacation to find a voicemail on our phone. Bill Gairdner had called from his home near Toronto to say he had been trying to reach me. Something had happened to The Prof, he said. I knew Bill was being discreet — the black tie — didn't want to say on the phone The Prof had died. He'd suffered a brain hemorrhage like his dad and fell to the floor of his TV room. The Prof's wife had died a year and a half earlier and he lived alone. His niece couldn't reach him and asked her husband to drive to The Prof's house. When he got there The Prof was lying on his back with his eyes fixed open.

I spoke at his funeral in a small chapel in the hills west of Palo Alto. I told the gas-can story and people laughed although inside I was crying. A few weeks later, I found out he'd bequeathed money for my youngest son's first two years of college. That was decades ago, and I no longer have an older friend to tell me what comes next, what to look out for and what it all means. I still don't know.

Chapter 25

My First Christmas Dinner

One Christmas Eve The Prof invited me to his house on the Stanford campus for what he called an intimate gathering. I was in my twenties and never had been to a Christmas party. Christmas didn't register for me.

A year before I had gone to the movies with a friend, also a Brooklyn Jew, to see all the *Planet of the Apes* movies on Christmas Day—there were only three *Planet of the Apes* movies at that time. When we got out—and weren't those ape costumes cheesy?—we were hungry and looked for a place to eat but every restaurant was closed. This was in Palo Alto. At first, we didn't understand, but then it hit us. In California they close restaurants on Christmas Day and do other unusual things we never knew about in Flatbush.

I went to The Prof's intimate gathering with my girlfriend, a Chicago Jew named Ruth who had studied journalism at Stanford. The people attending were The Prof, his wife, his mother-in-law, a professor and his wife whose names I don't remember, and an assistant professor of French named David, an L.A. Jew.

We ate dinner and had a good time, and when the meal ended, The Prof announced, "Now it's time to exchange presents."

Exchange presents?

What Ruth and I did was exchange horrified looks. We bore no presents. Why? Because in Flatbush where I grew up and in Ruth's Jewish Chicago neighborhood, West

Rogers Park, there was no Christmas, no lights blinking on and off from the house, no Santa and his reindeer ready to gallop off the roof, no carolers, no Virgin Marys gazing down at the blessed baby, no Christmas dinners with ham or goose—we went out for Chinese food. But there were Hanukkah menorahs in all the windows, menorahs proudly displayed.

Ruth and I didn't know the Christmas tradition of exchanging gifts. Everything in our upbringing fought against that, denied it. And my parents weren't much on giving gifts to begin with, except for a few bucks Hanukkah gelt. We sat there in The Prof's living room two schmucks. It was more than that. We were outsiders, outside the mainstream, just a couple of Jews who might have been living in the shtetl.

The Prof saw what was going on and played past it. Never would he embarrass us. He and his wife gave us our presents and pretended we had given them presents. He smiled the whole time. Even the other professor and his wife, people I never had met, brought presents for us.

The absolute killer was David, the L.A. Jew. He had presents for everyone which he brandished around the room—yes that's the word, brandished. He might have been one of Santa's elves. He gave me a hardback copy of Kenneth Grahame's *The Wind in the Willows* with an inscription on the title page David had written with a fancy fountain pen. I hated him for it.

How did David know this shit about Christmas presents? What larger world had he inhabited that I wasn't aware of? Maybe LA Jews were different from the rest of us. I mean, although David had graduated in French Studies from UC Berkeley and was currently writing his doctoral dissertation at Cal on the eleventh century French poem *La*

Chanson de Roland, his father was in the chicken business. But he knew about the present thing and Ruth and I didn't. Sellout.

But a funny thing happened. After I got over feeling mortified for bringing no gifts, I began to like the party. I can't speak for Ruth. I looked at what was really happening instead of what I was afraid would happen. No one spurned me for being ignorant of Christmas customs. No one tried to convert me. No one accused me of offing Jesus Christ. Everyone was on best behavior. Everyone was kind. The gifts meant *this is a night when we give you a present because we want to please you*. Nothing more. But that was enough, and it was new to me and, although I didn't want to be Christian, I had to give the Christians credit.

That was a first.

Chapter 26
Bill

Bill Gairdner, my best friend from Stanford, suddenly died of a stroke in Toronto in January 2024. We met in 1967 and shared an office and ran track together and we had remained close friends for more than 50 years even though we lived thousands of miles apart.

He was an extraordinary person, maybe the most extraordinary person I ever met. He was the Canadian champion in the decathlon and competed in the 1964 Tokyo Olympics, and after that he was a world-class 400-meter hurdler, and he got his Ph.D. in English from Stanford—he graduated with honors, and I merely graduated. He became a college English professor in Toronto but gave that up because it wasn't interesting or exciting for him—he had a tropism toward risk and adventure. He started a business which earned him millions and he sold it and retired at age 48. Who retires at 48?

And then he became a writer. He was a philosophical conservative, loved Edmund Burke, and wrote books and articles from a conservative point of view which made him famous and infamous in Canada. He was a brilliant thinker and writer and if I disagreed with him about politics or philosophy, I had to be careful, had to rehearse my arguments in advance—not that he ever embarrassed me, although he could have.

When he died his daughter Ruthann contacted me and said fly to Toronto immediately because we want you to speak at Dad's memorial service, so I booked a ticket San Francisco to Toronto and packed my bag and sat on the plane writing my speech—see below—which turned out to be humorous, more a celebration *than a dirge, I'm not sure why. And while I wrote it on the plane, I cried the whole time because I loved and missed Bill and now I couldn't laugh with him like silly boys or talk about what Heidegger meant by being, and because even more of my life was vanishing, and I was learning the difference between simple loneliness which I can accept, and utter aloneness, which I believe is the basic and final tragic condition of life. Bill would have had something to say about that.*

Here are the remarks, slightly edited, I made about Bill to a packed house in an auditorium outside Toronto.

Hi, my name is Lowell Cohn and Bill and I became friends in 1967 when we were first-year Ph.D. students in the Stanford English Department. That's 57 years of nonstop friendship. We were sitting next to each other in a class on the eighteenth century English novel and Bill, whom I did not know, whispered to me, "What do you think of this professor?" I said something erudite like, "He's a fucking old lady." As you can tell, I had a post-adolescent anti-intellectual streak which I hope I've outgrown.

Here's how smart Bill was. One question on the final exam in that class asked, "What is truth in *Moll Flanders* (a novel by Daniel Defoe)?" Are you shitting me? I had no idea what truth was nor how it related to Moll, but I looked over at Bill and he was furiously writing away with a smile on his face. I wrote some crap which the professor correctly didn't like. Afterward, I asked Bill what truth was in Moll Flanders and he said it's obvious, Moll judges everything by money, it's her truth. Right then I learned the difference between a first-rate intellect—Bill's—and mine.

Anyway, after I called the professor a fucking old lady, Bill got the giggles, and so did I and he invited me for a coffee at the student union. That's how we became friends. He did not come from a literature background, didn't major in English at University of Colorado, and I was the youngest in our program and we felt like outsiders. Once, he was taking a course in Elizabethan drama and asked me to sit in for one session and give my opinion of the class. So, I was sitting there, and the professor was talking about dating the play they were studying. He wasn't discussing the play itself. He was dating it—it's the kind of stuff they used to do in English departments, but I'm being unfair.

The professor said they knew the play was written after a particular date because a certain actor always played the lead in this playwright's plays, but he wasn't in this play, which meant he had died, which meant the play came after his death date. Without missing a beat, Bill raised his hand and said, "Maybe he played the ghost."

I loved Bill for that. His wit, his timing, Bill gently mocking authority. The professor got a kick out of it and said, "Oh, Mr. Gairdner."

Before I go on about Bill, I need to mention he introduced me to The Prof. One day Bill said, "I have a friend you've got to meet. He's a full professor in the French Department."

And that's how I met my second father, and The Prof was Bill's second father too, and The Prof called us *mes enfants*. Bill named him Prof and it stuck, and everyone called him Prof. Even his wife called him Prof.

The Prof was a political conservative, which made him suspect on the Stanford campus. He even created something called the Conservative Forum. Bill became deeply interested in conservative philosophy on the Stanford track running with The Prof. Bill would have found his way to conservative philosophy without The Prof, but The Prof became a profound and wise mentor to Bill, showed him how to think and what questions to ask. The Prof was Bill's Socrates. At the time, I knew nothing about politics, liberal or conservative. Bill and The Prof were my friends I ran track with, and that was enough.

If The Prof was my West Coast dad, Bill was my West Coast big brother. He was five years older than me, and he looked out for me. He always looked out for me. Twenty years ago, I had a medical emergency, and it seemed I'd need surgery. Bill phoned and said, "I'll pay for the surgery whatever it costs. I'll fly to San Francisco and be with you." I told him I had good medical insurance, and it turned out I didn't need the surgery. Bill was looking out for me.

Three years ago, my wife died, and Bill and Jean (his wife) said come up to Toronto. We have a private apartment in our home. We'll leave you alone. I said I'd come for three days because, face it, everyone wants a guest gone after three days. Bill and Jean were offended. "Stay longer," they insisted. "Stay as long as you like." So, I stayed, and I could see Bill stealing glances at me to make sure I was sane and Jean, bless her heart, did my laundry.

I want to get back to our years at Stanford if you'll bear with me. One day I was walking down a hallway in the English Department and way down at the other end, I saw Bill with his back to me. "Gairdner," I shouted. He whipped around and pointed his index finger at me like a gun. I already had drawn my index-finger pistol and we both shot each other, the gunfight at the Stanford corral. All those professors and Ph.D. students in that corridor, as silent as a cathedral, exchanged looks with each other like we were a couple of halfwits, but we loved the gunfight in plain view and for the next five decades we argued about who drew first.

Chapter 26

About ten years ago, Bill visited me in Scottsdale, Arizona, where I was covering baseball spring training. Bill, God love him, knew nothing about baseball. He didn't understand why the players for the Toronto Blue Jays weren't all Canadians. One day after we watched a game which Bill didn't comprehend and after I had filed my column, Bill said, "Let's eat dinner at the best Italian restaurant in Scottsdale."

We did some research and found the best Italian restaurant and decided to eat at the bar. From the bartender we ordered two plates of pasta and a nice Chianti. The bartender said, "Those are great choices. We have the most renowned Italian chef in the valley, and he'll make wonderful dishes for you."

Casually, Bill asked, "What's the chef's name?"

We expected the bartender to say something like Giancarlo or Giuseppe or Guido. What the bartender really said was "Sigfried."

Sigfried?

Bill and I looked at each other. And then we went hysterical laughing. Wine shot out my nose. The top Italian chef in Scottsdale, Arizona was named Sigfried? The bartender hustled away. Bill had tears of laughter streaming out his eyes. He slid his arm around my shoulders and kissed me on the cheek. I knew what the kiss meant. "Here we are together enjoying the absurdity of life just as we did when we drew on each other at Stanford." It meant although life is tragic, it is also comic, so remember that. It meant we will always have this Sigfried moment. I kissed Bill back.

Long before that, it must have been in 1968, Bill and I had worked out at the Stanford Stadium. On the way back to the gym for a shower we passed an outdoor swimming pool—

the Stanford campus has an inordinate number of swimming pools—and Bill said, "Let's go in there." So, we went to the swimming pool, and I got ready to jump in, but Bill said, "Not that. Let's do backflips.' He went first. He walked to the end of the diving board, turned around, tested the board with his toes, bounced up and down and jumped as high as he could. He turned over backwards in the air and seemed to hover way up there. Then he splashed into the water. He was laughing the whole time. For the next half hour, the two Ph.D. candidates performed backflips.

As I look back, I realize Bill loved to defy gravity in everything he did. When he ran hurdles, he left the Earth and flew across the hurdles. When he backflipped, he rose above the swimming pool, above the people there, above me. His whole life he flew above all of us. And that's how I always think of Bill. Bill is my friend who can fly.

Chapter 27

My Introduction to Linguistics

Where I came from everyone referred to condoms as scumbags. It's not only where I came from. It's also when I came from. In Brooklyn in the 1950s and early 1960s everyone I knew called condoms scumbags because the word was so descriptive and accurate and vivid. As time went on, the word scumbag has taken on a more metaphorical meaning, as in "Irving's a complete scumbag," implying the Irving in question is morally shaky or has a personality which makes him unfit for basic human intercourse. Some of my younger friends who currently use the word scumbag, always in reference to a person, have no idea of its linguistic origins. The loss of the original meaning is another example of the decline of the English language. Don't get me started.

I bring all this up because recently I was thinking about something that happened when I was fifteen. It was a Friday night and I was standing in front of my apartment house on Avenue L with my friend Stuie. Neither of us had anything to do, which was not unusual. We never had anything to do. The sun had gone down, and a chill swept along the avenue, and we couldn't decide whether to walk left or right when along came an older guy. He might have been sixteen or seventeen and his name was Kessler. He knew our names and we were flattered because no one knew us. For no apparent reason he said, "You guys want to see me buy scumbags?"

Stuie said yes sure definitely. And I nodded because I'd never actually witnessed anyone buying the items in question, least of all me who'd never laid eyes on the things and would have no need to see or buy that particular consumer aid for years to come. So, we walked along East 19th Street toward the drugstore on Avenue M, and Stuie asked why Kessler needed scumbags and Kessler, his chest puffed out, said, "Why do you think I need them?"

Stuie didn't say anything but I was impressed. I had no idea why Kessler invited us along and in my innocence was flattered by his hospitality. Then Kessler said he learned a new word studying for the college boards.

"Do you want to know the word?" he said.

"Yeah," Stuie said. "What is it?"

"Xenophobia."

"What does it mean?" I said.

"It means fear of farmers."

"Fear of farmers?"

"Yeah, fear of farmers."

"Why would anyone be afraid of farmers?" I asked.

"Beats me," Kessler said.

Just then we entered the drugstore called Musso and Michaelson's and as we walked inside, I was assaulted by the unique odor of drugstores, the cloying combination of perfume and oil of wintergreen and Juicy Fruit chewing gum and arthritis medication and plastic and rubber and God knows what else, so many smells mixed together they merged into a haze of smells.

"Watch me," Kessler announced as he walked toward the counter. We were alone, just Kessler and Stuie and me, and Michaelson the druggist who had round red cheeks and always smiled like everyone's favorite uncle. Stuie and I stood behind Kessler, and Kessler stared at Michaelson and suddenly he hesitated before the enormity of his request.

Chapter 27

Michaelson waited. He was a patient man. Finally, Kessler, his voice a little hoarse, said, "I'd like to buy prophylactics." I couldn't help noticing he had used the formal terminology.

Michaelson didn't react. I thought Kessler was in trouble. Maybe there was a law against the under-aged buying prophylactics. Maybe Michaelson at that very moment was pushing a hidden button under the counter to summon the police like a bank teller who'd just received a note: *Your money or your life*. But that wasn't it at all. Suddenly the warmest smile spread across Michaelson's kindly face and he said to Kessler, "Do you want them monogrammed?"

Kessler didn't get the joke, but Stuie and I, who always were in the smart classes, did. Along with Michaelson we laughed our asses off at Kessler, and Stuie and I walked out of the drugstore in hysterics, and to tell you the truth, I don't know if I ever saw Kessler again, and I don't know if he ever got to use his prophylactics that night.

But years later I was in a Kessler situation, God was I. I had moved away from Brooklyn and was a graduate student in the English Department at Stanford and in 1969 had won a fellowship to research Joseph Conrad for a year at the British Museum in London. London had more cachet than Avenue L and Palo Alto, and I felt like a big deal. At least I did at first. Although I was twenty-three, I was unprepared to be left on my own in a foreign city. The fellowship was called the Leverhulme Fellowship and a real lord administered it—Lord Murray to be exact. It wasn't until I actually arrived in London that I learned the Leverhulme Fellowship, which suggested to my youthful imagination sherry before lunch and cucumber sandwiches and castles with sprawling green lawns covered with croquet wickets, was endowed by Lever Brothers Soap. So, I was a soap fellow.

I had taken a room in a part of town called Kilburn because it was cheap. I lived right near the Bakerloo Line of the underground (subway) at the Kilburn High Road in a neighborhood which looked surprisingly like Brooklyn except older. And it occurred to me I had traveled all this way only to return to the beginning. Kilburn had small two-story run-down attached homes, and everything was foggy and wet and to be in London in those days was to look at the world though a dirty window. I later learned lots of Irish Republican Army terrorists lived in Kilburn, but no one ever tried to blow me up.

I shared a kitchen and a bathroom, which had a bathtub but no shower and it felt creepy sliding into a bathtub, naked skin to dirty porcelain, that perfect strangers used, and it made me feel I'd gone back to the 1940s. My room was large with a high ceiling that needed paint and, to heat the room, I had to drop shillings into a meter, each shilling giving me an hour of juice in a small electric heater in front of the bricked-over fireplace. The heater had one bar which gave off enough wattage to melt an ice cube. The meter didn't take enough shillings to keep the heat burning all night, so I'd wake up at three in the morning to find a low-pressure system pushing in through the water-stained wall. I could see my breath in the air, and I'd taken to wearing a beanie to bed to keep my brains from freezing.

I didn't actually know anyone in London. I was supposed to meet Lord Murray for lunch so he could praise me for being a Leverhulme fellow and discuss my research, something about first-person dramatized narrators and moral uncertainty in the fiction of Joseph Conrad. I wanted to tell Murray—I assumed we'd drop the lord business and be a couple of pals—well, I planned to explain to good old

Chapter 27

Murray that I'd made a breakthrough in the history of knowledge and then I'd lay my *Lord Jim* spiel on him. But I never got around to that. I never much got around to the British Museum, either.

I didn't feel what you'd call normal in London. Although the English were annoyingly polite, they never wanted to be friends like, say, New Yorkers who would tell you *go fuck yourself* and then invite you home to dinner. I wandered the streets of London like a ghost, never talking to anyone or doing anything worthwhile or thinking the least bit about Joseph Conrad or his dramatized narrators or, God forbid, his struggle with moral uncertainty. That was his problem. My problem was terminal loneliness and an irresistible urge to admit defeat and slink back to California and sunshine and people who knew me. Because I had no one to talk to, I had begun talking to myself, long monologues involving hand gestures and laughs and snorts. I would talk anywhere, my sense of social decorum having vanished.

And then one day I noticed on a bulletin board outside Queen Mary College, where I was theoretically enrolled, a notice that said concerned Jews were marching on the Soviet embassy to protest the treatment of Soviet Jewry. This was a subject I hadn't given much thought. Soviet Jews had their issues and I had mine. But this was an opportunity. Not just to meet a friend. It was a chance to meet a woman, the right woman from my heritage, someone sympathetic, someone wise and beautiful who would understand the depth of my solitude and restore me to life. Forget that I hadn't stepped into a synagogue in a decade, not even for the cheese and wine spread after a bar mitzvah.

The next day I walked into a drugstore in Kilburn for the proper accoutrements because I was sure whoever she was would fall in love with me on the spot and I wanted to be prepared. I was surprised how much the place looked like Musso and Michaelson's. I almost expected Stuie and Kessler to come strolling through the door. I wanted to ask the man behind the counter for what I needed but I was having trouble with terminology, with how not to give offense, with how to make myself clear without actually saying prophylactics or rubbers or, heaven help me, scumbags.

Several older women were hanging out near the counter buying hairspray and stuff like that and that didn't help either. I waited for them to leave while I hid behind the sunglasses rack, but they didn't leave. For all I knew this was the social hub of Kilburn and they'd be there for hours. So, I took a deep breath and walked over to the counter. The druggist, the chemist, whatever they call them, looked my way. His face had a helpful, inquiring expression. At the last moment, I received an inspiration and was glad of it. I said to him, "I need something for birth control." I noticed I had whispered the words as if I were trying to slip them past the women clinging to the counter.

The druggist stared at me, and for the longest while he didn't say a word. Then in a loud, clear voice he said, "Breath control?"

Breath control? Was this guy hard of hearing? A bolt of panic shot through my chest, although a part of me appreciated the concept. Breath control, people all over the world squirting anti-bacterial drops into their mouths for clean-smelling breath, a whole world free of halitosis. I tried again. I leaned over the counter, looked the druggist squarely in the eye and repeated, "I need something for birth control." This time he stared at the women who also had leaned toward me when I'd spoken. "Breath control," he announced to them. They all huddled up like the San Francisco 49ers gathering around Joe Montana. I heard the words breath control repeated several times. I saw heads shaking. Even though all of us were speaking English we were speaking a different language. One of the women said to me in a tone of accusation, "Are you Australian?"

I tried again. Slowly I said, "Birth control. I need something for birth control."

A light bulb of recognition beamed bright above the druggist's head. "Oh," he said, "You've got it all wrong, sonny. Birth control isn't for men. It's for women."

He turned to the women who were clucking their tongues and suppressing giggles. This was becoming a nightmare. I made one last desperate attempt to clarify. "Not for women," I said. "For me."

One of the women walked over to me and slid her meaty arm around my shoulder. "You mean condoms, dear," she said matter-of-factly. "Why didn't you say so in the first place?"

I wanted to explain I was having linguistic difficulties, but I was sure she couldn't understand. I walked out of there with a jumbo pack. I went home and took a greasy bath and washed my hair and combed it, although I never really felt clean in that city. It was as if centuries of coal dust had settled on my skin and turned it gray.

I met the Jews near a synagogue and a monitor walked over and politely handed me a lit candle. I said thank you. We began walking toward the Soviet embassy, a whole procession of outraged Jews and me. It was dark and the procession stretched for blocks and the candles flickered and glowed. It felt good to be part of a group. I noticed a young woman walking next to me, dark hair, dark eyes, long dark eyelashes. I was sure her name was Rachel or Ruth or Sarah, some fine Old Testament name. I knew she could understand me. She had ripe peaches for breasts, let me climb among the fruit. I smiled at her. Rachel or Ruth or Sarah smiled back. Her teeth were as white as liquid White Out. I leaned toward her searching for just the right thing to say. "Sure is a nice march," I intoned, breaking the ice. She smiled back. She didn't say anything. I got straight to the point. "What are you doing later?"

The monitor hurried over to me with a stern look on his face.

"What's up?" I asked.

And then the monitor told me. "This is a silent march."

"A silent march?"

"Yes, a silent march."

"You mean no talking?"

"Shush," he said.

I looked at Rachel or Ruth or Sarah for support. "Shush," she said.

I wanted to say to them, "To hell with your silent march. I need someone to talk to." Now more people were shushing me. A confederacy of shushers.

At the next corner I dropped out of the protest. I figured the Jews could get along just fine without me. On my way to the Bakerloo Line, I dumped my candle into a garbage can. A half hour later, I slumped into my cold dank room and sat on the bed and saw the water drops near the ceiling and took a deep breath. And from some place down the corridor of years, I'm not sure why, I retrieved the memory of Kessler and I apologized to him because I had laughed at him, which made me feel like—well there's no better way to put it—I felt like a real scumbag.

Chapter 28

An Honest Bloke

The cabdriver kept looking at me in his rearview mirror. Weird. I was going somewhere in London, can't remember where. He kept looking—I saw his eyes in the mirror. What was he staring at?

"You Jewish?" he said.

My father, sensing an anti-Semite, would have said, "What's it to you?"

Me, I said, "Yes."

"I thought so," he said. "You look Jewish."

My tribal honker.

I didn't say anything. Waited, vigilant.

"Me, too," he said. Almost bragging.

A *landsman*.

"I like to meet fellow Jews," he said, "someone like me. But you're not English. I hear it."

"I'm American here as a student."

"A student," he said, "a student all the way from America. You must be smart."

"I don't know about smart."

"My name is Mark," he said. "Call me Mark. I don't give just everyone my name, but in your case."

He looked over his shoulder, big grin on his face, spit at the corners of his mouth. Squirrelly guy. Hadn't showered in God knows.

"Hello, Mark," I said.

Before he turned back to the road, I saw a frown.

"I'm worried about you," Mark said.

Already he was worried. He knew me three minutes. He could have been my Uncle Irving, a world-class worrier. All Jews are worriers.

"It's the money," he said. "It's how people act over here. Take advantage of a young American like you, give you the wrong change. I'm telling you this. I wouldn't want anyone to cheat a nice Jewish boy. You understand how our money works?"

"I'm getting used to it," I said. "But when I'm in a hurry I get confused."

"See what I mean," Mark said. "See what I mean. Tell me what a guinea is."

"A pound and a shilling." Proud.

"Good, good. I could see right away you're smart. See you're smart. But you need to be careful. You give someone a five-pound note, a ten-pound note, count your change. Make them wait while you count your change. Cheat an American, oldest trick in the book."

I assured Mark I'd count my change.

"Good, good," he said, "Mark takes care of a smart Jewish boy from America. Takes care. My *zeyde* would be proud." (Zeyde is Yiddish for grandfather.)

He pulled over to the curb.

"Get out on the correct side," he warned. "Look the correct way. Americans get confused, get hit by cars. I've seen it."

I got out. Safe. He approved. He told me the fare. I gave him a five-pound note, told him the tip. He raised his hips off the seat, reached into his pocket, grabbed a wad of tired bills and made change, handed me bills and coins. Grinning the whole time. We had made a connection through our Jewishness. I counted the change. In my money ignorance I still knew he'd shorted me.

Chapter 28

"Mark," I said, deeply apologetic, "You gave me the wrong change. You owe me money."

"Oh, oh," Mark said, studying the bills and strange coins in my hand. "Oh, oh, my mistake. So sorry. It happens sometimes." His voice a groan.

He made things right. He wished me a happy healthy Sabbath and drove off.

And while I stood there in London, the big loud gray city rushing around me, I understood Mark the Jew had intended to cheat me the whole time. It's what he did, cheat American dopes. Couldn't help himself. Was wired to get a few extra cents. His way of life. Except for this colossal difference. Mark hated cheating a nice Jewish boy, hated himself for his inescapable inclinations. Felt disloyal to all our generations of circumcised men, wanted to look out for me. So, he'd warned me in advance, warned me against himself, pleaded for my help. And I'd helped him and now he'd have one fewer sin to atone for next Yom Kippur.

Chapter 29

Smart-Ass Jew

The guy said to me, "What makes you New Yorkers think you're so smart?"

I stared at him thinking there are all kinds of New Yorkers. Was he asking about all New Yorkers or just a particular group? Would the guy ask a Nigerian, "What makes you New Yorkers think you're so smart?" Or would he ask an Italian, a Pole, a Sikh, a Haitian, an immigrant from Yemen, a Korean, a Dominican, a Puerto Rican or an Albanian *what makes you New Yorkers think you're so smart?*

I sat there wondering if New Yorkers was code for Jew. I was sure of it. The guy, someone we'd call a no-good cocksucker in Brooklyn, was asking me, "What makes you New York Jews think you're so smart?" Meaning you Jews are an over-educated bunch of doctors, lawyers and college professors who condescend to regular folks like him. I'd heard Jew insinuations before but never from my editor at my first newspaper job.

Here's how the whole thing started.

I was in my early thirties working for the *Palo Alto Times* in Palo Alto, California, home of Stanford University. Not actually working *for* the *Palo Alto Times*. I was a freelancer, and I didn't make enough to live on. I supplemented my income by teaching Freshman English at community colleges and substitute teaching at local high schools, trying to keep the students from stabbing each other or me. And I wasn't a sports writer yet. I was a film and drama critic and was paid, get this, ten bucks for a review. After my first year, the Arts editor phoned me, said I'd done a great job and the *Palo Alto Times* was giving me a twenty-five percent raise. Twelve-and-a-half bucks, as in *bupkis* (Yiddish for *nothing*).

I went several nights a week to movie previews and little-theater productions where *Waiting for Godot* always seemed to be running. All that existential angst. Great play but overexposed to the theater-going public. Every time I hear the words *Waiting for Godot* my eyelids start to twitch. I bought a pen with a flashlight on one end and sat in dark theaters scribbling in a notebook. People in the audience must have thought a firefly got loose in the auditorium. I covered the San Francisco Film Festival and had lunch with Shirley MacLaine and Richard Benjamin, where I sat there thinking, "Holy shit, I'm having lunch with Shirley MacLaine and Richard Benjamin." When Benjamin thought the waiter was slow, he shouted, "Food!" across the restaurant for everyone to hear.

The *Palo Alto Times* and its sister paper, the *Redwood City Tribune*, were intelligent, stylish, sophisticated papers catering to the Stanford community and the rich, highly-educated people who live on the Peninsula, the swath of land down the Bayshore Freeway between San Francisco and San Jose. The art, music, book, theater and movie reviewers were mostly Stanford Ph.Ds. who, like me, had left academia and, like me, were eccentrics—kooks?—and like me weren't sure where they were headed.

The Arts editor at the *Palo Alto Times* liked my reviews and thought I showed promise as a writer. He gave me a weekly column—fifty bucks they paid me. Hoo-Hah! Shortly after I got the column, the Tribune Newspaper Co., part of the Chicago Tribune Group, bought the *Palo Alto*

Times and *Redwood City Tribune,* merged them into one paper, *The Peninsula Times Tribune,* a paper no longer containing the name of a city. Bad move considering it went belly up.

To run the paper, the Tribune hired C. David Burgin as executive editor. Burgin had a reputation for salvaging failing newspapers and launching new papers. About two weeks after his advent, his secretary phoned me at home. "Dave would like to see you."

This I welcomed. I was pumped to meet the new head guy, hoped he'd have something to teach me. I already had published in *Sports Illustrated, Sport Magazine,* and the Sunday magazines for *The San Francisco Examiner* and the *San Jose Mercury* but had lots to learn.

Burgin's office was a suite. In the outer office sat his secretary. There were chairs for visitors. I took one. Burgin was in his private office with the door shut. Our appointment was for 1 p.m. By 1:15 Burgin had not come out. Nor at 1:30 nor at 1:45 nor at 2. I asked the secretary if Dave knew I was there. She gave me a lukewarm smile, assured me he did. At 2:15 her phone rang, she nodded her head as she listened, hung up and said, "Dave will see you now."

I walked into Burgin's office feeling wilted—by now I needed a pee and a glass of water, and it was hot in there. I wondered why he made me wait so long. The room smelled of cologne. I expected Burgin to stand up, shove his hand across the desk and say, "Sorry for the delay. I'm settling in and things are crazy around here."

But he didn't. He was on the phone. He was telling some distributor what comic strips he wanted for the new, improved *Peninsula Times Tribune.* He didn't look at me. He raised his pointer finger and held it in the air like someone testing wind direction and velocity. The finger meant he'd get to me when he was ready. He didn't invite me to sit.

I studied him. His face was ghost white. And it was fat. His little beady eyes looked like marbles pushed into a giant marshmallow. He wore a white shirt with the top button open. Near his stomach, the two sides of his shirt didn't quite meet, and I could see his wife beater on top of his boiler.

When done with the comic guy, he motioned me to a seat with the finger. Didn't say a word. Stared at me. Out of the blue, he asked which columnist I liked in the local papers. This was a test. I said Charles McCabe, a star for the *San Francisco Chronicle*.

"He's a mere essayist," Burgin said.

What's mere about being an essayist, I wondered. *Was Montaigne mere?*

"I've been reading your column," he said.

"Yes." My voice hopeful.

"It's shit," he said.

"Huh?" I replied.

"It's shit," he repeated. "You don't do any reporting. You don't do any homework."

"Huh?" I replied.

"Is that all you have to say, huh?" His white face turned purple as a plum.

"Huh?" I replied.

He kept going. Ran me down. Said I had no business using the word "I" in my columns. I asked how I could write my experiences and opinions, which the Arts editor told me to do, without using I.

Bullshit, he said.

He said I was a crummy writer and might not have a

future. *Sports Illustrated doesn't think I'm a crummy writer*, I told myself.

No one had ever talked to me like this—not a professor or an editor or a boss or my friends or my father. I wanted to slide out of my chair, fall to the floor in the fetal position.

"You need to report," he said. "You need to do homework."

He was almost frothing. I thought he'd leap across the desk and squeeze my windpipe.

"Help me understand what you mean by reporting and homework." I said, my voice shaky. "I'm trying to learn. If you explain it to me in a calm voice, I'll do what you say."

He said, "You're from New York, right?"

From New York?

I said, yes, I was from New York.

And then he said it, the key line of this story. "What makes you New Yorkers think you're so smart?"

I was pretty sure this prick was saying, "What makes you New York Jews think you're so smart?" In his paranoia—who knows where it came from—he thought I was disrespecting him, and he was getting even.

"Well, you're not so smart," Burgin said, leaning across his desk at me. I sat there certainly feeling like a Jew. He told me he'd brought in a writer way smarter than me. This writer had tended bar where Burgin drank and now the bartender was a writer. Burgin said this writer's "I.Q. went right off the chart."

At which end? I wondered.

Burgin told me to get lost. Looked away and waved me out of his office with the finger.

That night I phoned my dad in Brooklyn, asked how he interpreted Burgin's smart New Yorker remark.

"He meant Jew," my dad said without prompting from me. "Of course, he meant Jew. He's a bum. Be careful with this man, Lowell."

Wanting to please Burgin, I tried reporting. I investigated local issues and interviewed people, and wrote columns which seemed to me stilted, almost like book reports. One was about the local weather. I had lost my tone, my style, my confidence. Burgin never helped me, although he'd mark up my columns in red pen, the red ink screeching what was bad. When he was done, my columns looked like Jackson Pollock's splatter stuff.

Sometimes he'd shout at me. Did this in front of the entire newsroom. He was an old-school editor who thought fear and abuse motivated journalists. If you couldn't take it, clear out. People who admired him—and some did—said he had "great shit detectors." I guess I was shit.

I have to get away from this lunatic, I told myself.

I had written a long feature that just appeared in *Sports Illustrated*. It contained plenty of reporting and homework, and SI paid me three grand for it. I sent the article to the *San Francisco Chronicle*, top dog in the market, and asked for a job. The executive editor liked my sports writing. Offered me a job as sports columnist. Fine by me. I had been perfectly happy at *The Peninsula Times Tribune* as a two-bit reviewer and once-a-week columnist until Burgin arrived. To escape him, I was entering the big time. I secretly thanked Burgin for driving me out.

But before leaving *The Peninsula Times Tribune*, I wanted revenge. You bet I did.

On a fine piece of stationery I bought for the occasion, I wrote:

Chapter 29

Dear Dave:

I am leaving The Peninsula Times Tribune as freelance reviewer and columnist. I hereby give two weeks' notice.

Cordially,
Lowell Cohn

That was it. No explanation. No thank you for breaking my chops about homework or belittling me. I was especially proud of the *cordially*, a polite way of saying drop dead.

I didn't tell him where I was going. I told no one at the paper where I was going. I knew that would burn him. He asked writers and editors at the paper where I was headed, was obsessed but didn't have the nerve to ask me himself. No one knew. No one needed to know. This was between Burgin and me—*High Noon* in Palo Alto.

Then it was my final night. I had seen a play and was in the empty, silent, fluorescent-lighted newsroom dutifully writing my review. It was past midnight. This was before computers. I wrote on a typewriter and would leave the typed sheets in a mail box for my editor who read copy in the morning—we were an afternoon paper.

After a few minutes, I became aware of Burgin. Hadn't known he was there. He should have been home in bed. He began to pace, his shoes sounding squishy under his heavy tread. He walked past me. I didn't look at him. He walked past me again.

I knew he wanted to confront me. Tell me I was a New York loser. Or ask where I was headed. Or say, sure, he'd been a bastard, but it was for my own good. I continued typing. Typed slowly. Dragged out the time.

He walked past me again and again. Then abruptly, he

sat next to me, our elbows almost touching. Scowl on his face. He was breathing hard. Gulping. Squirming. Sighing.

I kept typing.

He just sat there wringing his fingers. Silent.

I thought, *Ask me where I'm going, you son of a bitch. You ask, I'll tell.*

He didn't ask.

Read me in the San Francisco Chronicle, I thought.

He was muttering now. I never acknowledged him, remembered the hour and fifteen minutes he'd made me wait. Remembered the finger. Finally, he gave up—punked out we would say in Brooklyn. He slammed his hand on the desk, stood, squished to his office and sat down with a groan. I glided past him, walked out the front door, walked away from him forever.

Greatest fuck-you moment of my life. Don't mess with a smart-ass New York Jew.

Chapter 30

I Married a Shiksa

When Dawn agreed to be my wife, I sent my parents in Brooklyn a letter. I informed them I planned to be wed—*wed* was the formal word I used—and I invited them to attend the wedding on June 8, 1985 in The Brazil Room in Tilden Park, Berkeley.

I wrote instead of phoning because I did not want to catch my parents by surprise, fearing they might say something they'd regret and because I did not think the news would make them happy. I was marrying a shiksa (a non-Jewish woman).

A few days later, my phone rang. My mother. Her voice trembling.

"Your father and I will attend," she said, "as long as you're not getting married in a church."

Married in a church?

I heard my mother's sentence and felt her terror. Her good Jewish boy, her son who'd had a bar mitzvah in an Orthodox temple, had gone over to the Catholics with all those saints and no meat on Friday and that crossing maneuver over the chest and the poor guy hanging on a cross. And on top of that Dawn's goyish relatives would invade my parents' peaceful lives like a plague or, God forbid, my parents would have to give me up, exclude me, the apostate, the anti-Jew.

"Don't worry," I told my mother. "We're getting married in a beautiful park and a judge will perform the service. And, Mom, I'm still Jewish. Nothing has changed."

I could feel my mother expel her fear like helium hissing out of a balloon.

"We're coming," she said.

That was forty years ago. Bear with me. I need to slow down because I'm getting way ahead of myself. This story is about my wedding and my marriage, sure, but it's about more than that. It's about being an assimilated Jew, whatever that means, and still being a good Jew, whatever that means. And it's about going against Jewish tradition and everything I'd been taught, going for what I wanted. It was the greatest act of rebellion in my entire life.

It all started in the fall of 1979 when I was turning thirty-four. I was single, a freelance writer struggling to make my way, and I taught a creative writing class one night a week at Merritt Community College in Oakland, California, taught the class to earn enough money to support myself—my parents also sent me five hundred dollars a month because my teaching and freelance writing weren't quite enough.

I had taught the class for years. The first night the class was filled with eager writers, which was always the case on first nights. People like to think of themselves as writers, not realizing what writing is—hard work, opening a vein and letting it bleed. The first night of class there always would be one man wearing a beret. It would be a different man each first night, but there definitely would be a Beret Man. I knew this man played at being a writer but would disappear after the first assignment. It's easier to wear a beret than to write.

So, I didn't notice Dawn the first night in 1979. Way too many wannabe writers. But after a few weeks the non-writers disappeared, and she remained. In the meantime, the

Chapter 30

San Francisco Chronicle hired me as a sports columnist and Dawn came up after one class and told me she had read me in the paper and was impressed. I wasn't impressed with her, thought she was kissing up. In addition to Beret Man each class had a kiss-up, someone who thought getting on the teacher's good side made them a better writer.

But she wasn't kissing up. She challenged me in class, and she usually had a point, and she was the best writer in the class; she was funny and used vivid images and had stories to tell about her Italian-American family. Her *nonna* (grandmother) grew her own vegetables right there in her backyard in Oakland and raised chickens and wrung their necks with her bare hands and served chicken cacciatore that very night.

Dawn was also beautiful. I admit this meant something to me. She had full lips and her complexion was dark, and she was sultry and her hair was wild and all over the place and I just loved looking at her. I would tell the class, "Pick up your pens. I want you to do ten minutes of in-class writing." And I would give them some assignment or other, something that made them look down.

Why did I do this? So, I could gaze at Dawn. Okay, I'm shallow.

She'd be writing furiously pulling on her left eyebrow, a gesture I learned to love because it meant she was fully committed, and I wondered what it would be like to know her.

But I never approached her. I was merely the teacher. And when the class ended in December 1979, I told the students I wouldn't be returning because writing the *Chronicle* column took all my time. One student approached me and asked if I would meet with a few of them once of month and go over their writing in a seminar, do it for free. I felt this might be a pain in the ass until I said, "Will Dawn be in the group?"

"Yes."

"Count me in," I said trying not to sound eager.

The writing group met at various students' houses including Dawn's. Turns out she was my age, was going through a divorce, had a four-year-old son Brian. Finally, I worked up the nerve to ask Dawn out and she said yes.

I rarely had gone out with non-Jewish women, or girls as the case might be. I didn't know many shiksas, and I was worried about disappointing my parents. I respected their authority and wanted them to respect me and yet this was the first time I didn't worry about what they thought, not that I told them about Dawn, not at first.

She took me to real Italian restaurants where they cooked like her nonna. She made for me osso buco, which is veal shank, which I never heard of, which tasted amazing.

We went on dates I'd never dreamed of. On one, we took a hotel room in Mendocino County near the Pacific Ocean and lay in bed with a book of modern short stories. I would read a story to her, then she would read a story to me, and we had to guess who wrote the story, guess by the writer's style. And we were right almost every time—Bernard Malamud, John Updike, Saul Bellow and more. And when she got one right, she laughed a lusty laugh, a laugh of delight. And I listened to her laugh and thought *I never met anyone like you before* and *reading these stories with you is as good as sex*.

One time, she told me to meet her at a movie theater at a certain time. She came with a picnic basket—mortadella, prosciutto, sourdough bread—and we ate a picnic in the back row. She called dates like this *surprise-a-dates*. On an-

Chapter 30

other she booked us time at a spa where we got massages and took a hot tub, a complete surprise to me, as I'd never been to a spa or had a massage—way too exotic for a Flatbush boy. I don't recall a spa or a masseuse on Avenue M where my mother shopped at the butcher and bakery, got the seeded rye hot from the oven—although the man who owned the jewelry store got arrested for being a bookie, a *shonda* (disgrace) in the neighborhood.

Before I get to my marriage proposal, which is looming, I want to skip ahead a few years to give you a sense of Dawn, skip ahead to a memorial service for my friend Paula Satlow whom I had introduced to Dawn.

Paula was part of a group from my Stanford years, although she had gone to Cal. Many of Paula's friends from the old days were there including a former girlfriend of mine. Dawn was the outsider. One by one we went to the lectern and talked about Paula and then the ceremony was over. But it wasn't over. Dawn, who had not been scheduled to speak, walked behind the lectern. Some of my old friends saw her as an interloper.

"Paula once invited me to a Spanish delicatessen," Dawn said. "I was thrilled because I'm not part of this group and I want to be, and Paula was including me. We went in and she said she wanted to buy something special for me. She showed me beautiful pottery and special rice and wine. But she didn't buy me any of that. She walked over to the cans of tuna, to the Spanish tuna packed in oil. 'This is for you,' Paula said, and she picked up a can of tuna. At first, I was let down, but I got over it. 'If Paula wants me to be the tuna,' I said to myself, 'I'll be the tuna.' So, I want to introduce myself to all of you. I'm the tuna and I'm proud of it."

Dawn was the best tuna I ever saw or tasted.

Also, she was the Other. She was different from Jewish women I had dated, exposed me to a world larger than Flatbush, a world I wanted.

One time, years later, we were in New York, staying in a hotel on Third Avenue. She went out to Starbucks for a coffee and when she returned, she was laughing hysterically.

"You've got to hear this," she said. "I'm standing in the line at a Starbucks waiting to place my order when a crazy lady walks in."

"New York is filled with crazies," I told her.

"I know. This crazy lady looks at everyone in the line and then walks over to me. 'California bitch,' she says. And then she says it again, 'California bitch.'

Then Dawn said, "So, here's what I want to know. I'm a bitch. Okay, I'm a bitch. But how did she know I'm from California?"

"Beats the hell out of me," I said, and I kissed her full on the lips—the pure joy of being with her.

Sometimes after we were married, a copy editor at the *San Francisco Chronicle* would phone, usually at dinner time, with a question about my column. Instead of saying, "Hello, Dawn, may I speak to Lowell," he would say, "Lowell." That's it, just *Lowell* as if Dawn didn't exist. Responding in kind, she would push the phone to me over the penne bolognese and say so the copy editor could hear, "*Chronicle* asshole." Which said it all.

Dawn named things. Our Honda Accord was Kenny. Our portable air conditioner was Jeffrey, the toaster was Freddy, our long blue sofa was Sofia, our bedroom lamp that looked that the Eiffel Tower was Effie. She named things because they were alive to her and had a spirit of their own. Her world was alive.

Chapter 30

Dawn had an obsession with actor Philip Seymour Hoffman, thought he was the bees knees, ranked up there with Brando, but when she talked about him, full of fan eagerness, she would mangle his name. Sometimes he was Philip Sophomore Heman—she was unaware of saying that, but I took note. Or—and this was the living end—she called him Philip Hoffmour Semen. So, naturally, I injected Seymour Hoffman or whatever his name was as often as possible into our conversations, and Dawn would ask, "Why are we always talking about him?" And I would smile.

Now that you have a sense of the Dawnness of Dawn, let me take you back to my marriage proposal, or rather just before my marriage proposal. My parents visited me in California, and I tremblingly invited Dawn to have dinner with us. This was the first time they would meet her. My parents were polite. Formal. Cold. Dawn didn't notice or pretended not to notice. My parents thought she was a phase I would outgrow and they didn't want to encourage her.

Another time, I invited her to dinner with The Prof, my second father, my West Coast dad, at a sweet little trattoria in North Beach San Francisco. The Prof stared at her face and said she had the nose of Michelangelo's David. The Prof was able to welcome Dawn in a way my parents could not. After we married, Dawn told me what meeting The Prof had meant to her. "I knew you were serious about me," she said.

After that, I planned to ask her to marry me on a Friday night in the Napa Valley, among the beautiful places on Earth. We had drinks at Auberge du Soleil, a fancy resort we couldn't afford to stay at—these days deluxe suites can go for two grand a night—but we loved the bar, all Spanish-style and bare wood. I knew this was the perfect setting for my marriage proposal. And I almost came through, but I chickened out. I wasn't sure why.

We then drove for dinner at a place near the highway called Mustards. Mustards is a good restaurant but it's no Auberge and I felt like a schmuck for missing the moment. I was quiet at Mustards and Dawn looked at me with an enquiring look. Then I understood why I had chickened out at Auberge. This was the big moment, crossing my personal Rubicon, going against my background and my parents and everything I thought was right. The hell with all that. I reached into my pocket and produced the diamond engagement ring, handed it across the table and said, "Dawn will you marry me?" And she said, "Yes I will marry you." And then she said, giggling, "You were going to ask me at Auberge, but you lost your nerve, right?" I said I lost my nerve. "It would have been more romantic for you to ask me there," she said, "but what happened will be a good scene for your memoir."

"I'm going to write a memoir?" I said.

"Of course you are."

About a week later, we drove to a lovely hotel in northern Mendocino County called the Benbow Inn, a Tudor-style place with an elegant dining room. Dawn was wearing the engagement ring which I had not sized properly—we'd take care of that soon—and because she was dramatic and always made the dramatic gesture, she waved her left hand to emphasize a point and the ring flew off her finger.

"Don't anybody move," she cried out in the hushed dining room.

People stared at her. Maybe they thought gunmen had rushed into the room for a holdup. But Dawn said, "I lost my engagement ring and I don't want anyone to step on it."

Chapter 30

About forty people in suits and dresses fell to their hands and knees and searched under chairs and tables for the ring until a lady shouted, "I found it." And Dawn ordered champagne all around. She loved a community effort.

A few days after she accepted my marriage proposal, I casually said to Dawn—almost a throwaway line—"You'll convert to Judaism, right?"

Like it was expected. And in a way it was. My older brother Robert had married Nancy who was Catholic, but he insisted she convert, and she did. If it was good enough for my big brother, it was good enough for me. Plus, it's what my parents wanted.

So, again, I said, "You'll convert to Judaism, right?" And Dawn's eyes flashed, and then she said.

"You love me, correct."

"I love you," I said.

"You love me the way I am."

"I love you the way you are."

"Then why do you want to change me? I might change into someone you don't love."

I thought about what she said, thought for all of ten seconds.

"You're absolutely right," I said. "I don't want to change you,"

And the issue ended there and then—I could live with disappointing my parents yet again. But there was something else. Accepting Dawn on her own terms made me a better man. Dawn was the kind of woman who took a stand, defined her limits and it's why I loved her.

Dawn had a son Brian from her first marriage. He was not my son, but he became my son. I love him. He lived in my house, and I brought him up, although he has a father with whom he's close and his father and I are friends. When Dawn gave birth to our son Grant in 1988, twelve years after she had Brian, my mother and father flew to Oakland to take care of Dawn, who was exhausted. She was almost forty-two when she gave birth to Grant—she did that for me—and my mother seeing my wife so tired, said, "Dawn, you go to sleep, Dear. You need your rest. I will take care of Grant."

And there was my mother, Eve, an older lady, sitting on our couch all night holding crying three-week-old Grant in her arms, giving my wife peace. It was almost biblical what Eve did. And then she did it again the next night. During the day, my dad, who was dying but we didn't know it, sat in a rocking chair warming himself in the sun from the living-room window because he always felt cold. He would die eight months later, but he had seen his grandsons.

My parents understood that Dawn honored my Judaism. There were never crosses in our home. When our son Grant turned ten, Dawn said to me, "Are we going to send him to Hebrew School or not?" We sent him to Hebrew School. When he turned thirteen, she said, "Let's schedule his bar mitzvah. He needs to be a Jewish boy." He had a bar mitzvah.

After my father died in 1988, we flew to New York, Dawn, Brian, me, our son Grant eight months old. At the gravesite Dawn held our baby in her arms and quietly cried. The hearse driver took us back to my mother's apartment and we sat with her until it was time to fly back to California. We walked to the door of the old apartment which used to have so much life and now my mother was condemned to live in it alone. Brian and I went through the open door toward the lobby of the apartment building. I was holding

Grant. But Dawn didn't follow us. I looked back. She was hugging my mother, hugging my mother under the *mezuzah* at our front door, my mother's head resting on her shoulder. Loving her the way my mother had shown Dawn love.

"I love you, Eve," she said. "We will come visit you and you will come stay with us, and you won't be alone. I promise you."

And as I looked at Dawn and my mother and heard what Dawn said I thought of *The Book of Ruth*. How could I not?

Ruth, a Moabite widow, was speaking to her mother-in-law Naomi, a Judean, and she said the famous words: "Whither thou goest, I will go; and where thou lodgest, I will lodge: thy people shall be my people, and thy God my God."

Dawn didn't go all the way. She didn't become a Jew. But she loved my mother as Ruth loved Naomi. *Dayenu (it would have been enough)*. She cared for my mother. Dayenu. She kept a Jewish home. Dayenu. She raised a Jewish son. Dayenu. She may not have been Ruth, but she was Ruth enough for me. Dayenu.

Chapter 31

The Can

he can?"

Someone was shouting at me on the phone I had answered in the *San Francisco Chronicle* Sports Department.

"The can?" the voice repeated. It was a female voice. It was an interrogative voice filled with amazement and horror. "The can?"

I knew who it was. My friend Paula Satlow. She was calling me at the *Chronicle* where I had been working about a month in 1979. She wanted to see how I was doing.

"The can?"

"What's going on?" I asked Paula.

"Just this," she said. "I called the Sports Department and an older man answered."

I explained to Paula we didn't have private phones. If you were near a phone and it rang, you answered.

"I get that," she said. "But this wasn't just any answer. I asked to speak to you and the older man said, 'He's in the can.' Who says in the can? Who says in the can to a stranger on the phone?"

She meant the man who answered was barely civilized. Being civilized was important to Paula. She was Brooklyn Jewish like me, had attended Tilden High School, went to Smith College, spent her junior year in Spain and was bilingual English and Spanish. And she had a master's degree in architecture from the University of California, Berkeley. To the best of my knowledge none of the sherry-drinking, library-haunting Smith professors ever accused anyone of being "in the can." When Paula visited me at home and wanted to use the bathroom she never announced, "I'm going to the can."

I need to interject something about hygiene here. In our Brooklyn apartment, we had one bathroom for the five of us, also a bathtub and a stall shower, which seemed the tops in sophistication. When someone was in the bathroom, doing whatever, everyone else left that person alone out of respect unless there was an emergency like my sister needed to throw up, and then whoever was in there got the hell out fast.

So, we had decorum. Of course, when I was done in the bathroom, my mother always asked, "Did you wash your hands?" and then she would inspect them? (Did your mother do that to you?) I have been an obsessive hand washer my entire life. We never used air freshener. This was something else I didn't understand. My mom left a box of wooden matches on the sink, and we were expected to light matches before we exited the bathroom. The room forever smelled of sulfur.

Back to the *Chronicle*. I looked around the Sports Department. Only one other person there early in the day. Jack Fiske, the boxing writer. He was from the Bronx and he was old school, a throwback, a grumpy old journalist (nee Jacob Finkelstein). He was how you imagined a boxing writer—gruff, tough, plain-spoken, his voice an accusation. He took no shit, gave out tons of shit. He knew everyone there was to know in boxing and some famous people feared him. I told Paula to hold the phone a minute. I turned to Fiske.

"Why did you tell my friend I was in the can?"

"Because you were. You were in the can. What was I supposed to say?"

For him, in the can was a perfectly acceptable way of talking. He was who he was, wouldn't change. I wish I had said, "Jack, don't you have any manners?" But that's not what I said, which was, "Actually, Jack, I was getting a cup of coffee." And then I thought how silly of me to say I wasn't in the can.

Fiske shrugged and turned away. He had spent quite enough time on my bathroom habits, caffeine addiction, whatever.

I got back on the phone with Paula. "I guess that's how they talk around here." My voice an apology.

"My God," she said, "what kind of people have you gotten yourself mixed up with?"

Over the years I would find out.

Chapter 32

Horseshit vs. Bullshit

My father said I should talk to my Uncle Bob. My Uncle Bob lived on Long Island in a fancy house because he was an impresario of classical music and made lots of money booking headliners like Beverly Sills. Before that he was a writer, not a good one, and he had written comic books like Superman, but he did not invent Superman.

Uncle Bob invited me into his big study in his big house and told me, "Don't be a writer. It will only break your heart." He said my dad was worried about how I would support myself, if I'd ever have a future, success in writing being so rare. He said my dad would send me to law school, where my dad thought I should have gone in the first place. None of this Ph.D. in English Lit la dee da, which I already had achieved. My brother owned the doctor slot in our family, my sister the teacher slot and I was assigned the lawyer slot. I was the only one who had failed to meet expectations. In our Jewish family, like many Jewish families in the 1950s and 1960s, there were slots which allegedly led to success.

Thing is I didn't want to be a lawyer and learn about habeas corpus or bankruptcy or felonious assault, and I would have tanked the bar exam. I wanted to write mostly because I didn't know how to do anything else. I would have been a flop as a pipe fitter or orthodontist.

I politely told Uncle Bob I would try to be a writer. He left the room, and I heard him and my father whispering and when I joined them my dad looked gray.

I didn't want to be just any kind of writer. I chose to be a sports writer. This was not a frivolous decision. It was a strategy. I had grown up reading newspaper sports sections and I knew—believed—I could write as well as most sports writers, maybe even better. I was too ignorant to have self-doubt. I was in my late twenties and didn't have time to mess around—three years of law school was out of the question. I had to move fast. And I wanted action. I had spent almost my entire life in universities, buried in hushed dusty libraries. I wanted crowds and noise, to write on deadline and to read my stuff the next day in the paper. I needed the fix.

Almost immediately I published freelance articles for *Sports Illustrated*. Their editors didn't tell me to be a lawyer. And they paid me a lot. I leveraged my *Sports Illustrated* work to a job at the *San Francisco Chronicle* as a sports columnist, an almost unheard-of first job for a writer, one which made my parents *kvell* (burst with pride). But this story isn't about the *Chronicle* and me. It's about what sports writing meant to me.

There weren't many Jewish athletes, that's for sure. Aside from Sandy Koufax, Hank Greenberg and Al Rosen whom I knew and liked when he was general manager of the San Francisco Giants, the cupboard is mostly bare. But there were tons of big-deal Jewish sports writers like Dick Young at the *New York Daily News*, or sportscasters like Dick Schaap who edited *Sport Magazine* and became ubiquitous on television. I could be one of them, or so I thought. And I could bring a New York voice to the West Coast, irony and sarcasm and bluntness, stuff most writers in Northern California didn't know or practice.

And there was something else. Sports appealed to the

Chapter 32

intellectual side of me. Yes, the intellectual side. I had trouble understanding Hegel or Kant, still do, but I understood the basic structure of a game. I'm going to talk about baseball but what I'm about to write applies to basketball, football, boxing, you name the sport.

Baseball rules are simple and absolute. Three strikes you're out. Four balls take your base. Three outs to an inning. Nine innings to a game. Home team gets last licks. Fair is fair and foul is foul. Unlike real life, the whole thing makes sense, like the rules of courtship make sense in a Jane Austen novel. A baseball game is a self-contained drama with a beginning, a middle and an end. The literary critic in me loved this. A baseball game starts with a problem—who will win?—and as the problem gradually gets resolved the viewer experiences suspense, a resolution, and sometimes a catharsis—like me when Don Larsen no-hit the Dodgers in the 1956 World Series. A baseball game adheres to Aristotle's unities of action, time and place. You can look them up.

Baseball appealed to the Jew in me. It does not have Ten Commandments, but it has any number of uncodified rules, serious rules. You don't spike the shortstop sliding into second base. When you're in the batter's box, you don't peek at the catcher to see what pitch he's calling—well, that was before they started using a wrist-band gizmo which allowed the catcher privately to call for a pitch and location. Never throw at a batter's head. Don't steal a base when you're way ahead late in the game. Don't bunt to break up a no-hitter. Violate these rules and others and a pitcher will drill you with a fastball in the ribs. Baseball is distinctly Old Testament.

Baseball is fair. It rewards excellence—this goes for most

sports. Baseball's fairness was important to my parents and to me, born in 1945. My parents told me life wasn't fair because Jews got bad breaks. "We're discriminated against." They told me we couldn't get into certain colleges or country clubs or professions. The deck was stacked against us. But in baseball a home run is a home run no matter who hits it, and a win is a win is a win no matter who wins. Baseball was a corrective to the sense of injustice my parents lived with and passed onto me.

And baseball has a culture, an entire culture which, believe me, is different from the culture I grew up in. For starters it has a ball, a very hard ball, which is both a thing and a symbol. It is the focus of the action. The pitcher throws it, the batter hits it, the fielder catches it. A thing.

But it has meaning beyond that. When the manager walks to the mound to take out a struggling pitcher, he holds out his hand for the ball. This happens every single time. The pitcher hands the ball to the manager and walks off the mound and leaves the field. The exchange of the ball means the game no longer is in that pitcher's hands. He is out. Relieved. Dismissed. He doesn't own the ball or the game anymore. Handing over the ball is an enduring ritual in baseball, the most ritualistic of American sports.

If a starting pitcher gets sick on game day and the manager needs to come up with a quick replacement, he walks to the new starter's locker and places a ball in the new starter's baseball shoe. Meaning it is his ball and his game.

The ball is the conch in *Lord of the Flies*.

I love the symbolism of the ball and I love the words of baseball. These words were new to me when I started covering the sport. A fastball is heat, cheese, gas. A batter looking exclusively for a fastball is looking dead red. A curveball is the hook or Uncle Charlie. Other words for pitches—spitter, splitter, screwball, knuckler, beanball. A strikeout is a punchout. A base hit is a knock. Baseball players use all these words and more and they are more colorful than lawyer words like exculpatory, and they mean more to me than words I studied for the SAT—my mother bought us a book of SAT words—like audacious.

Baseball is a linguistic wonderland for a Brooklyn boy.

But one word more than any expresses the culture of baseball. Excuse me for writing this and if you are sensitive, please stop right here, but the most important, most fundamental, most descriptive word in baseball is horseshit. I learned this to my astonishment in the 1980s. Every major league player you remember or who currently plays understands the nuances of the word and has employed it many times.

What follows is a serious analysis of horseshit. I am not trying to be crude. I want to educate and initiate you into the language of baseball, a language I came to as an adult.

I will talk about Frank Robinson, who was a connoisseur of horseshit, but he is representative of every baseball player. Robinson was a Hall of Fame outfielder and manager of the San Francisco Giants, when I met him. If Frank didn't like a column I wrote, it was a horseshit column. Sometimes he called me a horseshit writer, which I took in stride. At least we were communicating. If he objected to a reporter's question he'd shoot back, "That's a horseshit question." This I heard hundreds of times. If one of his outfielders threw to the wrong base, it was "a horseshit play." If the postgame meal served on large trays in the clubhouse didn't appeal to him, it was "a horseshit meal."

Horseshit was Frank's go-to pejorative, as it is in every

clubhouse in the big leagues. One day Frank didn't like the positioning of his fielders during batting practice. Too many near the middle of the field. So, he yelled, "Spread out the horseshit," as he waved his arm indicating where he wanted his players to move. Horseshit becoming a noun. A versatile word.

My enduring fondness for the word is strange considering I didn't grow up with it. I grew up with bullshit. And that in itself is strange because in Brooklyn there are more horses than bulls. I checked the internet and Brooklyn has horse stables and riding academies galore. I couldn't find a single reference to bulls. So, horseshit should have been our preferred curse word in the 1950s, but bullshit was. Which means I was a late convert to horseshit.

What does horseshit mean?

According to Merriam-Webster's Collegiate Dictionary Eleventh Edition horseshit is a vulgar term meaning "nonsense, bunk." Let me stop here and admit I should have gone to the OED for a fuller explanation. Now you see the level of my scholarship. I'm a horseshit scholar and that explains why I fled academia and ended up in the sports pages.

Anyway, I disagree with Merriam-Webster's definition, which I consider a horseshit definition. Bunk and nonsense are closer to bullshit than horseshit. Bullshit is phony stuff, and a bullshitter is a phony and a liar.

Horseshit is an all-purpose term of condemnation, especially the way it's used in baseball. It denotes displeasure, unhappiness and scorn. Something that is no good. It is not nonsense or bunk.

I don't blame the folks at Merriam-Webster's for getting

it wrong. How many of those word geeks spent any time in a big-league clubhouse trying to scrounge a quote off a pissed-off player after a loss? Merriam-Webster's knowledge of horseshit is strictly second-hand, probably from what their editors have read or been told. Did Billy Martin ever rush into the offices at Merriam-Webster and scream, "Your definition of *cosmology* is horseshit"?

If this were an academic essay, the kind I learned to write at Stanford, I'd pause right here and summarize before moving on.

Summary:

Horseshit is a simple, direct, aggressive term conveying displeasure, annoyance, anger. Anyone who says horseshit is seriously pissed off. When Frank Robinson said I was a horseshit columnist he was not accusing me of nonsense or bunk. He couldn't have cared less about nonsense or bunk. He was saying I suck, plain and simple, probably because I had criticized him in print. For me, he was speaking a new language. When I failed a test, my father never said, "That's a horseshit result." He said, "You need to do better to get into a good college."

What is bullshit and how does it differ from horseshit?

Merriam-Webster does better with bullshit than horseshit. As a noun the dictionary defines bullshit as "nonsense: foolish, insolent talk." As a verb Merriam-Webster comes up with: 1. "to talk foolishly, boastfully or idly. 2. to engage in a discursive discussion: to talk nonsense with the intention of deceiving or misleading."

For further elucidation on the word bullshit, please read Harry G. Frankfurt's delightful little book *On Bullshit* (Princeton University Press) which should be required reading at every American university and in Congress and the White House. I am not kidding. This book really exists.

So, what's the point of all this? When I was introduced to the word horseshit in the 1980s, a whole new world opened up to me, the Goyish World populated by big-league baseball players from America's Heartland—the South and Midwest and Texas, guys who chewed tobacco and spit on the dugout floor or collected the spit in empty Coke bottles to avoid spitting on the clubhouse carpet. Johnnie LeMaster, a Southern Baptist who lives in Paintsville, Kentucky, and used to play shortstop for the Giants, once asked my religion. "Guess," I said. He said, "Protestant." I said, "No." He said, "Then you must be Catholic." I smiled and said, "I am Jewish." He looked confused. He wasn't aware of Jews, couldn't imagine what a Jew looked like.

But baseball talk united Johnnie and me and all the ballplayers. When they called my writing or my question or my clothes horseshit, we were speaking the same language, the lingua franca of baseball. I had come from grandparents who grew up in the shtetl and spoke only Yiddish, from parents who spoke Yiddish at home and English in the New World, and I had learned Hebrew at age eight, but through the linguistic idiosyncrasies of baseball—I'd call them linguistic glories—I learned to talk American. To be American. I am American.

Chapter 33

I Take on the Hearst Empire

This is how the whole thing started. Whenever Helen Green phoned, my mouth went dry, and my scrotum tightened. From fear.

Helen Green was the kindest, gentlest woman I knew, but she was Bill German's secretary. German was executive editor of the *San Francisco Chronicle*, a card-carrying sadist, and when my home phone rang and Helen said in the sweetest voice, "Bill would like to see you," I wanted to throw up. Just about everyone at the *Chronicle* felt that way. Without knowing it and without knowing why, Helen Green was the Angel of Death.

German took pleasure in humiliating people, loved doing it to their faces, loved telling people they were replaceable—the *Chronicle* would go on without them. This was especially true when anyone asked for a raise, God forbid. German would run that person down like a road-paving truck. When you walked out of his office, you wanted to refund your salary.

I didn't expect German to be this way. He had hired me in 1979, hired me as a sports columnist although I never had written sports columns. He apparently saw something in me.

So, I thought German was a reasonable man, in my corner. Then the Helen Green calls started coming along with the cold sweats. *I got rid of Dave Burgin at* The Peninsula Times Tribune, *I thought, but Bill German is a bigger lunatic.* On this occasion, Helen told me what time German wanted to see me. I showered and drove to the office. I couldn't eat. German made me wait in Helen's office just outside his. Made me wait a long time. It was like throwing a double-murder suspect into an interview room and making him sweat for hours to soften him up.

German was a short stocky man—a little Rod Steiger. And he was mostly deaf, so he never actually listened. He declaimed. Loudly. I often felt myself sliding down the chair toward the floor under the verbal barrage. I wondered if the visitor's chair was slightly sawed off at the front legs so suckers like me would slide forward and feel disadvantaged.

When he finally summoned me to the inner sanctum, he reached onto his desk—all papers in sharp piles, the edges like the blade of a knife—and he held up that day's sports section. Held it by the corner as if closer contact would contaminate him. He pointed to my column on the front page.

"This is a piece of shit," he explained.

It was a boxing column, boxing a sport I knew something about—I had written about boxing for *Sports Illustrated*—and I honestly didn't know why the column was shit. With German there always could be a subtext. Maybe he thought I required taking down. Maybe he needed a victim for venting. Always a possibility. Maybe he really thought it was shit. And maybe it was.

"Why is it a piece of shit, Bill?"

"I don't have to tell you," he said.

Didn't have to tell me? This was a grownup talking—German must have been sixty years old. Something snapped in me. My father, a formidable man who could have knocked German out with a left jab, always explained things to me. He had encouraged me to ask questions, think for myself, challenge him. At Stanford I had brilliant professors and they always answered direct questions, saw it as an obligation.

"That's not an acceptable answer," I told German. "I taught writing at Stanford. If a student asked why something didn't work, it was my job to have an answer. Give a suggestion. That's what you should do."

German sat back in his chair, appalled. Apparently, no one ever asked him to explain himself.

"OK," he said, his voice condescending, like he'd explain the obvious to a moron. "It's a piece of shit because it doesn't flow."

And that was it. The piece of shit doesn't flow.

"It's bad when a piece of shit doesn't flow," I admitted. "In what sense doesn't this piece of shit flow?"

He leaned forward, his chair snapping behind him. His face was near mine.

"What do you mean?" he asked.

"If this piece of shit doesn't flow, I'd like to know how it doesn't flow."

"It just doesn't flow," he said. Pissed.

"Do you mean I don't develop my thoughts adequately? Do you mean I randomly skip from subject to subject? Do you mean the prose is inelegant? What do you mean? When I criticize student writing, I always give specific examples. It's important to be specific, Bill."

"I don't have to be specific. It just doesn't flow and it's a piece of shit."

"With all due respect, Bill, I think you should have been better prepared for this meeting."

His face took on the deep purple of beet borscht. He aimed his fist at the office door.

"Get out," he shouted.

It never occurred to me what absolute chutzpah I showed in speaking to German that way, a man with power, me with no power. The *Chronicle* had put my face on billboards and on the sides of buses, and my ego became as big as Alaska. I had not learned that following ego is always a mistake and I felt invulnerable. I left his office thinking *screw German*. I had married a year earlier, my wife with a young son from a previous marriage. I earned only $42,000, which made it hard to support my new family, but after getting thrown out of his office, I couldn't ask German for a raise. Which led to this.

I phoned William Randolph Hearst III. He was grandson of William Randolph Hearst, the newspaper big deal and the model for *Citizen Kane*. Hearst 3—people called him Will—was publisher of the *San Francisco Examiner*, an afternoon daily located directly next door to the *Chronicle* where I worked on Mission Street in San Francisco. Afternoon papers were beginning to fail—this was before all newspapers began to fail—and, as *Chronicle* boxing writer Jack Fiske liked to say, The Ex was "sucking hind tit."

Will Hearst was trying to revive the *Examiner*. I heard he was looking for a sports columnist to make a splash.

Hearst took my call in his office. Said, yes, yes, sure, he was interested in meeting me. Very interested. Said he would call me back. A few minutes later, my phone rang. He told me to meet Frank McCulloch, the *Examiner's* managing editor, a giant in West Coast journalism. Everyone in the business knew about McCulloch, a shrewd, honest, uncompromising man with the highest standards. Hearst mentioned an out-of-the-way restaurant for lunch, didn't want anyone from the *Examiner* or *Chronicle* to see us. Hush-hush stuff.

Chapter 33

It was a winter day in San Francisco and the rain came down in waves, filling my thin loafers with water. When I walked into the restaurant, I could feel my socks squish. McCulloch was waiting at a table. He was bald and tough-looking, reminded me of a cut man in a boxing ring with a cotton Q-Tip shoved behind his ear. I was thinking of the legendary boxing trainer Whitey Bimstein. I imagined McCulloch drinking Guinness at a bar. But when he rose to shake hands, he was courtly. Said he admired my work. Went into great detail. Had studied my writing. Said I'd be great for the *Examiner*.

No one at the *Chronicle* ever treated me like this. The *Chronicle* had a pervading attitude—*If you work for us, you suck. So, don't ask for anything, especially money.* That's how I interpreted the place, and I wasn't the only one. I felt excited talking to McCulloch but also guilty because the Chron had given me my shot. McCulloch said Will Hearst would be in touch.

Hearst phoned me, said come to his house in San Francisco. Frank would be there, too. When I arrived, Hearst asked me for a favor. Could I drive him to the dry cleaners? He had to pick up some shirts. I drove Will Hearst to the dry cleaner and double parked on a busy street while he ran in. He came back with shirts in plastic wrap. Even though he was a multi-millionaire and had private rooms at the Hearst Castle in San Simeon, the detour to the laundry made me feel Will was a regular guy just like me. When we returned to his house, McCulloch was there. On a table in the living room, I saw a framed photo of Hunter S. Thompson.

Hearst, about my age, wildly enthusiastic—someone who'd discovered his purpose—said he wanted me for the improved *Examiner*. I would team up with their current sports columnist Art Spander. Art and I would be a dynamite duo. On this Hearst and I agreed. We discussed money there in his living room. He offered $82,500, a big number for 1986 and almost twice what I earned at the *Chronicle*. I was thrilled. I told Hearst I would tell the *Chronicle* about his offer, and as a courtesy, give the *Chronicle* a chance to respond. Hearst said, of course.

McCulloch, who had been quiet, said I should meet with their sports editor, whom I knew casually. I got the impression the meeting was a formality, and when we met things seemed to go well.

I phoned my parents, told them the news. Then I phoned my older friend Alphonse Juilland (The Prof), chairman of the Department of French and Italian at Stanford. He asked when I would sign the contract. I said what contract? "Newspapers are a handshake business," I explained. "It was that way at the *Chronicle*. That's just how it is."

He was quiet for a while. "I find that unusual," he said. "When I came to Stanford, I signed a contract with the university."

I said he didn't know journalism. I explained journalism was different. He said *if you say so.*

A few days later, I was in Bill German's office. He wore a tie, slightly undone, his top button unbuttoned. His sleeves were rolled up. This maneuver of mine had moving parts, things I'd never dealt with. But one thing I knew, and I knew this going in: German had given another columnist a raise after the columnist got a competing offer.

German was cheerful when I told him I had another offer.

"Was it from *The Wall Street Journal*?" he asked, his tone amused.

CHAPTER 33

"The *Examiner*," I said.

He stiffened in his chair and a bullet slammed through his heart. Pure hatred in his eyes. One thing I didn't know was German's feelings about the *Examiner*. It was The Other. The Competitor. The Hated. Any other paper, German could have lived with. Not the *Examiner*, even though the *Chronicle* had seduced writers from the *Examiner*. He ordered me out of his office. I wasn't receiving any counter offer from German. *The hell with him*, I thought. *I'll go to* the *Examiner*.

A few hours later, my doorbell rang. I opened the door and a well-dressed man said, "Courier letter." He handed me a letter in an envelope containing the words *San Francisco Examiner*. I never had received a courier letter. I eagerly took out the letter, assuming it formalized our deal. I felt great. The letter said *The Examiner* was withdrawing forthwith from our arrangement and would not hire me. I'm sure the *Examiner* lawyers got Hearst off the hook, phrased it to show there never was a formal agreement to begin with. It's what I would have done.

I thought I would suffer a heart attack. The blow was that hard. I felt like an innocent in the world, a violated innocent. Competing with that feeling was the thought I'd contributed to my downfall, playing two giant corporations against each other, and got what I deserved.

I called my father. He said, "The relationship between you and the *Chronicle* is ruined."

The *Examiner*'s managing editor Frank McCulloch phoned me, said meet him for lunch. On the drive over, I tried to understand what happened to queer the deal. One of two things. Maybe the meeting with the *Examiner* sports editor had been serious, a deal maker or breaker. I had no idea. I certainly couldn't understand the sports editor overruling the publisher, and I had been polite and cordial in that meeting. Or maybe—and this one intrigued me—German had put the muscle to Hearst. *Keep your hands off my guy.* All these years later I still don't know.

I arrived first at the restaurant. McCulloch walked in with the sports editor. They were businesslike, fast-paced. McCulloch announced there was no deal. I sat there silent, had no idea what to say. My silence made McCulloch uncomfortable. He said I could phone Hearst, try to revive things. It was up to me. I said Hearst had sent him and the sports editor to reiterate I was history, right? McCulloch said, sure. I said what was the point of phoning Hearst. McCulloch didn't say anything.

The waiter brought menus. Having gotten business out of the way, McCulloch was hungry. He studied the menu, said, "Let's order."

"Let's order?" I said. "I don't want to eat with you." I walked out.

Now I had screwed things at the *Chronicle* because of the *Examiner*, but there was no *Examiner*. I was doubly screwed.

I phoned Alphonse Juilland at Stanford. Almost weeping, he said, "I should have made you sign a contract."

I phoned the *Chronicle*'s Bill German. Got Helen Green. Long pause. He came on the phone.

"Yeah."

I said I was staying at the *Chronicle,* where I was protected by a union contract. He hung up. Years later, the *Chronicle* sports editor told me German immediately called him into his office. German told him I was staying. German was compulsively rubbing his hands together and grinning. This is what the sports editor, now at another paper, told

Chapter 33

me. I'm not sure what the rubbing meant—something about getting even? I thought of a Dickens character displaying his deep-down desires through a grotesque physical gesture.

A few days later, I was walking into the *Chronicle* building at Fifth and Mission when I bumped into Hearst on the street. This never had happened before. I told him he was a coward. I used the word *coward* several times. I'm not sure what I meant. Maybe something about having his henchmen kiss me off, him staying away. Maybe the courier letter. Maybe not standing up for me.

Hearst allowed me to call him coward. I think he was being kind, letting me blow off steam. He told me if the *Chronicle* forced me out, he would find a job for me—not as a columnist—something lesser. In spite of everything he was a good guy. At that very moment, the *Chronicle*'s publisher Dick Thieriot, scion of the deYoung Thieriot family which founded the *Chronicle*, came strolling around the corner. Dick Thicriot saw us and frowned. I imagine he and Hearst disliked each other, rich boy competitors. Looking at me, Thieriot said, "Don't talk to this guy." Usually when someone says that he's joking—"Hey, don't talk to *this* one." But Thieriot wasn't joking. Hearst didn't laugh. Thieriot really meant don't talk to Hearst. And I never talked to Hearst again. I never talked to Thieriot either.

They both walked away, and I was left at the corner of Fifth and Mission in San Francisco, me a throw-away by two of the oldest, richest, most entitled families in San Francisco. Carrion. I hadn't understood the world could be that cutthroat. Nothing in my over-protected Flatbush upbringing had prepared me for anything like this, and if I were being honest, I had brought destruction on myself.

At the *Chronicle*, German systematically diminished me,

enjoyed doing it. Started running my columns inside the sports section instead of page one. Hired other sports columnists whom he featured. He told me my writing wasn't good. Maybe it wasn't. I found it difficult to write for a hostile place. This process of getting discarded went on for years. The sports editor—a new guy—was rude to me. Once he was rude to my wife on the phone. He had no reason to be rude. German's attitude gave the sports editor license. That's how I saw it.

Eventually, they took away my column. In a late-night phone call. I had to walk into the bedroom, tell my wife I'd be covering Stanford sports, a minor beat. Losing my column was a public comedown and I felt it deeply, although I never showed it. San Francisco Giants manager Dusty Baker phoned me at home. "Whatever happens," he said, "keep your head high. They can go fuck themselves."

I did Stanford football and basketball. I half-assed it because I didn't know what I was doing and didn't care. I saw a psychotherapist and drank too much, and both helped. My wife told me *look at the positives in our lives*. I found that difficult. She said we had each other, had our son, Grant, six years old, and my stepson, Brian, eighteen. She said I wasn't alone in this. She was supportive, although I was distant and preoccupied, and my moods wore on her.

I told my wife I would look around for another job.

"Does this mean we might have to move from the Bay Area?" she asked.

"Yes, it means we might have to move."

"Why?" She was scared.

"Because I refuse to feel like I'm dying."

Her son Brian from a former marriage, whom I loved like my own son, lived with us during the week, with his father on weekends. She didn't want to break the connection between Brian and his dad. Her mother was in the early stages of dementia. What would my wife do about her son and mother if we moved away? I said we could work that out. We would bring her mother with us. My wife didn't speak. She just looked away. I wondered if my marriage would survive.

We went to the movies, saw *Heavenly Creatures*, a film about mystery writer Anne Perry as a teenager murdering her friend's mother. My wife wept through the entire film.

A few days later, my phone rang. The caller said he was the sports editor of the *Santa Rosa Press Democrat*, a paper I was vaguely familiar with. Santa Rosa is an hour north of San Francisco in the Sonoma County wine country. The sports editor, Jim Jenks, said the *Press Democrat* heard I was unhappy at the *Chronicle*. *No shit*, I thought. He said he had an opening for a sports columnist. Would I be interested? He reminded me the *Press Democrat* was owned by *The New York Times*. I was interested.

I walked into our bedroom and told my wife the *Santa Rosa Press Democrat* wants to talk. I expected her to be happy, but she barely registered what I said. Her eyes had a glazed look. She had been living with bad news for years, was habituated to the negative. I told her again. "The *Santa Rosa Press Democrat* wants to interview me for a columnist job." She stared at me.

"Why couldn't you have waited until today?" she said.

"What?"

"Why couldn't you have waited until today before telling me about leaving."

She meant if I'd waited until today none of the anxiety about her son and mother would have afflicted us—I never would have brought up the subject of moving elsewhere. I said I didn't know the *Press Democrat* would phone me today. What she said didn't make sense until I realized the terror she'd been holding in, the terror of leaving and all that meant, the terror of living with a lunatic—me.

I drove to the *Press Democrat* where editors interviewed me one after another. This was a *New York Times* practice, I was to learn, and it was exhausting and went on all day into the evening. They wanted to see how I'd hold up, if I'd contradict myself. The *Press Democrat* had a smaller circulation than the *Chronicle*, but it was a well-written, well-edited, ambitious newspaper and took every hire seriously. And it was part of *The New York Times* chain, a big deal in my universe.

Before going to the interview, I read a book about job interviewing techniques—I really wanted this job, wanted out of Purgatory or hell or wherever I had fallen. The book said in one of the interviews someone will ask about money, ask how much I want. The book said never answer that question. Death trap. Say something like, "We're just getting to know each other, to see if you like me and I like you. Let's allow the process to unfold and talk about money at the very end if we get that far."

My second interview was with Bob Swofford, the managing editor, whom I didn't know. His manner was severe. Stern. Frightening. His very first question was how much I expected to earn. The *Press Democrat* was not the *Chronicle*, he said, and couldn't pay what I earned over there.

So, you're the one the book warned me about, I thought. I was prepared. God was I prepared. I said, "We're just getting to know each other, to see if you like me and I like you. Let's allow the process to unfold and talk about money at the very end if we get that far."

Chapter 33

Swofford relaxed and smiled. Asked me smart journalism questions about my methods—later he would be one of my advocates at the paper. We are both retired and are friends.

The *Press Democrat* offered me the job, said I didn't have to move to Santa Rosa, could stay in Oakland near the sports teams. But the *Press Democrat* offered less than I could live on. I phoned Swofford, explained my position. He listened politely. He called back. Raised the number, even gave me a signing bonus. An anvil fell away from my heart and the world went from gray to all the Crayola colors.

Sports editor Jenks called me, said we had a deal, welcome aboard, can't wait to get started. I said I want it in writing. He said newspapers are a handshake business. *My ass*, I thought. I insisted on a written document. He faxed me a letter of employment which I signed and faxed back. A few weeks after the *Press Democrat* hired me, they hosted a party in my honor at an exclusive San Francisco restaurant. Most of the paper's bigwigs drove down from Santa Rosa and we celebrated with wine and a gourmet meal. Managing editor Swofford, who was seated across from my wife, Dawn, and me, grinned, stretched out his arms toward us and said, "Lowell, we are so happy to have you."

To which Dawn replied, "Bob, we are so happy to be had."

When I signed the papers at the *Press Democrat*, I learned we had a stock plan with *The New York Times*. This stockplan business was new to me. When I went to New York for *Press Democrat* work, *The Times* gave me an identity card which allowed me into *The Times* building, gave me a desk and phone. Instead of a hotel, *The Times* put me up at a private club when I wrote a follow-up to 911 a year after the attack. At the *Chronicle* writers were shit—my interpretation. At *The Times*, we had value. *The Times* gave me discount cards to all the big New York museums. Three weeks into my employment, *The Times* flew out an editor to meet me, take me to lunch. Management at the mother ship wanted the rundown on the new sports columnist. No one at the *Chronicle* ever took me this seriously. In my first few years there, the *Press Democrat* won a Pulitzer. And later it won another.

There's more to the story; this part is almost surreal. As ballplayers would say, you can't make this shit up. The publisher of the *Press Democrat* was Mike Parman, a big, strong, smart, welcoming man. He was behind the *Press Democrat* hiring me. And as I grew to know him, I grew to love him. He knew how to run a paper—like no one I ever met. He made the hard decisions, some unpopular, but he decided for the right reasons. He was not a wimp who hid in his office or behind other people. He was accessible and he listened, and I admired him as I admired my father and mother.

Mike Parman, who saved my life, was Frank McCulloch's son-in-law, the son-in-law of the man at the *Examiner* who almost ruined my life, who wanted to order food when my world was exploding. But Mike Parman gave me a job, gave me license to write whatever I wanted, gave me raises without my asking. He worked hard to keep me happy. He was married to McCulloch's daughter Dee Dee, who became my friend.

Mike Parman and I never discussed McCulloch and Hearst, but Mike knew what happened. Must have known. We were having lunch one time and Mike dropped a sentence into the conversation, dropped in a non sequitur,

"Frank and I are best friends." Then he continued whatever he was saying. He had drawn a boundary, something like, "No matter what happened between you and Frank, this is a topic we don't discuss, and you never badmouth my father-in-law." And I never did. Never wanted to.

And then Mike Parman was dying of pancreatic cancer and had to retire. In Sonoma County and at *The New York Times* Mike Parman's retirement was big news. There was a party for Mike at the Chalk Hill Winery, a castle on a hill. Buses drove us to the winery from the parking lot down below. An invitation-only crowd jammed the lavish events room, among the guests Arthur Sulzberger Jr., publisher of *The Times*. He came to pay homage.

Only a few people were invited to speak, Sulzberger, the new *Press Democrat* publisher Bruce Kyse and me. There may have been a few others. The *Press Democrat* honored me in allowing me to honor Mike Parman. I spoke about Mike from the heart and, at the end, looked at him from the stage and said *I love you, Mike.*

When I walked off the stage, I saw Frank McCulloch far away, there for his son-in-law's farewell. I had not seen him for years since the kiss-off in the restaurant. I didn't feel angry. I was happy now. It was blood under the bridge, and it was years ago. And McCulloch had acted for Hearst, was a good soldier. I'd come to peace with that. But I didn't approach him. That would be too much. As I stood with my wife, my back to the stage, a shadow appeared. McCulloch in front of me. He looked stooped, frail, old. And he looked guilty—or maybe I read guilt into him.

"Hello, Lowell," he said.

"Hello, Frank."

We stared at each other.

"You came out all right," he said.

I told him I came out all right.

That pleased him, made him feel relieved. I'm sure it did.

He looked down and scraped his shoe on the wood floor. He seemed to be searching for words, for something he needed to say. I wasn't sore at him, but I wouldn't help him.

"That was the worst day of my life," he said, his voice sincere, sorrowful.

"Worst day of *your* life?" I said. And I almost laughed.

He nodded his head sadly and looked me in the eye. He shook my hand, turned and walked away and passed out of my life yet again.

Frank McCulloch was correct—I came out all right. Better than all right. I flourished. I've had this feeling, one I can't prove, one that may seem ridiculous. The disaster with the *Examiner* and *Chronicle* was something I needed, although I didn't know it. It made me grow up, become a serious person—serious about life. It involved suffering—learning how much suffering the world can inflict—and getting past it, moving on, keeping my dignity. I went to the bitter end before I could earn peace. Even now the peace comes and goes. It's like that for everyone. I learned that too.

Chapter 34

Jew 'Em

My son Grant was two, maybe three years old. He looked at my mother, visiting us in Oakland from Brooklyn, looked at her with the face of an angel.

"Does Grandpa sleep with Jesus?" he asked in his innocent voice about my dead father.

My mother almost fell off the couch.

Her husband sleep with Jesus?

Meaning my father, a Jew, had gone over to Jesus after he'd died. Slept in Jesus' arms. Became a Christian. Started believing in all those saints and martyrs, believed in swallowing the blood and body of Christ.

My mother shot me a frozen look. Not exactly hatred. Extreme condemnation. The look meant, "This is what comes of marrying a Catholic." The look meant, "This is what comes of having a Catholic mother-in-law who's trying to convert my grandson with talk of a dead Jew sleeping with Jesus. Behind our backs she teaches him about the Father and the Holy Ghost and the Son of God getting nailed to a cross and dying for our sins and getting buried and rising from the dead and going who knows where. What kind of nonsense is that?" The frozen look meant, "You turned your back on us by marrying a shiksa and now your son—my grandson, for God's sake—believes in Jesus, Jesus as the Messiah, Jesus the No to every Jewish Yes."

I expected my mother to start reciting the Shema right there in our living room. The Shema is the most important prayer for Jews. *Hear, O Israel, the Lord is our God, the Lord is One.*

My mother defined the world as Jewish and non-Jewish. Simple as that. When we'd meet someone new and she couldn't tell Jew or not a Jew, she'd whisper to me, "Jewish?" I still organize the world that way. I walk into a room of people I don't know and instantly I'm inspecting noses, chins, posture, regional accents—I'm on the hunt for Jews. And I'm pretty good at finding them. Frankly, I have a Hall-of-Fame batting average. Call it *Jewdar*.

What my son said about my dad and Jesus confirmed to my mother, Eve, what she always feared. That we put up a Christmas tree. Which we did. My wife didn't see the tree as a religious symbol. She loved the tradition of it. The tree made her feel connected to her parents and grandparents, something I could relate to. But my mother didn't understand that. She thought Christmas tree and she immediately locked onto the birth of Jesus, God help her, and those manger scenes with the wise men and the little baby, and the goyim singing carols and blaming us for the death of Christ.

Our tree was extra tall because we have a sunken living room with a high ceiling. It was always a Douglas fir that we called the King of the Forest. (See *The Wizard of Oz.*) One time we bought our tree and the guys at the tree farm tied it to the top of my Honda Accord and we were driving home on the freeway when we heard ripping and roaring and tearing on the car roof and the tree fell off onto the freeway. Luckily, we were in the slow lane. We exited onto the shoulder and stared at the freeway. The tree was very much there. Cars whizzed around it at 65 miles an hour.

"Get the tree," my wife said.

"Get the tree?"

"Oh, please," she said.

I waited for a break in the traffic while my wife alternately yelled, "Get the tree!" and "Don't get hit by a car." I ran onto the freeway, grabbed that sucker and yanked it back. I tied it onto the car roof, better this time, and thought, *I almost got killed for a Christmas tree.* What would Eve Cohn have thought about that?

Our tree had ornaments by the ton. I never knew from ornaments until I married: little sleds, tiny gingerbread homes nestled on snow, mini-Corvettes, Santa Clauses, angels in poofy dresses, and round oblong colorful things that refracted the light from the strings of lights I wound around the tree. And I liked the tree. God forgive me. I liked Christmas.

"You bring a child up with two traditions, he gets confused," my mother managed to say.

Me, I didn't manage to say anything. My wife managed.

My wife, RIP, was a lapsed Catholic. I will use present tense. Don't get her started on the nuns in Catholic high school, Sister This and Sister That. Don't get her started on Sister Mary Xavier who refused to give my wife her diploma at high school graduation for failing to return a library book, humiliating my wife and her father and mother. Don't ask my wife why she had to eat fish on Friday, and if she didn't it was a mortal sin, but that rule suddenly vanished and the mortal sin vanished with it. Or why there can't be women priests. Don't ask her about the bad things priests have done to children. Or what some popes did to Jews. She still loves the look and feel of a church and the sound of Gregorian Chant, loves the good things about Catholicism. When we used to visit Italy, we sat quietly in church in every town we stayed in.

"We keep a Jewish home," my wife told my mother.

Eve was finally able to breathe.

"We're bringing up our son Jewish," my wife said.

And we were. On his eighth day of life, we gave him a *bris*, the ritual circumcision, a rite for Jewish males that has survived through the generations. I'd be damned if my son ended the tradition, although the *mohel* said we had a dissenting marriage—what a cruel term—and performed the bris as a pediatrician, not as a mohel. A Reform rabbi who was a fan of my sports writing performed the service in our living room. Later, our son would attend Hebrew School and have a bar mitzvah and be a Jew. But my mother would suffer from Alzheimer's by then and didn't know what was what, although she had seen the mezuzah we put next to our front door, a mezuzah we bought in the Jewish ghetto in Venice. And my wife cooked borscht and brisket and latkes and potato kugel for my mother and my Aunt Sarah, and at Passover my wife assembled the *seder* plate and made her special Venetian haroset recipe from chestnut paste, figs and pine nuts. She tried so hard.

After a cooling-off period, my mother felt reassured my son and I were sufficiently Jewish, even though my mother-in-law had tried to make an end run around Judaism. The two ladies actually became friends. My mother never mentioned the Christmas tree. We always got rid of it before my son's birthday, January 13, when my mother and Aunt Sarah would visit. We recycled the tree and vacuumed up the evidence, including every single pine needle and stowed the Christmas decorations in the basement. My mother would have plotzed if she knew we bought the King of the Forest every year, a monster tree that scraped the living-room ceiling.

Chapter 34

And there things stood until one Christmas at my mother-in-law's house in San Leandro just south of Oakland. My mother-in-law was named Ann, her maiden name DeMarco. Not Cohn or Goldstein or Levy. DeMarco. She was a happy, sweet woman and she cooked great Italian food.

We were seated around the table, my wife and I, my mother-in-law, my wife's uncle Oscar DeMarco and his wife, Jeannette. My wife happened to mention she would go shopping soon for something or other.

"Don't pay full price," my mother-in-law said. "Be sure and Jew 'em down."

My heart clenched. My mother-in-law had just said, in front of me, *Jew 'em down*. She must have believed every myth about Jews being cheap and shifty and driving cruel bargains and controlling the world's economy. Maybe she believed we murdered Christian kids and used their blood to make the Passover *matzoh*.

My wife stared at me and grimly shook her head, which I took to mean, *Please don't freak out right now and ruin Christmas for everyone. We'll talk later.*

So, I kept my mouth shut and ate the penne with Ann's meat sauce and packed a phony smile onto my face, but I kept thinking, *How do I handle this because I have to handle this.* My mother and father would demand I handle this.

After the meal and after my mother-in-law washed the dishes and after we'd all exchanged gifts, I asked my mother-in-law if we could talk privately.

"Sure, dear," she said. She looked puzzled.

I led her to a back room.

"Ann, when you said that thing about Jew 'em down that was offensive. You know that, right?"

"Oh, no," she said. "'Jew 'em down' is just an expression. Everyone uses it."

Oy vey.

"I get that," I said. "But it's an expression that has a meaning."

She didn't understand my meaning about meaning. I had been an English major in college, and she never went to high school and didn't think about words.

"Try this," I said, being patient. "Surely, you know I'm Jewish."

"Of course, I know you're Jewish."

"Well, saying 'Jew 'em down' is a put-down of Jews."

"Don't be silly," she said. "It has nothing to do with Jews."

And then I brought out the heavy artillery.

"Let's reverse positions," I said, striving for a teaching moment. "What if I say to you, 'You're just a dago?'"

She laughed a throaty laugh.

"It's true," she said, giggling. "I am a dago."

That was it. She was a dago, and I was a Jew.

"Ann," I said, "There's no problem between you and me. I love you."

And I did.

Chapter 35

Gravestone

A few months after my father's death, my mother and I went on an excursion. I had come to New York from California to visit my mom and see how she was doing. We drove to the cemetery to visit my father's grave. It didn't have a stone yet. Although we knew for several days we would be making the trip, we felt nervous. I brought a tape recorder and asked my mother to tell me how she met my father. It was to keep her occupied, but it was more than that. I wanted her voice on tape and I wished I had done that with my father, asked him to talk into a recorder about his life. To preserve his voice. Their voices.

My father was the youngest child in his family, almost twenty years younger than his sister Anna and that led to an odd circumstance. Anna had a son named Bernie, only fifteen months younger than my father. They grew up like brothers, but my father was Bernie's uncle, and Bernie is the key to this story.

"How I met Dad was very interesting," my mother said as we crossed from Brooklyn into Queens.

My mom had a friend named Tessie Pomerantz who drove a Packard and to drive a Packard in those days meant you were comfortable. *Comfortable* was the word my mother used. Bernie and Tessie started going around together and, out of the blue, Tessie said to my mother, "I met Bernie's uncle. Eve, why don't you have a date with him?" My mother said, "A date with the uncle? He's an old man." Tessie said, "No, he's Bernie's friend. They're like brothers."

"So, I met him, and I was not enough sophisticated for him," my mother told me. "I was not kissed until I was eighteen. He had no use for me. I must have been very babyish to him."

Three couples went on the date and, going to the restaurant, my mother had to sit on my father's lap in the taxicab. She remembered he wore a coat with a velvet collar and a derby. When the evening was over, he said he would call her, but he never did.

A year later, my mother found herself in a group going to the Midwood Inn, "a very nice little restaurant on Flatbush Avenue near Midwood Street." My father showed up with a woman named Helen Carp and my mother was with no one. At the Midwood Inn my father sat near my mother, and he leaned over to a friend and my mother heard him say, "Would you take Helen home? I want to take Eve home."

"He was a beaut," my mother told me with pride.

My father walked my mother home from the Midwood Inn and when he got to her house asked for her phone number.

"I'm not giving you my phone number," my mother said. "You promised to call me, and you didn't. I'll never give it to you."

And my mother, God love her, walked inside.

At that moment, her older sister Irene came along. My father said, "May I have your phone number?" Irene gave it to him. This happened in 1932 and my parents married in 1935. My mother always admired the way my father went after what he wanted.

We pulled into the cemetery, under an old tan brick arch, and I went into the office to get directions to the grave.

Inside a watchdog barked insanely. We drove along a road with large monuments on either side and stopped where we thought my father lay. My mother waited in the car because it was cold outside. I ran up and down the rows of headstones searching for the grave. All the rows looked alike. I hurried down a row called Cypress and there they were, the graves of our family. It was like being lost in the woods and wandering into a familiar meadow. Aunt Irene, who had died after they discovered cancer in her inner ear, lay next to her husband, Reuben, a big good solid quiet man who developed cancer in his stomach and lost so much weight his clothes hung on him like tents before he died. My uncle Bob, who died a few months after my father, was buried there, the dirt on his grave fresh.

And there was my father. No grass grew on his grave. Too early for that. The earth was a dull brown, the color of partly-baked meat, the only marker an index card, something you find in the library card catalog. Emanuel Cohn, died September 28, 1988. I walked back to the car and led my mother to her husband. She stood in front of the graves looking from her sister Irene to Reuben to Bob to my father to the space reserved for her.

"Let's go home," she said.

That was it? We had not been there two minutes. We walked slowly away from the grave. Neither of us spoke. On the way home, my mother cried quietly in the car.

I flew to New York a few months later for the unveiling of my father's gravestone. The night before the unveiling I lay awake in my bed in the family apartment. It was the same twin bed I slept in as a boy, but now I was married with a wife and two kids in California. On the other side of the wall, I could hear the springs creak in my mother's bed and from time to time a moan would seep through the wall.

I thought about the last time I had seen my father alive—September 10, 1988. I had flown to New York to cover a game between the San Francisco 49ers and the New York Giants. A few nights before the trip, my mother phoned. Said my father was ill. It didn't seem to be anything serious, she said, but my father had been admitted to the hospital merely as a precaution. Her voice had the tone of forced nonchalance she used to persuade herself everything would be okay. Before she hung up, she asked if I had an electric razor. "Dad is having difficulty shaving himself with a blade," she said.

When I got off the phone, I searched the bathroom cabinet and found an old Norelco shaver I had been given for my bar mitzvah. The plastic traveling case had begun to disintegrate and the zipper didn't work. I hadn't used the razor in years, but I held onto it because it reminded me of when I thought I became a man.

When I arrived in New York, I drove to Brookdale Hospital where my father would die and rode the elevator upstairs to his room. My brother had driven in from Philadelphia and was talking with my mother. My father lay in bed, his eyes closed. A stubble had formed on his sunken cheeks. I took out the razor and gently placed it on his cheek. When the buzzing began my father's eyes fluttered open and he stared at me without recognition. "Lowelly?" he finally asked. The name he had called me as a boy. "Yes, Dad." I kissed his face.

As I shaved him, he would go in and out of consciousness. A huge abscess had formed inside his body—he was septic—and he wasn't up to fighting the infection. When I finished shaving him, I drove to a hotel near Newark Airport, closer to where the 49ers would be playing.

My father had twice defeated cancer and he had beaten Addison's disease, but he was an old man and he had been fighting the infection for months, although we didn't know it. He died eighteen days later.

Through the wall I heard my mother moan again. I got up and turned on the light. The paint on the ceiling was chipped and peeling away from the plaster. I took another blanket from the dresser because I always was cold in that room. I found an old copy of *Oliver Twist* in the bookshelf and tried to read but couldn't focus. Lying in that bed I always had looked ahead to the future. This was the first time I was looking back.

I remembered going to the Golden Gloves fights at Madison Square Garden. My dad took me to the Golden Gloves every year before I went to college. We saw the fights in 1962, my senior year of high school, and afterward we walked to the subway. My father was in a good mood, walking slightly ahead of me, talking to me over his shoulder. The way I saw it my dad was heading directly for a telephone pole. There were maybe ten feet between him and the pole. It occurred to me he might walk smack into it. But I dismissed the thought. My father was legally blind but he got around Manhattan every day without walking into poles. He kept talking. The distance between him and the pole narrowed. I said to myself, *He's going to hit that pole.* But, still, I didn't warn him. I never had told my father what to do. He was the father and I was the son. It seemed presumptuous to give my father an order — "Look out for the pole." At least it did then.

After his head hit the pole, his hair fell into his eyes and a huge ugly welt formed on the left side of his forehead. My father leaned against a car. Breathing hard. I had tears in my eyes.

The next morning my mother said, "How did your father get that bump on his forehead?"

I couldn't look at her. I didn't say anything. My father put his hand on my shoulder. He told my mother we enjoyed the fights.

It's funny the things you remember. My mother spoke in her sleep, but I couldn't make out the words. I turned off the light but never fell asleep. My mother stopped moaning. At the first signs of morning, I sneaked down the hall toward the shower to get ready for the gravestone service. I peeked into my mother's room to make sure she was sleeping peacefully. Her bed was empty. I walked into the living room. She sat in a straight-backed chair, already dressed in a dark suit. In her lap she held her purse.

I drove my mother to the cemetery again for the unveiling of my dad's gravestone. There we met my sister and brother and their families and my cousins and aunts. We covered the inscription on my father's headstone with a clean white handkerchief and we recited Hebrew prayers which my brother and I translated into English.

> "God, full of mercy, who dwelleth on high, cause the soul of Emanuel Cohn which hath gone to its rest to find repose in the wings of the *Shechinah* (the presence of God), among the souls of the holy, and pure as the firmament of the skies, for they have offered charity for the memory of his soul; for the sake of this, conceal him in the mystery of thy wings forever, and bind up his soul in the bond of life; may the Lord be his inheritance, and

may he repose in his resting-place in peace, and let us say, Amen."

My sister put her arm around my mother's shoulders. Then we took the handkerchief off the stone and each of us knelt down and picked up small pebbles. We carefully placed the pebbles into the grooves on the tombstone formed by the letters of my father's inscription, into the "E" of Emanuel, the "C" of Cohn. A way of showing we had visited, borne witness.

The group broke up. Car engines coughed to life. I lingered at the grave, staring at the clean, new marble. I could accept it now. My father was under the stone, but he was in me, too, always would be.

I felt someone gently grasp my hand. My mother. We held hands.

"There's no grass on Dad's grave," I said, offended. "The ground is still bare."

"Don't worry, Lowell," my mother said, and we turned toward the car. "It will grow in the spring."

Chapter 36

The Prisoner of Waldbaum's

It was 1989 and I flew from California, where I had lived more than twenty years as a student, writer and teacher, to visit my mother in Brooklyn. She still lived in the family apartment, Apartment 1B, where I had grown up. My mother was alone—my father had died the previous year.

The first morning, I told her I had an appointment in Manhattan, and I'd be back for dinner. Typically, she became worried. "You're going to the City by yourself?" she asked. I reminded her: (1) I was an adult with a wife and family in California. (2) I had grown up taking the subway from Brooklyn to Manhattan.

"Well, if you think it's safe," she said. I got ready to leave, but my mother stopped me. She noticed I had placed my wallet in the right rear pocket of my pants.

"It's a mistake," she warned. "They're out there waiting for you. They're bastards."

She did not say who the bastards were, but they were everywhere, and they were specialists at lifting wallets from dopes who kept cash in their right rear pockets. She made me pull out my wallet and stuff it in the front pocket of my trousers. The wallet felt stiff and bulged over my right thigh and caused me to walk with a limp. My mother smiled. "That's more like it, dear."

I limped out of the apartment house, but the minute I hit the street I shoved the wallet in my rear pocket. I'd deal with the bastards if I had to. I crossed Avenue L and walked through the playground where I had played as a kid. On

Avenue M, I made my way to the subway station and climbed the stairs because in my part of Brooklyn the train is elevated.

I glanced around the station platform and noticed a man who looked vaguely familiar. In his late thirties, he wore a cream-colored suit and a tie and cream-colored pointy French-toe shoes and he looked like a pimp and surely was one of the bastards. But his chubby face recalled someone from my childhood more than a quarter century ago. It was the Duck.

The Duck's name wasn't really the Duck. It was Phil. But the tough kids in our neighborhood, for reasons I never understood, went by a variety of animal names. In addition to the Duck we had a Turtle, Weasel and a Rabbit.

I glanced at the Duck shyly, then looked away. We never had been friends. I played ball with him and the Turtle and the others in the playground, but I was known as a kid who did well in school, never got suspended. There was no reason to believe the Duck would remember me. There wasn't any reason to talk to him.

What are you so shy about? I scolded myself. *You're a sports columnist for a big-deal West Coast paper. Go up and talk to him.*

And that's exactly what I did. I went up to the Duck and said, "Excuse me." I almost said, "Excuse me, Duck," but I didn't want to presume familiarity after all that time. Plus, he might not like the name.

He stared at me.

"Yeah," was all he said. The Duck's tone was hostile, like, "What the hell do you want?"

I pushed on. "Phil, you may not remember me, but my name is Lowell Cohn and we grew up together."

Chapter 36

The broadest grin spread across the Duck's broad face. "Sure, I remember you and don't call me Phil. I'm the Duck."

That settled, we boarded the train and sat together, and the Duck asked where I'd been the past twenty years. I told him I'd gone to school in California and stayed there. "No shit," he said, and he looked amazed as if I owned a condo on Mars.

"Where have you been, Duck?"

"Jail mostly."

Jail? As I asked Duck about other guys we'd known it turned out quite a few had served time. Bobby B. was currently in the joint, Duck said. He had squealed on some guys and probably wouldn't live much longer. Pete W. already was dead, stabbed in prison because he was a jerk. Big Sal lost his mind. Duck thought he might be in an institution, and Little Sal was driving a truck.

I found that bit of info about Little Sal startling. I pictured Little Sal as the neighborhood psychopath. He was handsome—blond hair and blue eyes, unusual for an Italian. And he had a warm manner. But he liked to fight and bit fingers and noses, and once you got into it with him it was never over until he bashed you over the head with a pipe or baseball bat or a hockey stick. He might wait a year. With Little Sal there was no time limit on revenge. I made it my business to get along with him. The fact that he of all people wasn't locked up reminded me life is surprising.

I always had considered Little Sal stupid. He never took algebra, and he got crummy grades and thought school was for losers. When we were in high school, I went with him to see the western, *One-Eyed Jacks*. Marlon Brando plays the good guy and Karl Malden the bad guy. But Malden becomes the sheriff of a town and pretends to be good and halfway through the film I figured out the meaning of the title—I had learned about symbolism in my advanced literature classes. I turned to Little Sal with a feeling of complete intellectual superiority and said, "Sal, tell me why they call this film *One-Eyed Jacks*."

"You brainless scumbag," he explained. "It's because you only see one side of his face, you know half of his personality."

Way to go, Sal.

Duck and I were on the Manhattan Bridge now and, from the train, we could see Brooklyn and Lower Manhattan and the East River. My mind cruised back over all those years, and I remembered when Big Sal's father died. One day, the old man was in the house weighing three-hundred pounds, smoking Lucky Strikes by the carton, and suddenly he was gone.

"He had to go to the hospital for a rest," Big Sal told me. A few days later, Big Sal's father was dead, and we all had gone to a strange neighborhood for an open-casket Catholic service.

Years later, Howie King told me the story of his death. It turns out Big Sal's dad had a craving—an addiction is more like it—for halvah, that Turkish, dry, sweet pastry they sell in candy stores all over New York City. When he went into the hospital, they put Big Sal's father on a strict diet, took away his Luckies and told him under no circumstances could he touch halvah. Well, the big guy could live without his sausages and his peppers and his smokes, but halvah deprivation was driving him nuts. He was in the hospital a few days, getting better, until one of his friends sneaked in a gross of halvah. Big Sal's father downed the stuff in one

Chapter 36

sitting and when the night nurse came on duty, she found him stone dead. As far as I know, he's the only person ever to O.D. on halvah.

I told Duck the halvah story and he said it sounded like bullshit. By now the train had crossed the East River into Manhattan and disappeared underground. The dark acted like a soporific on the Duck, who closed his eyes and began peaceful snoring. I remembered as a kid he had a sleep disorder and would snooze against the handball wall while the Sals threw balls at his head.

The Duck woke up and was stretching as we approached Canal Street. He smiled at me.

"Why are you going to The City?" I asked.

"I'm running an errand for Nathan Hershberg," Duck said. (Nathan Hershberg was not his real name.)

"Nathan Hershberg?" I said. "Why would you run an errand for that creep?"

The Duck eyeballed me. "He's only one of the most important guys in Brooklyn."

Talk about life being surprising. When we were kids, Nathan Hershberg was the biggest geek. He wore glasses with tape on the frame and he had a bulging Adam's apple and he talked with a pre-pubescent buzz. While the rest of us played ball, he played chess with the Yiddish-speaking old folks at a picnic table. And now Nathan Hershberg was a big deal?

"What do you mean one of the most important guys in Brooklyn?" I said.

"He runs the numbers racket."

"Nathan Hershberg?"

"Yeah, he's only the toughest Jew I ever met."

I couldn't understand a world in which Hershberg

became boss of the tough kids. I would have gone more deeply into the subject, but Duck said, "We're having a party Friday night. Everyone's going to be there. They'll all be glad to see you." Duck said Nathan Hershberg would attend and he named several other sociopaths and I wondered how I'd fit in.

"So, are you coming?" the Duck wanted to know.

"Yeah, yeah, sure. You bet."

"You won't give us the high hat, will you, Mr. West Coast writer?"

"Of course not."

He gave me the address, and as I got ready to leave the train, Duck said, "Do you do drugs?"

"No."

"That's right, you was always a good kid." As the words escaped his mouth, I realized he wasn't praising me. *Good*, for him, meant someone on the other side. I guessed I would be the only good kid at the party and that could turn out bad.

That night over my mother's overcooked brisket and boiled potatoes and limp broccoli, I said I had bumped into the Duck. My mother said she recalled him and asked what he'd been doing. "He's been in jail mostly." I told her he invited me to a party, and I mentioned other names from the guest list. She set down her fork and shot me a look.

"You're not going, so forget it."

It was the second time that day she'd given me an order. I opened my mouth to argue but stopped. It was exactly what I needed her to say, what I was pulling for. No matter how old you are, sometimes you need your mommy. I skipped the reunion, apologies to the Duck.

Next morning, I took my mother shopping along with

her older sister, my Aunt Sarah. They were in their eighties, frail, stooped over, their posture resembling a couple of apostrophes. Waldbaum's, the neighborhood supermarket, was several miles away. I would call from California and tell her take a cab and she would say, "The walk does me good." But my mother was once mugged on the way to Waldbaum's, and I didn't see the walk doing her any good at all.

I drove her and Aunt Sarah in my rental car to Waldbaum's and parked a block away. I am not fussy about supermarkets, but this place shocked me. People pushed and shoved each other in the narrow, crowded aisles, and gridlock formed near frozen foods. Next to the door people were feeding bent aluminum cans into a dispenser for the deposit. Others waited impatiently for them to finish. Getting returns on cans was big business. Shoppers, mostly old Jews, fought over grocery carts. There weren't enough of them. This I never had seen before.

When I'm in California I miss New York, but when I'm actually there in the middle of the turmoil, whether I'm on the subway or stuck in traffic or just shopping in the neighborhood grocery store, I want out. I gazed around Waldbaum's. I wondered how my mother lived with this chaos.

The moment my mother and Aunt Sarah entered the store, they started planning strategy for nabbing a cart the way Rommel must have planned a route through the desert. My mother spotted an old man waiting on the checkout line. She walked over to him and said, "May I have your cart when you're done?" She waited on line with the man ten minutes. That seemed typical. During that time, several other shoppers asked the man for his cart, but he gallantly pointed to my mother shadowing him and said, "I promised it to this young lady."

The carts were of a hybrid form. Because New Yorkers steal shopping carts by the ton, Waldbaum's had attached a long vertical pole to each cart to prevent it from clearing the exit door. With their long poles the carts resembled bumper cars. And I had no doubt as I watched these shoppers smashing into each other that no kid in a bumper car has greater malice in his heart than these senior citizens.

When she finally nailed her cart, my mother wheeled through the store like Mario Andretti at the Indy 500. She made a pit stop near cheese just in time to see one Jewish Orthodox woman in a wig scream at another woman for blocking her way to the deli. The second woman was so startled she swerved her cart sharply, hitting a bottle of Cheez Whiz with her pole. The Cheez Whiz flew from the shelf, hitting the wigged lady a glancing blow on the head. Then the bottle broke into pieces on the floor, leaving a gooey blob in the aisle. My mother maneuvered past the wreckage into dairy and asked a teenager who worked there for six eggs. In California it is common procedure to divide a box of a dozen eggs in half, but the boy stood his ground.

"You can't do it," he told my mother.

"Why?" my mother asked.

"It's a rule."

"I wouldn't want to break a rule," my mother said like the good former elementary school teacher she was. She bought the dozen eggs even though she hardly ate them because they were murder on her cholesterol. In the meantime, Aunt Sarah was trying to buy vanilla ice cream. The ad in the newspaper said Breyers was on special. But no matter how hard Aunt Sarah looked, she couldn't find Breyers. She went in search of the store manager and when

Chapter 36

she returned told us, "The coupon's for Breyers but you can substitute Sealtest."

By now my mother and Aunt Sarah had lost their coupon. They spotted torn newspapers on the floor and, although they received lucrative retirements from the New York City Board of Education, the two old ladies got on their hands and knees and searched through the ads until they found a Breyers coupon.

I made sure my mother bought plenty of toilet paper and cleanser and other essentials to last until my next cross-country visit. We had to bag our own groceries. Maybe I'm spoiled but I've come to expect some smiling California teenager in a neat uniform to suddenly appear and bag groceries and put them in the cart and ask if I need help to my car. No way. I asked the checkout lady if we could bring the shopping cart to the car a block away. She stared at me as if I'd suggested kinky sex. "You have to leave something behind as security," she decreed.

We considered leaving a bag of groceries, but finally decided on leaving Aunt Sarah, who had great respect for law and order. One of the indelible memories of my childhood is Aunt Sarah being pulled over for driving through a stop sign and telling the cop, "Don't give me a ticket. I'm a New York City school teacher and I'd never do anything wrong." The cop gave her the ticket.

When I tried to leave Waldbaum's the cart wouldn't clear the top of the door because the pole got in the way. So, I tipped the cart back on two wheels—actually popped a wheelie on the shopping cart—which gave me just enough clearance. Unfortunately, the dozen eggs started sliding past my arm and would have crashed to the floor if my mother hadn't made a great running grab.

When we reached the street, I looked back into the store and there was Aunt Sarah waiting patiently by the checkout stand. To the end of her days, she never once complained about being the Prisoner of Waldbaum's.

Chapter 37

The Flood in 4B

Another visit to my mother in Brooklyn, but I also was going to meet Johnny Saxton, a former welterweight champ, for a book I was writing. My mother was supposed to get a call from a guy who knew a guy who knew where Saxton lived.

I saw only glimpses of my mother now, twice a year, snapshots of her aging. She no longer dyed her hair. Because she had no one to dress up for she wore what she called a *shmata*, Yiddish for a raggedy piece of clothing, in her case an old housecoat. When she was a schoolteacher, she was a snappy dresser and, in her classroom wore red shoes like Dorothy's and she never took any shit. One day she was in the hall between classes. She must have been laughing—she had a hearty gleeful lusty laugh—when the principal, Bernie, yelled at her in front of her students, "Eve Cohn, you shut up."

Told her to shut up. Told her in public.

She cut him dead. My mother always stood up for herself, she could erase people from her life, and I admired her for that. Bernie would try to make small talk at staff meetings or in the teachers' cafeteria, but she would turn away. He simply did not exist. Bernie was losing face before the entire staff. This went on a year until one day he summoned my mother to his office. When she shut the door, he walked over to her, dramatically fell to his knees and said, "Eve, you're the queen. What can I do? Please forgive me."

"Get up, Bernie," my mother said. "You're making an ass

of yourself." And she walked out of his office, walked out with schmucky Bernie still on the floor. Whenever I experienced rudeness from athletes, I told myself, "Be Eve." And I was.

Another time—I must have been eleven or twelve—my Hebrew School teacher, Mrs. Klayman, phoned my mother about me. My mother and I were in the kitchen. My mother listened patiently. My mother said, "Hmm." My mother said, "We're very proud of Lowell." My mother said, "Thanks for calling, Mrs. Klayman." My mother hung up the phone but didn't say anything to me.

"What was that about?" I asked.

"Mrs. Klayman says you don't have the stick-to-itiveness of Robert." Robert was my older brother. "Don't worry about it," my mother said.

Mrs. Klayman had broken several rules.

Her sins: She complained about me with incomplete evidence. What was stick-to-itiveness anyway? From my mother's point of view, I had plenty of it. My grades were good and my teachers liked me. Maybe Mrs. Klayman couldn't keep me interested. And there was this. Mrs. Klayman had compared two of my mother's children. My mother and father never compared us, loved us for who we were.

So, I was flying from San Francisco to New York to see my mother, flew on TWA—you remember TWA. I changed planes in St. Louis, where I had a two-hour layover and bought a copy of *Zorba the Greek* and read about Zorba who also didn't take any shit and had mastered the key to life— be totally involved in the moment no matter what. Experience the miracle of being. Experience the wonder of things as if you were just born. No one enjoyed the divine simplicity of life—wine, food, women—more than Zorba. The life-thrill encouraged Zorba to take risks, seek adventure.

Be like Zorba, I told myself, although lately I had lost confidence, even in my writing. Things were going to hell for me at the *San Francisco Chronicle* and I constantly heard a black dog barking in my brain.

When I arrived at Kennedy Airport the baggage area was crowded with people who had that uniquely drained, angry look of airline travelers. The bags started spilling onto the turning metal belt and people pushed and shoved and were rude in a New York way I understood. I would be the same when my bag appeared. Gradually the crowd thinned out, and then I was alone. That forlorn feeling of no suitcase. I walked over to the lost-baggage counter where a guy in a uniform stood, but he wouldn't look at me. I was another pain in his ass.

"Excuse me," I said.

"Can't you see the counter's closed?"

"But my bag didn't arrive and I need my bag."

His toupee had slipped off the top of his head and leaned on his left ear. I wanted to say, "If you're going to wear a fucking toupee have the decency to wear it right." But this guy was the kind who'd send my luggage to Beirut. So, I shut up. I filled out forms and asked when TWA would deliver the bag to Brooklyn, and he shrugged and said by midnight if I was lucky.

When I rang the bell to the apartment my mother shuffled to the door and peeked through the peephole to make sure I wasn't a neighborhood lunatic and when she saw it was me, she undid all the locks and slowly pulled open the door. And I almost started crying. So much older. Frail. My mother who just a few years before had seen worry in my face and asked why, and I said serious problems between me and my newspaper, and she said FEA and I knew immediately what she meant. *Fuck 'em all.*

I walked in and felt how abandoned my mother was in an apartment that once had so much life, three kids and my strong loud confident father, and all that talking laughing arguing yelling. Once I heard my father choke and sputter in the bathroom. He had grabbed the Brylcreem I used to coagulate my two-inch-high pompadour. He thought it was the Colgate because he was partially blind and couldn't read the tube. He began brushing his teeth. He coughed and spat and then he yelled at me, and then we all laughed. And now on the carpets I could see dirt spots that never would come out and paint peeling off the walls. It had come to this, my mom in a rent-controlled shithole, not seeing or knowing or even caring.

"I made nice tuna salad for you," she said. She emphasized the word *nice*. I almost vomited. My mother always bought the cheapest tuna, whatever off-brand cans were on sale at Waldbaum's. And when had she forgotten I don't eat fish? I told her I had a swell meal on the plane, a lie, and planned on eating the crummy snacks they threw at me on the flight, the nachos or whatever I'd shoved into my backpack.

I walked deeper into the gloom of the apartment and asked about the guy who knew the guy who knew the boxer who was supposed to phone her. "I'm sorry, he never called," my mom said. That made her feel useless, and I gave her bony body a hug and kissed her thin translucent cheek and said don't worry about it. We sat at the kitchen table, and I looked over at Nellie, the phony parakeet in the phony gold cage that had hung on the wall from my childhood, and I saw dust on Nellie's head.

"I reread *Middlemarch*," my mom said. Right. My mother was sophisticated. She admired brains. When I was a kid and said, "Mom I'm bored," she said, "Go read a book." She didn't say go change the spark plugs in the car, not that we had a car. Read a book.

She taught sixth grade when I was in sixth grade at a different school and on a Friday, they made us take the standardized IQ Test to see if we were college material and now it was the next day and I was rushing out to play ball when my mom said, "Are you feeling relaxed?" I said, "Yeah sure why?" Pulling papers out of a large manila envelope, she said, "You see this?" And I said, "Yeah sure why?" And she said, "It's the test you took yesterday."

"You mean the IQ Test?"

And she said, "Yes, the IQ Test. I want you to fill it out exactly as you did yesterday. Don't change anything. Got that?"

So, my IQ was known to our family. It was high and my mother liked that. And that made it sad, or do I mean ironic, when Eve Cohn lost her mind to Alzheimer's, which eventually killed her. Once, she pointed to my brother and said to me, "I'd like you to meet a nice man," no longer understanding we were brothers, or even what brothers were.

But that was to come years after this visit. Right now, we were in our apartment and my mother asked if I wanted to sleep after the long flight. She had made my bed, she said. She was talking about the twin bed in the old cold bedroom I had shared with my brother and sister. But I told her it was only 6 p.m. in California and she said she was tired and I heard her wash in the bathroom, one bathroom for a family of five, and when she walked out she had big gobs of white cream like Crisco on her face and her mouth had caved in because she took out her teeth and put them in a coffee cup in the bathroom and she kissed me good night.

I lay down on the living room couch and waited for TWA to call about my bag and for the guy to call who would connect me with the former boxer Johnny Saxton which I knew would never happen. Waiting became a metaphor for the messages you send out in a day or in a life no one receives or answers. Just filler. Life as filler.

I read some *Zorba* and wondered why the narrator, the part Alan Bates played in the movie, didn't make it with the sexy dark mysterious available widow played by Irene Papas. I was lying on the couch getting frustrated with Bates, a writer, a man who lived in his head, and frankly cheering him on, when I heard the sound of cascading water. Now, you hear many sounds at night in Brooklyn. You hear the sounds of kids breaking into cars. You hear drunks telling each other go fuck yourself. You hear battalions of cockroaches invading the linoleum kitchen floor and you hear cars crashing and sirens screaming and car alarms complaining, but you most definitely do not hear water cascading. I do not know if there exists a place in the entire borough where fresh water flows runs falls meanders or cavorts. Most of Brooklyn has been cemented over and if you live there, you lose sense of what came first and lies beneath.

So, water was cascading. At first, I didn't pay attention. I was silently giving Alan Bates an atta boy, but the water got louder and I decided I'd deal with Alan later. I followed the sound to the bathroom. A small river flowed across the bathroom floor, but it wasn't coming from the faucet or the

Chapter 37

shower or the toilet or any of the usual water places. It gurgled through the bathroom ceiling, snaked down the wall and landed on the cracked floor tiles. The floor was soaked with two inches of water. My first impulse was to wake my mother. It's amazing what going home does to your maturity. I was in my forties, but I never had taken care of my mother. In this apartment I always was just a son. I began to tiptoe into her bedroom and whisper, "Mommy, there's a leak in the bathroom."

No, I scolded myself. Grow up. Handle the crisis yourself. Be Zorba. I went to the linen closet, such a musty old-people's smell, grabbed a fistful of towels and spread them around. But the leak in the ceiling had turned into a torrent. I walked into the kitchen and placed my ear to the wall. Aside from all the Brooklyn sounds, there was one more sound I was familiar with, the sound of shouting.

Next door lived my boyhood friend the super. When we were kids his father had been the apartment house superintendent and now with the dad retired and living in Florida, the son had inherited the job. Like the men in that family were in a super's guild and this apartment house was their domain. There I was with my ear to the wall. The super stayed up late arguing with his wife. This I knew. They had humdingers you could hear in our kitchen, the super calling the Mrs. a worthless whore and the Mrs. asserting he was half a man and him telling her he'd pull her blond hair out by its black roots and her screaming just try it. I was hoping they had one going tonight. That way I could knock on their door, confident I wasn't waking them up.

Mr. and Mrs. Super didn't disappoint. As I heard him shout miserable cunt, I knocked on their door. A quick silence and then a final fuck you. The super yanked open his door, red anger in his eyes and was shocked to see me in Brooklyn because I had gotten out, was supposed to be in California.

"How's the Mrs.?" I asked.

"Great just great a real sweetheart," he said.

And then, I'm not sure why, I told him, "I think somebody upstairs died."

"How the hell did you know?" he said. "The man in 4B died tonight and the cops found $59,000 under his bed."

That explained something. We lived on the first floor in 1B so whatever went on in 4B, happened in an identical apartment several floors over our heads. I led the super to our bathroom, and he inspected the flood and whistled low between his teeth, the kind of manly-man whistle you associate with guys who know how to frame houses and gut fish.

"I'll go up to 4B and see what's the matter," he said.

About midnight the super reappeared. When he'd entered 4B he noticed someone, probably a cop, had washed his hands and left the water running. The shock of the fifty-nine grand. After flooding 4B, now vacant, the water had made its way down to 3B, which is exactly what the super did. He climbed down the fire escape and knocked on the bedroom window of the startled tenants who naturally were asleep. The super identified himself and they let him in and, sure enough, their bathroom was a lake.

After that the super checked out 2B, also vacant. About half the apartments in the building were unoccupied. The place used to bustle with kids, but they had moved away. The parents were senior citizens, and the owner was warehousing the apartments until the old people went to nursing homes or dropped dead and he could turn the building into a co-op. At least, that's what I thought was happening. When the super entered 2B he found water dripping down the entire B line of apartments. So, while I had waited, he'd gone on a quest that involved death and hidden treasure right there in Brooklyn. He told me he turned off the faucet in 4B but the water probably would drip until morning.

After he left, I lay down on the couch and dove back into *Zorba* and cheered on Alan Bates who finally came through with the widow. "Good for you, Alan," I told him, "although it would have been nice if you kept the crazy townspeople from murdering the widow after you got yours."

I couldn't sleep that night, needed to be awake to cushion the shock before my mom walked into the bathroom. I lay on the couch and heard the D Train of the subway rumble outside my window all night long and I thought about maturity, how in fiction the young protagonist often has a life-changing event and, boom, he's mature. Life isn't like that. You're forever fighting for your maturity, and you gain it by inches and sometimes you fail and fall back into dependency and childishness. Until the day you die you struggle to be grown up.

In the morning when I heard my mother moving around, I peeked into her bedroom and tried to be cheerful. "Small adventure last night, Mom."

I led her to the bathroom. The floor was drenched and the walls were streaked. My mom stared with a look of disapproval on her face. Or was it defeat? She never said a word, although she groaned a long low groan. Looking at her looking at the ceiling, cracked and old and wet, I imagined she asked herself when the whole thing would just fall down.

She sat on the toilet seat while I got on my hands and

knees with a bunch of towels and soaked up the wet. It took half an hour and when I was done, I leaned back against the bathtub and looked up at her. For a crazy instant I almost told her I was reading *Zorba the Greek,* a book she knew, and asked whom she thought I was, Alan or Zorba. But I resisted. I knew she would turn the question back on me. "Whom do you think you are, Lowell?"

TWA brought over my suitcase later that afternoon.

Chapter 38

Alimentary Jew

I am an alimentary Jew. I experience my Jewishness through my mouth, tongue, salivary glands and stomach. I live in the San Francisco Bay Area, not a hotspot for Jewish food like New York or Los Angeles. I never eat right—that's what it feels like.

I grew up with kosher dogs and sauerkraut and deli mustard and sour pickles from a barrel, and kreplach soup and stuffed cabbage and potato knishes. There was more, the non-Jewish Jewish food—Cantonese Chinese and pizza. Forget Proust and his little cookies. This was real food.

My God, New York pizza, the quintessence of pizza, the Platonic ideal by the slice. There is nothing, and I mean nothing in the Bay Area like New York pizza.

I went walking around the old Flatbush neighborhood a few years ago with my boyhood friend Stuie Kucker who now lives in Queens, who grew up across the street from me in Brooklyn, who's been my friend since we were nine. It's something I do every few years, fly from San Francisco to New York and walk the neighborhood, walk past my past, walk past my apartment on East 18th Street near Avenue L and wonder who lives there now, probably Russian-speaking Jews. I wonder if I dare ring the buzzer at the big heavy front door of the six-story building.

Would I be buzzed into the lobby? Would I walk to my apartment on the building's ground floor? Would I ring the bell and explain who I am, walk into what my mom called the apartment's *foyer*? Some foyer that was. Two steps and you were through it. Once in, what would it be like? Would I still feel the leftover life of my family, the life of my mother and father and sister and brother and me? Would I feel the accumulated years of being together, my father smoking his pipe and listening to Brooklyn Dodgers games on the radio, my mother watching the *College Bowl* quiz show on television and trying to answer questions along with the host Allen Ludden and the college hotshots, all of us inhabiting those rooms and corridors? Or is it all gone?

I so want to enter, to feel things as they were when I was a child. I want to go home, but how can I go home when there is no home to go home to? I never buzz the buzzer.

Stuie and I sat on a bench in the playground where we had played as kids. Now we were the old people sitting with old people. The old folks used to speak Yiddish in the playground, which we called the Park although it has only a few trees. Now they speak Russian—all those Russian Jewish immigrants to Flatbush. Before she died, my mother, God love her, renamed the playground Gorky Park.

While Stuie and I sat in the playground I thought about two of my dreams, one recurring, the other a one-shot deal.

In the first dream, one I must have dreamt a hundred times, I return to the apartment on Avenue L. I don't know how I get there. I don't fly on a plane. I simply show up, although in one version of the dream I enter an elevator in San Francisco and when the door opens for my floor, I'm on the street in Brooklyn facing our apartment house. I have a key to the big heavy front door of the building, and I let myself into the lobby. I turn left, climb a few steps and walk to our apartment,1B. Somehow, I have the key which I insert into the lock and open the door.

What makes the dream strange is that in real life my

mother is dead, died years ago. I know for sure another family lives there, but still, I enter the apartment. No sign of the present occupants. No children's toys or new furniture or cooking smells. My mother greets me and gives me a warm hug. It occurs to me I am living an alternate reality, that the new tenants and my mother inhabit the same apartment but don't know about each other, don't see each other, never interact. I am no fan of science fiction, but I dream this dream.

My mother and I sit at the kitchen table and gab and laugh and I fill her in on my family and what I'm writing, and she says she's proud of me, says she always was proud of me. I love this arrangement. It means I can visit my mother any time I want, and no one will disturb us. Our lives will go on like this forever.

In the other dream, the one-shot deal, it's three in the morning and I am in the backyard of our apartment house, and I am holding a hardcover book. It belongs to an old girlfriend in California. We had an awful breakup, mostly my fault and, even though I'm happily married to someone else, I still feel guilty for acting like a *putz*. I want to return the book to her. I owe her that.

I look up at the sixth floor of the apartment house and I see the window of her apartment, absurd because she never lived there. I don't know how I can return the book because, in this dream, I don't have a key to the building. I am letting her down yet again.

And then a miracle occurs. I sprout wings. Strong big wings from my shoulder blades. I try them out, pump my wings. They feel good. And I begin to fly. I fly in the gray light, fly over the chestnut tree in the backyard, fly toward the sixth floor. Feeling the power.

I fly to her window, book-ready, and because it's a warm

night, the window is open. I climb inside, gently place the book on the kitchen table, fly out the window. Mission accomplished.

This is the place in the story where I interpret my dreams even though a writer should not interpret his own work. That's for the reader to do. So, I'm breaking a rule, but I have a reason.

The book is obvious, right? In the dream I am closing the book on that old relationship. I can't make the breakup any better, but I can move on. In real life, I already had moved on.

But there's a more important element in both dreams. I'm sure you agree. Both take place in Brooklyn, at my apartment house even though I haven't lived there in more than half a century.

Why?

For me our Brooklyn apartment house is where, deep in my heart, I feel secure. It is the source of all judgments, where I measure my actions against the standards my parents gave me. I carry that place within me.

* * *

Stuie and I remained in the playground twenty minutes then walked to Avenue J, one of the shopping streets in our neighborhood. The old Brighton Line stops at Avenue J, a local stop on the subway, although it's no longer called the Brighton Line. My Orthodox synagogue was on Avenue J — the famous boxing ref Ruby Goldstein was a member of our congregation. Our temple is long gone, taken over by Hasidim.

Stuie and I walked past the library, walked past where

the Midwood movie theater used to be, the theater where Woody Allen spent his afternoons as a kid, and we stopped at the corner of Avenue J and East 15th Street. Stopped in front of a nondescript shop and gazed at the line of people spilling out the door and snaking down the street. No place has lines like New York. If it's good there's a line. In New York you learn to wait.

Over the front door the sign said: *Pizza,* and in smaller type, *Italian Heros.* This was Di Fara's Pizza, the most famous pizza joint in the city, maybe in the entire United States. *Joint* being the operative word. I grew up with joints. I love a joint.

Domenico De Marco opened Di Fara in 1965. I called Domenico De Marco *maestro* because he was a pizza artist—he died in 2022. People happily pay five bucks a slice at Di Fara. Who cares? You pay a fortune for a Silver Oak cabernet. You pay a fortune for a Di Fara slice.

"Do you want to wait on this line?" I asked Stuie.

He said, sure he'd wait. Di Fara was a big part of this reminiscing day, the glue—well, the cheese—of our relationship. We couldn't miss the experience. We waited on the slow-moving line, hung around almost an hour while the maestro handmade every pizza. As I waited, I wondered why New York pizza is better than pizza in the forty-nine other states. My sister, who now lives near Philly, once was in another Brooklyn pizza place and asked her friend why New York pizza is the tops. The pizza maker heard her and, trying to be helpful, said, "It's de wawdah."

Translation into standard English: "It's the water."

Which may or may not be true.

When Stuie and I finally slid through the door, we stood at a small counter and placed our order with a young man.

De Marco, lovingly creating pizzas, had his back to us. Stuie and I ordered two slices apiece, just plain, nothing on them except tomato sauce and cheese and whatever spices De Marco sprinkled on top. In New York you don't need accessories like pineapple in Hawaiian-style pizzas or grilled chicken. A New York slice of pizza speaks for itself. Putting pineapple or chicken on a Di Fara slice would be a desecration.

When we got our slices and two cans of soda, we looked around for a place to sit. Good luck. Di Fara's is a hole in the wall with only a few tables. We walked outside unsure what to do. Where to place the slices and the sodas? I saw a large console television on the corner of Avenue J and East 15th Street, a piece of junk furniture someone dumped. Nothing unusual about seeing a discarded TV on the corner. In Brooklyn you see all kinds of things on all kinds of corners. The TV was a big brown sucker with a busted screen, but it was level across the top which formed a little table, say twenty inches by twelve inches—call it a mini-counter.

"Let's put our stuff on top of the TV," I told Stuie.

He agreed it was the most civilized thing to do.

So, we're eating pizza and slurping soda as we used to as kids, using the TV as a tabletop and we're looking at all the noisy exciting life on Avenue J, hearing the car horns—why do people honk so much in New York? Other people are eating pizza leaning against cars or Di Fara's wall or sitting on the ground. A woman walks over and she's grinning. Despite their reputation for being rude, New Yorkers are the friendliest people. They want to know your story and want to tell their story. New York is a verbal paradise.

"Please stand right there," the woman says to Stuie and

me. "I have to get a photo of you two eating pizza off a TV set. This is priceless."

We pose holding twenty bucks' worth of slices to our mouths. She adjusts her cell phone and aims. I say, "Lady, you want to know something? I just flew three-thousand miles to eat this slice of pizza off this abandoned TV set."

She snaps the photo.

Chapter 39

Jewish Intellectual

Sitting at a bar in San Francisco. Foggy night. Warm inside. With me a beautiful woman some would call a babe. Platinum blond hair, deep dark eyes, long eyelashes and a body that never quits. We're discussing my years as a Marine, which thrill her but bore me. I don't like talking about them. Civilians never understand that life.

Guy walks over, lays his mitt on her shoulder. She flinches.

"Take you hand off her," I say, voice calm, controlled.

He takes his hand off her but pokes me in the chest.

"What you going to do about it, Four Eyes?"

I say, "Don't touch me. Apologize to the lady."

He pokes me in the chest a second time. Doesn't apologize to the lady.

I say, "You poke me again you'll suffer."

He laughs. "I'm peeing myself, asshole. I'll be in her pants in half an hour." He pokes me again.

I don't say anything. I study him. About twenty-nine. Big. Probably played high school football. Already turning flabby. I can take him out in two seconds. He thinks I'm frightened, about to lose the babe's respect. Thinks we'll go outside and fight for her. Guy like him believes there are rules. But there is only one rule—that there are no rules. It's the no-rule rule.

He tries to poke me again. I grab his index finger, snap it like a twig. He screams like a baby. I butt my forehead into his nose. Breaks on contact. You never punch a moron like him. Jaws break fingers. He falls to the floor, blood smearing his face. I kick the side of his head, not enough to kill him — I know about killing stupid guys on the floor. He'll be unconscious ten minutes, wake up with the headache of all headaches. I toss a fifty on the bar, tell the bartender, "This should pay for our drinks and his."

I take the babe by the arm. Sixty people staring at us. No one makes a move. We walk into the cold San Francisco night. She grips my hand, squeezes it.

"Your place or mine?" she asks.

What I just wrote is complete bullshit.

I never had a fight as an adult. I never was a Marine. I never impressed a woman, let alone a babe, by fighting. I measure five-seven-and-a-half on a good day. The flabby guy, if he ever existed, could wipe me out.

But since my wife died and I'm alone and I'm in my seventies, I read tough-guy fiction. I am obsessed with tough guys.

Why do I read tough-guy fiction?

Because tough guys make things turn out right. I want to make things turn out right. I want to eliminate my heartache and loss and get back what I had. How I used to feel. I used to feel happy.

Who writes tough-guy fiction?

Elmore Leonard, Lee Child, Dashiell Hammett to name a few.

What do their tough guys do?

Take matters into their own hands. Don't ask for help. Get things done. Live without fear. I am especially drawn to Leonard's and Child's tough guys.

What does it mean for a tough guy to take matters into his own hands?

Chapter 39

Think about what fictional Lowell did at the San Francisco bar. He didn't beg the bartender for assistance. He didn't call the cops. He didn't say to the lady, "Let's avoid an unpleasant situation and leave. It's for the best."

The hell with that. Fictional Lowell did what real Lowell never could do. He gave flabby guy a chance to apologize and stop poking him. Gave him several chances. Then he disposed of the problem man to man. *A man does what a man has to do.* It's the ethic of the Wild West and it's what Gary Cooper does to the Miller Gang in *High Noon,* although Cooper lies to himself and says he's protecting the town. Absolutely not. He's standing up for himself, defending his honor in the most elemental way. Sure, his Quaker wife, Grace Kelly, saves his bacon at the end, one of the reasons *High Noon* is a great movie. It shows the weakness of the tough guy. I should have such weakness.

The tough guy operates outside the law, feels hemmed in by law. Does it all on his own. Think of Raymond Cruz in Elmore Leonard's novel *City Primeval: High Noon in Detroit,* an underrated work in Leonard's canon.

Raymond Cruz is a big-city cop who can bring down by legal means Clement, the bad guy, a typically fascinating Leonard scumbag. Drawn gun, handcuffs, Miranda Rights, the full *shmear*. But he doesn't do that. What's between the two men is personal and Cruz handles it that way. You draw your gun, I draw mine. To the death.

As Clement looked up, Raymond shot him three times. He fired seeing Clement's eyes and fired again in the roomful of sound, still seeing the man's eyes, and fired again as Clement was slammed against the couch and almost went over it with the momentum but collapsed into cushions and lay there, denim legs stretching to the beer bottle on the floor with foam oozing out of it, his hands holding his chest and stomach now as though he were holding his life in, not wanting it to escape, his eyes open in stunned surprise.

Many of Leonard's tough guys are cowboys even if they aren't cowboys. The meanest, fastest, coldest, most effective man wins. Raymond Cruz is a cowboy at heart. And so is Leonard's famous hero Raylan Givens, a modern-day marshal who even wears a cowboy hat. I love those guys. In my fantasies I am Raymond Cruz or Raylan Givens or Lee Child's hero Jack Reacher who kills without remorse and never feels guilt and never loses a fight.

Jack Reacher is the ultimate tough guy. He gouges eyes, shoots people in the head and watches calmly as the head explodes. And then he moves on. He explains why he's a loner vigilante.

"Sooner or later it's us or them. That's how it is. That's how it always is. Why pretend any different?"

The opening scene of this essay in the San Francisco bar is a rip-off of Jack Reacher and an homage to Child.

Which brings me to Hamlet. Doesn't everything always come down to Hamlet? Hamlet is not a tough guy. That's his problem. He is a great character, maybe the greatest character ever written, but a very bad tough guy. Imagine Jack Reacher in Hamlet's position. Ghost of his dad tells him his uncle Claudius murdered him and is screwing Hamlet's mother (okay he married her). The ghost demands revenge.

What would Reacher do? He'd break Claudius' legs for starters. Then he'd pull out an eye or two, kick him in the head and leave him dead. He'd do this in front of his mother, Gertrude, and Polonius and Ophelia and the whole gang. He'd spare his mother. Send her to a small cottage by the sea with one servant to live out her days in penance.

Chapter 39

Any number of Elmore Leonard heroes would knock off Claudius. Think Roberto Valdez in *Valdez is Coming*, Leonard's best cowboy novel. Valdez challenges Tanner, the bad guy, to draw his gun.

"*See if your gun is as good as mine. What do you think of something like that? You and I, that's all, uh? What do you need anybody else for?*"

Tanner, surrounded by paid bodyguards, hesitates.

"*Not today,*" *Tanner said.* "*Another time.*"

Valdez shook his head slowly "*No, that was your time. You get one time, mister, to prove who you are.*"

Valdez doesn't kill Tanner, is satisfied to humiliate him. Oh, and Valdez steals his woman.

But Hamlet isn't Reacher or Valdez. He's a thinker, not a doer. You don't want this intellectual in a foxhole with you. You want Donald Westlake's sociopath hero, Parker, who meets Shevelly, a guy from the other side—a bunch he has a beef with—and after the confab in a car, Parker pulls a gun.

Parker leaned far to the right, aiming the pistol out at arm's length in front of him, the line of the barrel sighted on Shevelly's head. Shevelly read his intention and suddenly thrust his hands out protectively in front of himself, shouting, "I'm only the messenger!"

"*Now you're the message,*" *Parker told him, and shot him.*

Hamlet is no Parker. He's so *farmisht* (Yiddish for stressed out) he kills all the wrong people starting with bigmouth Polonius and then Laertes, and he arranges for the murders of Rosencrantz and Guildenstern. His weird behavior leads to the death of Ophelia and Gertrude. Because Hamlet cannot confront the real issue—get revenge on Claudius—he wastes time killing a bunch of ancillary characters. Hamlet lacks focus, lacks the cold-eyed, straight-ahead killer instinct of Cruz or Reacher or Parker. He finally kills Claudius at the end of a very long play, but by then he's made a mess of everything.

Why do I love fictional tough guys? Because I'm not a tough guy. I cannot settle things man to man. I cannot make life turn out right. Ghost comes knocking on my door, I'm Hamlet.

I am a Jewish intellectual. I was taught to settle arguments with words. I am a smart talker and a good debater. I am aggressive with my mouth, and I talk to win, to kill an opponent in a metaphorical sense. I use irony. Sarcasm. I come from a verbal Jewish culture—think of all those wise-guy Jewish comedians. And I respect the law and expect it to defend me. Reacher has no patience for the law. He has two fists.

Boxing was my favorite sport to cover as a sports writer. Ultimate tough-guy sport. Two men in a ring depending on themselves. No teammates. No mediation through ball, bat or net. Better man wins. The best boxing writer was A.J. Liebling. Wrote *The Sweet Science* which *Sports Illustrated* named the greatest sports book of all time. Liebling loved the fights. Understood what was at stake. Wrote about "low" characters like corner men and gangsters. Chubby guy. Connoisseur of French cuisine. Intellectual. Wrote for *The New Yorker*. A Jew.

The guys who created Superman were Jerry Siegel and Joe Shuster, couple of Jews. Superman is the ultimate Jewish man's fantasy, mild-mannered newspaper reporter who can kick your ass. Kick everyone's ass.

I'm saying Jewish intellectual men—some of us—are fascinated by the American tough guy—a man of few words, a man of action, brutal action.

Chapter 39

Next time you see me slouched on a barstool downing a shot of whiskey no water, don't lip off or I'll break your jaw and bust your nose.

In my dreams.

Chapter 40
Why Judge Judy is Essential

I am in love with Judge Judy. I don't mean physically in love—although she's kind of cute that gal even at age 82. I mean I love her style which is Brooklyn Jewish style which is my style.

I am a 79-year-old widower and I watch Judge Judy reruns several hours each day and experience a thrill every time she tells a litigant on her TV show don't fuck with me, although she never actually says don't fuck with me. She's too much of a lady for that. She says it in other ways:

You're a moron.

I don't want to hear you unless I'm looking at you and asking you a question.

You didn't keep your promise. You get dippity doo-dah.

If you say one more thing, I'll throw your case out.

Um is not an answer. It's either yes or no.

You have to understand one thing about Judge Judy. She's from my part of Brooklyn, mostly Jewish at the time we grew up, and even if her parents didn't speak Yiddish—I bet they did—they were influenced by the Yiddish language which has many words for fool: *shlemiel, shlimazel, shmendrik, schmuck, putz,* etc., etc. So, when Judge Judy calls someone a fool, she's being true to her roots, to a culture in which we called a schmuck a schmuck even to his face. Because telling the truth was important.

What some people—like the great Judge Joseph Wapner—saw as rudeness in Judge Judy was her acting natural. To use a cliche *telling it like it is.*

Judge Judy Sheindlin—nee Judy Blum—attended Madison High School on Bedford Avenue in Flatbush Brooklyn. My high school Midwood, also on Bedford Avenue, was Madison's rival, and I had many friends who attended Madison. I probably knew kids who knew Judy Blum. Famous alums of Madison are Carole King, Chuck Schumer, Bernie Sanders, Ruth Bader Ginsburg. Chris Rock went there but didn't graduate. My alma mater Midwood has one famous alum—Woody Allen.

Judy Blum would have grown up saying—or merely thinking—some Madison students were morons or idiots, and unlike most of us, she gets to call people idiots in her job. I envy her that. I had several morons for editors, but I had to be polite or keep my mouth shut. Calling them morons wasn't good for job security. But calling people morons assures Judge Judy of job security because people love her rudeness because she says what they are thinking.

More Judge Judyisms:

Don't speak.

Get your hand off your hip. There's only one attitude here and that's mine.

That's a ridiculous argument.

Do I look like an idiot to you?

If she's a neurotic broad you picked her and you chose to make a baby with her.

In Judge Judy's court you can't fold your arms across your chest or keep your hands in your pockets or have too many shirt buttons unbuttoned or chew gum. Heaven help you if you talk while she's reading a document. *Shh!!!!* she shouts and gives you the death stare. When you speak you must look her in the eye. You better stop telling a long narrative and get right to the point. *I don't want to hear the whole story from the Creation. I want to know why you didn't pay him back the two thousand dollars bail.*

And you must have the police report. If you don't, you're in trouble. *Why are you here? Did you think you were going to the beach?* She wants documentation. *Let me see the letter* (pronounced letta).

I love her power and how she solves things in a few minutes. I wish my life were like her courtroom. I've found my life has more questions than answers and precious few solutions.

Hers is a small claims court, maximum judgment $5,000. In one case a man broke off an engagement because he said his fiancée was having sex with a midget. In another a renter got evicted for having a nine-foot python that got away in the building. There was the plaintiff who sued the leader of an underground rock band for vomiting on her dress—Judy agreed and called it an assault and awarded her 500 bucks. There was the plaintiff who sued his roommate for spraying urine on his bed—judgment for the plaintiff 1,700 bucks. In yet another case a kid borrowed his girlfriend's car saying he needed to get clothes from home for high school choir practice but blew off practice and went cruising with another girl and crashed.

Cases involve people who get stopped driving without auto insurance—Judge Judy won't tolerate no car insurance—sisters or mothers, or husbands and wives, or lovers who dispute whether the money was a loan or a gift—Judge Judy leans towards loans in her judgments—dogs who bite people, neighbors who fight over noise or broken fences. There are dozens of cases about people who left a home or apartment in a huff and ask for return of property left there but the other person claims there's no property—Judge Judy

can't stand the drudgery of these cases. To many of these people she says:
I don't look stupid, do I?
Because if you think that I'm stupid I resent it.
Well, that's stupid. Then your answer is stupid.

Judge Judy clearly doesn't appreciate stupid. She imitates people who make faces by making faces back at them. When she's bored, she says,
Listen to me, I don't care. I don't care.

Why do I love Judge Judy? Because her world is orderly—it has rules, and it makes sense, and she is the enforcer of order. She insists people take responsibility for their actions, demands they support themselves, if able, and she won't accept excuses. When litigants weep, she has no sympathy. *Do I look like Dr. Phil?* And she lectures people on the immorality of their behavior:
If you tell the truth, you don't have to have a good memory.
That's what happens when you act like a jerk.
I don't think you're cute as a matter of fact. If you're trying to be charming with me trust me it's not going to work. Better looking and richer people than you have tried to charm me without success.
You are no gift. You are a 20-year-old unemployed person who takes from young women because he thinks that he's God's gift. I mean you're not even good looking. Judgment for the plaintiff.
That means that you're a baby and a bully. Maybe it's because you're short of stature.
Don't look up to God. God is not going to help you, Jimmy, not here.

And when she's heard enough or had enough, she often ends with a loud flourish bordering on a shout as she

straightens the case documents and rises from the bench about to leave the courtroom/studio:
>*Your case is dismissed.*
>*We're finished.*
>*We're done. Done. Goodbye.*
>I need Judge Judy in my life.

Chapter 41

Poland

Was I a real writer, not a daily newspaper scribbler but something more? This was a life question I asked myself after I retired in 2016. I was in my seventies and still searching for the meaning of my life.

I had gone to visit my sister, Carylann, who lives near New Hope, Pennsylvania. She asked what I would do in retirement. I looked at her, my mind blank. Her husband, Henry, a doctor long retired, said I need a focus. He was clear on this because he had a focus. He rode his bike long distances every day and was healthy and one of the happiest people I knew.

He said a focus was different from a specific project. It was more or less a state of mind. I was distinctly focusless. When I returned to California, I told my wife *I need a focus* and she said *Write a book.* I swallowed hard. *Don't write about some sports figure,* she said. *You're done with that. Write about what you know, write about your life in sports, write a sports memoir.*

Which, of course, scared me to death. I should write about me?

Okay, I would try. When I was hired at the *San Francisco Chronicle* almost forty years earlier, my dad had said, "This should only be the beginning," a Jewish dad wanting his son to achieve even more. I didn't think the *Chronicle* was the beginning. I thought it was the living end. Now I had something bigger in mind and maybe newspaper writing was only a beginning after all. Even if I flopped, I would have a focus, better than taking afternoon naps to kill time.

As I wrote every day—focus, baby—a scene from the far-off past drifted into my memory.

Early 1980s. I was invited to a book-launch party, and I went, not something I often did. When I arrived, I knew I made a mistake. People doing literary talk in the back room of a San Francisco restaurant. People holding wine glasses. Chardonnay.

I drifted to the side of the room, something I usually do in crowds. This drifting to the side dated back to my childhood. My parents would invite guests to our Brooklyn apartment, and I'd hide in my bedroom along with my sister and Aunt Sarah.

I found a seat near the wall of the restaurant, took a deep breath, and looked around. Seated across from me was an older man. Kind face. He too was a side drifter. Maybe he had an Aunt Sarah. He smiled at me and I smiled at him and we made small talk about how awkward we felt in large gatherings, and we were getting along fine when he asked in a gentle voice, "What's your name?"

"Lowell Cohn," I said.

Well, this kind older man almost levitated.

"Lowell Cohn," he gushed. "It's an honor to meet you. I read you every morning in the *Chronicle* and I love your writing."

I took it in stride. I allowed the kind older man to shake my hand and praise me. Then, as a matter of courtesy, I said, "What's your name?"

"Lawrence," he said.

"Lawrence what?"

"Lawrence Ferlinghetti."

Lawrence Ferlinghetti! I almost plotzed. *The* Lawrence Ferlinghetti, the cofounder of legendary City Lights Bookstore in San Francisco. In college I had devoured his poetry collection, *A Coney Island of the Mind*. Here was a writing giant praising me. I must have turned red in the face.

"Please don't praise me like that," I said.

"Why?" His voice soft and encouraging.

"It embarrasses me."

"Why?"

"Because you're Lawrence Ferlinghetti and I'm not."

As I wrote my sports memoir, I would remember Lawrence Ferlinghetti and my embarrassment. But there was something else. Ferlinghetti, in the few minutes I shared with him, took me seriously as a writer. And I wanted to remember that. And I also wanted to remember The Box.

The Box was about Stanford and English Literature and me. When I wrote analytical essays, mostly about Joseph Conrad, I used the most stilted prose. I cringe to read my stuff now with phrases like *in the final analysis* or *in this study I plan to* or *thus we can see*. Any writer who resorts to *thus* is screwed. When I finished my doctorate and left Stanford—focusless—I began reading for the pleasure of it, not because I was assigned *Tristram Shandy* or *Ulysses*, God help me. I read *Lolita* and giggled at the sheer beauty of the words. And I read Bernard Malamud, devoured his stories about people like my parents, people from my neighborhood, his English sounding like a direct translation from the Yiddish.

And then I started to write about sports—Goodbye, Joseph Conrad, nice knowing you—and words came out that didn't include thus or in the final analysis, and I realized I had been living in The Box which I sometimes imagined as a steamer trunk, and in this Box I wrote a certain way because I thought that's how intellectuals wrote. The words in the Box were black and white and gray, and when

I finished graduate school and leapt out of The Box and was free and finally could breathe, the whole world opened up to me, the words all the colors of the rainbow. And I loved them. And I could write them.

So, there I was writing my memoir in 2017 with Lawrence Ferlinghetti cheering me on, encouraging me not to report but to go inside myself to find stories. I finished my memoir two years later and called an editor at a major New York publishing house. He was brilliant and had been my editor on a previous sports book. I didn't expect him to take the call right away. *He's in a meeting. May I have your number and he'll get back to you?*

But he took the call even though we hadn't spoken in years. We had worked well together and liked each other. We made the obligatory small talk. He was living in Brooklyn. He told me about his neighborhood and its advantages, and the weather and I was nodding on the phone deciding when to end this bullshit when he finally said, "So, why are you calling?"

"I finished a sports memoir," I said.

"We don't do well with sports memoirs," he shot back.

Now I knew where he stood.

"If you don't want it, can you suggest where else to send it?"

He sighed deeply which I took to mean, *why did I take this fucking call?*

He named some names, said I should market it as stories about famous people, not stories about me.

The whole goddamn book was stories about me.

I began to think, *why did I make this fucking call?*

"But you'll have trouble publishing your memoir," he said. "Most editors feel the way I do."

CHAPTER 41

It was then I made my big mistake. It must have been wounded pride, the little Jewish boy wanting to be chosen for the softball team.

"Listen," I said too forcefully, "I'm one of the most famous sports columnists in the San Francisco Bay Area."

He didn't miss a beat.

"That's like saying you're the most famous sports columnist in Poland," he shot back.

It was a great putdown, one of the best ever. I sure felt put down and ended the call quickly. *Let's stay in touch, blah, blah.*

Thing is I published that book—*Gloves Off: 40 Years of Unfiltered Sports Writing.* Was proud of it. So, here's what I learned. If publishing a memoir means moving to Poland, sign me up. That's what I call a focus.

Chapter 42

Spaldeen, Meet Paul Tillich

I brought a Spaldeen to Palm Springs, California. If you don't know what a Spaldeen is, I'll tell you in a moment. No big secret but it was the key to my childhood.

I flew from Oakland to Palm Springs in April 2023 because it was my wife's dream, her dream before she fell in our kitchen, broke seven ribs, collapsed her lungs, spent five months in hospitals and a nursing home and died of a heart attack. We had been married thirty-six years.

What was her dream?

That she and I would rent a mid-century modern home in Palm Springs—she loved that style architecture of clean geometric lines with no clutter and large windows merging indoors and outdoors—and treat our two sons and their wives and our two grandchildren to a week in the sun and warmth, that we would bring the family together, host our family, be a family. Family meant everything to her.

The home had a pool. I made sure of that. I even paid extra to heat the pool somewhere near eighty-five delicious degrees. This is where the Spaldeen comes in. I need to tell you what a Spaldeen is.

A Spaldeen is a tennis ball without the fuzz, a naked tennis ball. It's made by the Spalding Company but because we Brooklyn kids in the 1950s didn't talk so good, we pronounced it Spaldeen, accent on the second syllable. Everyone called it a Spaldeen. Spalding even trademarked the name Spaldeen. For me Spaldeen means a certain era, a certain culture and feeling. It means belonging to our group, being one of us.

The Spaldeen is pink, an unmistakable pink and on the round surface are the words HIGH-BOUNCE BALL. It smells like rubber mixed with bubble gum, like the hard slab of bubble gum covered with pink powder that came with a pack of Topps baseball cards. That sucker could bounce, at least our version of the Spaldeen could bounce. According to *The New York Times* a Spaldeen could withstand 500 impacts against a hard surface at 50 miles an hour before flattening out. *The New York Times* said kids in Brooklyn pronounced Spalding Spaldeen as if we were the only people who said that, but Robert Rubino, my friend from Queens, said they also called it Spaldeen where he lived. Spaldeen brought together an entire era of New York City kids.

Spalding first produced Spaldeens in 1949. Initially Spaldeens were reject tennis balls, but they caught on with kids like me because we needed a ball that would bounce on our asphalt playgrounds and city streets. There wasn't any grass, or very little, and Spaldeens connected us to our environment. Spalding eventually created a separate line to produce Spaldeens—they no longer were rejects. The balls went out of fashion in the 1970s—oh, dear—and Spalding stopped producing them, but old timers pined for Spaldeens and the company reintroduced them in 1999.

I prepped for Palm Springs by buying a four-pack of Spaldeens from Amazon for $11.88, that's $2.97 a ball. When I was a kid, I bought Spaldeens at Estroff's variety store on Avenue M. They cost twenty-five cents.

When the package of balls arrived from Amazon, I checked out the pink color and it seemed legit. On the rubber I read Spalding HIGH-BOUNCE BALL.

CHAPTER 42 317

So far so good.

But the smell was off. Not quite as sweet as I remember. I could live with the smell. I could live with the fact the new Spaldeen didn't bounce as high as the old model—although Spalding says it does. Maybe they're right. Memory is fickle and flawed and romantic about things that really mattered. I even could live with the small print that said, "made in Vietnam." Nothing against Vietnam but come on.

What the hell? It was a Spaldeen. It fit in my hand just right and the feeling of ball in hand brought back a thousand scenes from my childhood.

The first day in the pool at the Palm Springs vacation home I told my thirteen-year-old grandson Sam we would play Errors. Any kid who grew up in Brooklyn in the 1950s knows Errors. You space yourselves a sewer apart in the street or between two handball walls in the playground and you throw grounders to each other, real burners. The kid who first commits ten errors loses.

We couldn't throw grounders in the pool, so we threw line drives. Whipped that Spaldeen to each other. And Sam was good, very good. Could catch one-handed if a throw went to his side, and soon his sister Camila, ten years old, joined us. God, she could catch and throw. And then my sons Brian and Grant, who had played Errors with me as kids, got into the act. And then Brian's wife, Carolyn, was playing Errors with us. Great hands, wicked line-drive thrower. Grant's wife, Swasti, was the official scorer. And if my wife had been there, she would have played her ass off, tried like hell to beat us. She could catch—she had her own mitt as a kid—and she threw hard and she would have been laughing and splashing, her hair wet, her eyes glowing.

We played Errors hours every day. Funny thing, the kids

could be whiny and difficult at dinner, arguing over who sits where, what kind of pizza they wanted, but in the pool, intent on the game, they were gracious. Never argued if we called an error on them. Even called errors on themselves. The Spaldeen made them polite and well-behaved.

We upped the difficulty. Someone would stand above the deep end of the pool. At the word "Go," he or she would jump into the water. On the way down, one of us would throw the ball, and Brian or Sam etc. had to catch it in the air. Hard to do. Sam got so good, he could catch the Spaldeen and do a three-sixty before crashing into the water. I caught exactly one the entire week. But I caught it, went to the bottom of the pool, and swallowed a quart of water.

The Spaldeen and Errors made our week. Next to the house itself—a beauty—the Spaldeen was the most important element of the vacation.

Which didn't surprise me.

For me growing up, the Spaldeen was the ground of being. Bear with me here. The great German-born theologian Paul Tillich (1886-1965) popularized the term *ground of being*. As far as I know, it was a synonym for God. Meant God is the source of everything we see and experience and feel. The miracle of life. The miracle of being.

In the twentieth century most Anglo-American philosophers had lost sight of being and endlessly debated logic and the meanings of words. More than anyone, Martin Heidegger, the greatest Western philosopher of the twentieth century and a Nazi sympathizer to his everlasting disgrace, reintroduced being into philosophy, and Tillich borrowed from him.

What do Tillich, Heidegger and the ground of being have to do with the Spaldeen? The Spaldeen was our ground of

Chapter 42

being in Brooklyn in the 1950s. It literally hit the ground, hit it hard, and bounced high. It lived between down and up. The Spaldeen was the basis of every street game we played, often on hot humid days, all of us sweating through our T-shirts and wearing out our Keds, and playing, oh gosh, stickball, punchball, slap ball, one-wall handball (I was very good, even with my left hand), hit the penny and stoopball. The games gave our lives purpose and the Spaldeen was the means of that purpose.

For me Spaldeen was even more personal. When I was a young man, a struggling freelance writer hardly making a dime, I sold a piece to *Sports Illustrated*. It was the first article I sold them—there would be more—and they paid me six-hundred-fifty bucks, a fortune to me. The piece was about playing punchball across the street from our apartment house in the Avenue L playground.

In punchball you throw the ball over your head and swing down on it with your fist like a tennis serve and then you run around the bases painted on the asphalt. The good players could punch a ball hundreds of feet. I can still hear the smack of fist on ball, and the ball was a Spaldeen.

Bringing a Spaldeen to Palm Springs took me back to my childhood but also to my start as a writer. If a Spaldeen was our ground of being, it was also my ground of becoming. The editors at *Sports Illustrated*, God love them, sent an artist to my Brooklyn playground and along with my story I saw drawings of a kid playing punchball with a Spaldeen. *Sports Illustrated* even identified the ball as a Spaldeen in the drawing.

The Spaldeen brought us together. Having a catch, throwing a ball between Mark Barich and me, was a form of communication. (What became of your life, Barich?)

Throwing and catching is a silent conversation, and sometimes silent conversations are the deepest. You and I cooperating, no subtext, no misunderstanding. We spoke through the Spaldeen at a time—maybe, I was eleven—when I had everything I needed, my world complete. A loving family. Good friends. Games which gave meaning to my life and still do. I never have felt that way again because I have learned anxiety, uncertainty, self-doubt, disloyalty, guilt and tragedy.

Was the Spaldeen God in the sense Tillich meant ground of being? Of course not. I choose to think of it as God's angel, God's gift to New York kids looking for the glue of life. To use Tillich's terminology, the Spaldeen was a symbol of God, something pointing to God—all the God we needed back then. On the final day in Palm Springs, I told my grandson Sam to stand on the pool's upper edge above the deep water, said this was the last throw of the day and it was his job to catch it. I said *on your mark, get set, go*. He dove forward. Didn't jump into the pool. Dove. Looked at me as he flew parallel to the pool. I hit him square in his outstretched hands before he smashed into the water headfirst. He caught it, grinned, went under.

When he came up, I said, "Sam, if you were with us in Brooklyn back in the day, my friends would have liked you." He grinned a pleasure-all-over grin and then he threw the ball to me right on the money. He was honoring his dad's generation and my generation and the generation that came before me. The Spaldeen generations. He was honoring the unbreakable bond of our family.

And the whole time I felt my wife in the soft kiss of the breeze and the gentle smile of the sunshine.

Chapter 43

Heaven

After my wife died in 2022, I went to stay with my sister Carylann, three years younger than me. She and my brother-in-law Henry live near New Hope, Pennsylvania, about an hour from where I went to college. I knew they would leave me alone because I needed to be alone, but while I was alone, I needed to be near people who love me.

I stayed in a darkened upstairs bedroom and read or looked out the window or cried. One day Carylann said we (meaning me) should get out of the house. I mumbled something. She said we should drive to Pinewood, or where Pinewood used to be.

Pinewood was the Jewish bungalow colony we went to as kids, happy kids. It had about forty cabins for about forty families with names like Friedman, Weingarten and Schiff out there in the rural, country part of New Jersey. It had woods and tennis courts and handball courts and a baseball field and a cement swimming pool oblong-shaped and as large as a lake, and a camp we attended during the day. For ten summers we were sunburned carefree children who escaped the heat and stink of New York in July and August.

My sister and I had not been to Pinewood in sixty-five years. We knew it had been sold, no longer existed as a bungalow colony, but we didn't know anything else. We set out in her car on a pilgrimage of discovery—it felt like a pilgrimage in space because we were driving there but also a pilgrimage in time because we were visiting our past.

Near Carylann's house, we crossed the Delaware River into New Jersey and drove about an hour to a small, rustic New Jersey town called Mendham. We remembered Mendham because we got haircuts there and bought shoes and bathing suits. Carylann and I thought Pinewood was located somewhere between Mendham and Chester, about eight miles west. We knew there was a turnoff to Pinewood on the road to Chester, but we didn't know where. We drove toward Chester.

But we didn't see a turnoff. All the roads were unfamiliar. Who were we kidding we'd find Pinewood after all these years? Carylann said we should grab lunch in Chester and drive back to her house, but I told Carylann I wouldn't give up so fast. I had been a journalist and I always made the extra phone call to a source or interviewed one more person for an article. I learned perseverance — actually relentlessness.

Carylann doubled back toward Mendham while I worried if I was being a pest, if she saw me as a pest. I asked her to go slow. And then to our left I spotted a sign Old Mill Road which seemed vaguely familiar. We drove past it, but I asked Carylann to turn around and drive up Old Mill Road. Which she did. She had no idea about Old Mill Road. I wasn't sure I did either.

I said, "If this is the right road, we'll cross the Ten Ton Bridge in a few minutes." Ten tons being the load limit of the bridge. After a few minutes we crossed the Ten Ton Bridge, and I felt my heart quicken. As kids we threw stones into the water below the bridge and climbed down the banks and waded in the brook. We drove on. I said Pinewood would be on the left. We drove to the end of Old Mill Road and didn't see Pinewood.

Chapter 43

"At least they would have built homes there," Carylann said, "but I didn't see any homes."

We drove back down Old Mill Road and came to a county park called Meadowood. I said, "That's our best shot. Let's turn in there."

We drove into a parking lot for Meadowood Park, looked around. This couldn't be Pinewood because all the cabins were gone and so was the pool and the tennis courts and the big casino where on Saturday nights the parents would put on shows and socialize without us kids. The casino had a soda shop where we ordered frappes—it's where I learned the word *frappe*—and we would sign a slip and charge the frappe to our bungalow.

The place was now a large wood. Nature had taken over, reclaimed the land, but there was a sign by a visitor kiosk which said Meadowood used to be a day camp. It didn't name the day camp. If this was the site of Pinewood, the sign wasn't entirely accurate. Pinewood was more than a day camp. It was a community of refugees from New York and Philadelphia, the men wearing bathing suits over their skinny legs and pot bellies, the men playing softball and the women wearing sequined bathing suits and playing mahjong. Even my mother played mahjong.

Carylann and I tried to walk into the woods, but the paths petered out and we were afraid of roughing it because of poison ivy. Oy, did I remember feeling miserable from poison ivy and all that Calamine Lotion looking like Pepto Bismol on my arms and legs and face. (Do you remember the 1959 song "Poison Ivy" by the Coasters?)

After a while we drove back to Carylann's. I went up to my room and searched online for Pinewood. Then it happened. I came upon a half-hour video about the history of

Meadowood Park. The video said Meadowood started as a nudist colony in the 1930s—can you imagine that? It was called Nature Lovers Club. And then it became Pinewood, yes Pinewood, and after Pinewood closed, Mendham Township took it over in the 1970s, burned down the cabins so it wouldn't have to pay taxes on them and made Pinewood a public park.

I called downstairs to Carylann, and we watched the video together holding hands. We had rediscovered our past and we had done it together and doing that with my sister was the greatest gift she ever gave me. Because everyone else in our family was dead—our mother, father and brother. We were the only two left. While we watched the video, I felt our family gather around us, experienced them as a warm glow in my chest and arms with gladness in my heart. And I felt the people of Pinewood—all that life all those years ago. Gone. Certainly, all the parents were gone. And some of our friends too.

I had stayed in touch with two friends from Pinewood, only two, Barbara Forman and Barry Hornstein. That was it. I remembered kissing Barbara in her bungalow one Saturday night when her parents were at the casino, remembered the feel of lips on lips—no tongues—and her smell. A girl smell. I loved that smell of girls then and still do.

I remembered one summer Rosh Hashanah came early. The men wearing yarmulkes turned the casino into a synagogue and chanted the prayers in Hebrew. I remembered how much they knew, almost like rabbis and how seriously they took their responsibility.

Pinewood was a garden with all those acres of trees and a babbling brook bordering the property—literally a babbling brook. But it was more than that for Carylann and me

Chapter 43

and, I guess for Barbara Forman and Barry Hornstein, too. It was our Garden of Eden, our paradise. It's where we were innocent. Where we knew nothing except happy families and good friends and life in the sun and water.

And it's the place we all left because Pinewood got sold, because we grew up, because life changed as it always does, because we were obliged to face the hard real world. For Jews the story of Adam and Eve is not about original sin. We have no concept of original sin. You need to understand that. To me the Adam and Eve story explains why life is tough, sometimes brutal, sometimes beautiful. It explains why we don't live in innocence with everything gifted to us. It explains why we work hard and suffer and grieve and die. It explains how human beings became part of history.

I always thought Adam and Eve got a raw deal in the Garden of Eden. God is the instigator in that one. He put two innocents (children really) in a special place and told them *have a blast but don't dare eat from this one tree.* Sure enough they were going to eat from that tree. I would have. God set them up. Set all of us up.

So, we all got expelled from Eden/Pinewood because life demands expulsion from paradise. Expulsion is the precondition of life.

And that brings me to heaven. One way to look at heaven—there are many—is to imagine you, me, us returning to the Garden of Eden, to innocence, paradise, a state of grace. Getting back what we lost. I think about heaven all the time because I want to meet my wife again, be with my wife, spend eternity with her in a place like the Garden of Eden.

But I have a big problem. I don't believe in heaven. No way. The whole idea of heaven seems improbable to me, a fantasy, a wish fulfillment. When I was eight, a Catholic family moved onto our block. There were two sons about my age. While we were playing in the street, they told me if I sinned, I'd go to hell which was a smelly fiery place presided over by the Devil, but I could make up for that by asking God's forgiveness. Then I'd qualify for heaven. They scared the shit out of me.

I ran home and knelt by my bed as they suggested. I held my little hands together and told God I had led a bad life up till then, but I wanted to repent and go to heaven where the angels lived. After a few minutes I felt like a phony. I wasn't such a bad kid and the God those kids talked about seemed like a serious sourpuss, so I got up, walked into the kitchen, grabbed a glass of milk and never thought about heaven again.

Until now. I hope there is heaven, an actual place with meadows and deer frolicking and lions not eating the deer because God provides, but it's hard for a Jew to believe in heaven.

I went to Hebrew School from age eight to thirteen. Never once did my teachers mention heaven. I learned about Abraham and Sarah, Isaac, Jacob, Moses, Queen Esther. I learned about poor overmatched King Saul. I learned about David and Jonathan. I learned about the Torah, Job, Noah. But I never learned about heaven.

If heaven is a concept in Judaism, it isn't central, although the religion talks about souls of good people enjoying peace on earth after the Messiah appears and time ends. Not in heaven. On Earth. But no one ever stressed this to me or even talked about it. Christianity, a Platonic religion, stresses life after death, believes the afterlife is more real than this life we live. Some of my Christian friends say they can't actually picture heaven because it's spiritual and therefore vague, but one friend told me she knows when she enters heaven she will be in the presence of Jesus and they will talk. That's why Christians, trying to be kind to a grieving person, say So-and-so went to a better place—because heaven is better than life on Earth. Heaven is the best place. To Jews here is the best place. That's how I understand it, and if I'm wrong, I apologize.

I want there to be a physical heaven where I rejoin my wife. It feels naïve to admit this, but I admit it.

My nephew Eric told me this story. After his father—my brother—died, Eric was out to dinner with his wife, Kristin. Eric said he had thrown out my brother's dated medical books and felt guilty about that. Kristin began laughing and Eric asked what was so funny and she said my brother was standing there at their table smiling. Kristin could see him, but Eric couldn't. My brother told Kristin he didn't care about the books, and she should tell Eric not to worry.

That made Eric feel better, and my brother's wife, Nancy, took comfort in what Kristin said. I don't know if I understand what Kristin experienced, but if she did see my brother, really did, does that mean there's a heaven with smiling ghosts sending messages through people with special sight? I hope so.

After my wife died, my oldest son Brian said to me, "You're such a Jew but because of Mom you want to believe in the Christian idea of heaven."

No kidding. I want to believe although I don't believe. I hope. I'm not becoming a Christian in my old age. I am a staunch and proud Jew. When I got inducted to the Northern California Jewish Sports Hall of Fame, the organizing committee asked how Judaism influenced my sports writing. I said Judaism didn't merely influence my writing. It *was* my writing. I wasn't a sports writer. I was a Jewish writer. I'm a traditional Jew merely hoping for a little wiggle room in the Jewish idea of heaven, a wrinkle, an extra benefit.

What would heaven be like?

It goes along with something that happened after I had spinal surgery a few years ago and spent two weeks in the hospital relearning how to walk because nerves in my left leg had been damaged. There was a chalkboard in my room and on the board the nurse was supposed to write down my goals. I told her my goals were to be well enough to do the laundry and put away the clean dishes from the dishwasher.

She eyeballed me. "*Those* are your goals?" she asked. Meaning my goals were mundane. Maybe she thought I wanted to climb Mount Everest in my seventies or write the great American novel. I said my goals extended no further than the wash and laundry because my wife's health was failing, and I wanted to do things for her, do everything for her. That was my idea of happiness. And that relates to how I see heaven which doesn't necessarily include God in the equation. If I get to bask in God's presence that's a bonus.

When I die my wife, Dawn, is waiting for me. She looks and sounds like herself. She is smiling. Her hands are outstretched toward me. She welcomes me to heaven. Welcome is the key word, like I'm being admitted, and she is my guide. We walk to a place which is our house, the house she found for us when she was alive, the house she decorated. We sit in the family room, and I ask if she'd like a cup of tea. "That would be lovely," she says. I make the tea and put in two Splendas and a little milk and bring it to her. She tastes it and says, "You make a perfect cup of tea." I smile and run my hand through her hair which has turned white and is beautiful.

At night we lie in bed and watch British mysteries on Public Television as we always did—*Inspector Morse, Prime Suspect* and *Poirot* and all the others—and because we always forget who committed the murder, we watch like it's the first time. We watch holding hands. Her left hand in my right hand, our palms touching, our palms warm. We watch and hold warm palms for hours.

I want to do that every day in heaven. I don't care if a council of rabbis decrees I'm a heretic. It's all the heaven I want, and if there's no heaven after death, I already did heaven right here on Earth.

Recently, I went to Friday night services at Temple Sinai, a Reform synagogue in Oakland, California, where I live. My youngest son celebrated his bar mitzvah at Temple Sinai, and I had not gone back in twenty-two years. I don't know why I went that night. I felt a need, vague but it's the best I can do.

I prefer a Reform synagogue to an Orthodox shul where I prayed as a child. The Orthodox was serious and grim to me as a boy, but Temple Sinai has music—Ilene Keys is the cantor who sang beautifully at my son's bar mitzvah. Someone played the piano, someone else played the flute and guitar. This never happened at my Brooklyn temple. Much of the Temple Sinai service was in English—impossible at an Orthodox place.

I sang along when I remembered the words. Other times I clapped my hands. I recited the prayers I knew. Then the rabbi said she would end with a *Yizkor* service. Yizkor is a service for the dead. The word Yizkor means *May God remember*. There are only four Yizkor services a year and I had wandered into Temple Sinai on one of them, Shavuot, which celebrates the revelation of the Torah to the Jewish people on Mount Sinai. I did not know it was Shavuot, but I was meant to be there.

The prayers were somber. The rabbi asked members of the congregation to say names of departed loved ones, to remember them out loud. I heard Isenberg, Goldstein, Lurie. I said, "Dawn Cohn." Her name was there for everyone in that room to hear and for people not in that room — my parents, her parents and our ancestors going back millennia. Her name rang in my ears, and I felt her presence near me, encouraging me, looking out for me. And I said Amen.

Acknowledgments

Thanks to Eric Kimmel for giving this book a focus and direction—for explaining to me what the book is all about.

Thanks to the following for reading early versions of these chapters: Sally Barnett, Grant Cohn, Carylann Dauber, Chere Douglas, Carolyn Finnegan, Barbara Forman, Gary Furness, William Gairdner, Stuart Kucker, Michael McKinstry, Matt Rowe, Robert Rubino, Brian Strauss, Camila Strauss, Fred vonAppen.

Thanks to Matt Sieger for editing my manuscript.

Thanks to Sam Strauss for formatting my manuscript and for his editorial suggestions.

Special thanks to Dawn Cohn, my wife. Without her editing and encouragement there would be no book.

"My Introduction to Linguistics," Chapter 27, first appeared in *Switchback*, the literary journal of the Master of Fine Arts in Writing Program of the University of San Francisco.

ABOOKS

ALIVE Book Publishing and ALIVE Publishing Group
are imprints of Advanced Publishing LLC,
3200 A Danville Blvd., Suite 204, Alamo, California 94507

Telephone: 925.837.7303
alivebookpublishing.com

www.ingramcontent.com/pod-product-compliance
Lightning Source LLC
Chambersburg PA
CBHW031313160426
43196CB00007B/515